Consumer Protection Through Mass Awareness: New Challenges and Opportunities

Consumer Protection Through Mass Awareness:

New Challenges and Opportunities

Arvind Sahani

CYBER TECH PUBLICATIONS
4264/3, Ansari Road, Daryaganj, New Delhi-110002 (India)
Ph.: 011-23244078. Fax: 011-23280028
E-Mail: cyberpublicationsdelhi@yahoo.com

CONSUMER PROTECTION THROUGH MASS AWARENESS: NEW CHALLENGES AND OPPORTUNITIES

Arvind Sahani

First Edition 2009

Published by :

G.S. Rawat for **Cyber Tech Publications**
4264/3, Ansari Road, Daryaganj, New Delhi-110002 (India)
Ph.: 011-23244078. Fax: 011-23280028
E-Mail: cyberpublicationsdelhi@yahoo.com

Printed at : **Amit Enterprises**, Maujpur, Delhi, (9810878184)

Preface

Traditionally, the pace of legal change was such that a lawyer or a business professional could learn the law as applied in the real world by referring to a book or other sources; the expectation was that the rules would remain stable and predictable for some time. With the advent of e-commerce, we saw a deluge of case law and new statutes and transactions, leading to the need for a new book explaining them and how they fit with existing principles.

The incredible pace of change that has continued in electronic commercial law has led to this second edition. Some of the areas that have seen the most significant changes are data protection/ privacy, data security law, online copyright systems, changing concepts of property, and the continuing plethora of inconsistent state laws and regulations. We address these and other areas of ongoing change in this second edition, and we identify the considerations that attorneys and business professionals need to follow in practice.

The goal of this book is to provide an explanation and understanding of the rapidly developing law associated with the use of electronic (digital) systems in commerce and as a form of commerce. We take the new cases regarding electronic commercial transactions and juxtapose them to traditional law and transactions so that similarities and differences can be discerned. We explain brand new statutes and highlight potential problems, some of which can be solved and some of which cannot. In short, we seek to explain the law of electronic commercial transactions.

—Author

CONTENTS

1

Introduction

Consumer protection is a form of government regulation which protects the interests of consumers. For example, a government may require businesses to disclose detailed information about products—particularly in areas where safety or public health is an issue, such as food. Consumer protection is linked to the idea of consumer rights (that consumers have various rights as consumers), and to the formation of consumer organizations which help consumers make better choices in the marketplace.

Consumer interests can also be protected by promoting competition in the markets which directly and indirectly serve consumers, consistent with economic efficiency, but this topic is treated in Competition law.

Consumer Law

Consumer protection law or *consumer law* is considered an area of public law that regulates private law relationships between individual consumers and the businesses that sell those goods and services. Consumer protection covers a wide range of topics, including but not necessarily limited to product liability, privacy rights, unfair business practices, fraud, misrepresentation, and other consumer/business interactions.

Such laws deal with credit repair, debt repair, product safety, service contracts, bill collector regulation, pricing, utility turnoffs, consolidation, personal loans that may lead to bankruptcy and much more.

In Specific Countries

United States

In the United States a variety of laws at both the federal or state levels regulate consumer affairs.

Among them are the federal Fair Debt Collection Practices Act, the Fair Credit Reporting Act, Truth in Lending Act, Fair Credit Billing Act, and the Gramm-Leach-Bliley Act.

Federal consumer protection laws are mainly enforced by the Federal Trade Commission and the U.S. Department of Justice.

At the state level, many states have a Department of Consumer Affairs devoted to regulating certain industries and protecting consumers who use goods and services from those industries.

For example, in the U.S. state of California, the California Department of Consumer Affairs regulates about 2.3 million professionals in over 230 different professions, through its forty regulatory entities.

In addition, California encourages its consumers to act as private attorneys general through the liberal provisions of its Consumers Legal Remedies Act, Cal. Civil Code § 1750 *et seq*.

California has the nation's strongest consumer protection laws, partly because of rigorous advocacy and lobbying by groups such as Utility Consumers' Action Network[2], Consumer Federation of California and Privacy Rights Clearinghouse.

European Union

The European Union has been very active in the field of consumer protection, producing a considerable volume of Directives which require member states to regulate consumer protection to a particular standard (which may or may not allow a higher standard of regulation).

A very important innovation has been the Unfair Commercial Practices Directive. Also Directives on Unfair Contract Terms (93/13/EC) and Electronic Commerce

(2000/13/EC). There exists a European Commissioner for Consumer Protection, a post currently held by the Bulgarian Meglena Kuneva.

Germany

The Federal Republic of Germany is a member state of the European Union and is bound by the consumer protection directives of the European Union.

Thus a large part of German consumer protection law has been enacted pursuant to European Directives (e.g. the directives on door-to-door sales, consumer credits, distance selling, package tours, product liability etc.). In 2002, a large part of this legislation was integrated into the German Civil Code ("Bürgerliches Gesetzbuch").

A minister of the federal cabinet is responsible for consumer rights and protection (*Verbraucherschutzminister*). In the current cabinet of Angela Merkel, this is Horst Seehofer.

When issuing public warnings about products and services, the issuing authority has to take into account that this affects the supplier's constitutionally protected economic liberty (article 12 Basic Law, see Bundesverwaltungsgericht (Federal Administrative Court)Case 3 C 34.84, 71 BVerwGE 183.

United Kingdom

The United Kingdom is a member state of the European Union and so is bound by the consumer protection directives of the European Union.

Domestic (UK) laws originated within the ambit of contract and tort but, with the influence of EU law, it is emerging as an independent area of law. In many circumstances, where domestic law is in question, the matter judicially treated as tort, contract, restitution or even criminal law.

Consumer Protection issues are dealt with when complaints are made to the Director-General of Fair Trade. The Office of Fair Trading will then investigate, impose an injunction or take the matter to litigation.

The Office of Fair Trading also acts as the UK's official consumer and competition watchdog, with a remit to make markets work well for consumers, and at a local, municipal level by Trading Standards departments. General comsumer advice can be obtained from Consumer Direct or via a local branch of the Citizen's Advice Bureau.

Other Commonwealth Countries

In Australia the corresponding agency is the Australian Competition and Consumer Commission or the individual State Consumer Affairs agencies. In New Zealand, the corresponding agency is the Ministry of Consumer Affairs and the New Zealand Commerce Commission.

2

The Consumer Protection Act, 1986

(68 of 1986)

24th December; 1986

An Act to provide for better protection of the interests of consumers and for that purpose to make provision for the establishment of consumer councils and other authorities for the settlement of consum-ers' disputes and for matters connected therewith.

BE it enacted by Parliament in the Thirty-seventh Year of the Republic of India as follows:—

PRELIMINARY

1. Short title, extent, commencement and application.—

(1) This Act may be called the Consumer Protection Act, 1986.

(2) It extends to the whole of India except the State of Jammu and Kashmir.

(3) It shall come into force on such date as the Central Government may, by notification, appoint and different dates may be appointed for different States and for different provisions of this Act.

(4) Save as otherwise expressly provided by the Central Government by notification, this Act shall apply to all goods and services.

2. Definitions. -

(1) In this Act, unless the context otherwise requires,—

(a) "appropriate laboratory" means a laboratory or organisation—

(i) recognised by the Central Government;

(ii) recognised by a State Government, subject to such guide-lines as may be prescribed by the Central Government in this behalf; or

(iii) any such laboratory or organisation established by or under any law for the time being in force, which is maintained, financed or aided by the Central Government or a State Government for carrying out analysis or test of any goods with a view to determining whether such goods suffer from any defect;

(aa) "branch office" means—

(i) any establishment described as a branch by the opposite party; or

(ii) any establishment carrying on either the same or substan-tially the same activity as that carried on by the head office of the establishment;

(b) "complainant" means—

(i) a consumer; or

(ii) any voluntary consumer association registered under the Companies Act, 1956 (1of 1956)or under any other law for the time being in force; or

(iii) the Central Government or any State Government,

(iv) one or more consumers, where there are numerous consum-ers having the same interest;

(v) in case of death of a consumer, his legal heir or representative; who or which makes a complaint;

(c) "complaint" means any allegation in writing made by a complain-ant that—

(i) an unfair trade practice or a restrictive trade practice has been adopted by any trader or service provider;

(ii) the goods bought by him or agreed to be bought by him; suffer from one or more defects;

(iii) the services hired or availed of or agreed to be hired or availed of by him suffer from deficiency in any respect;

(iv) a trader or service provider, as the case may be, has charged for the goods or for the service mentioned in the com-plaint a price in excess of the price –

(a) fixed by or under any law for the time being in force

(b) displayed on the goods or any package containing such goods;

(c) displayed on the price list exhibited by him by or under any law for the time being in force;

(d) agreed between the parties;

(v) goods which will be hazardous to life and safety when used or being offered for sale to the public,—

(A) in contravention of any standards relating to safety of such goods as required to be complied with, by or under any law for the time being in force;

(B) if the trader could have known with due diligence that the goods so offered are unsafe to the public;

(vi) services which are hazardous or likely to be hazardous to life and safety of the public when used, are being offered by the service provider which such person could have known with due diligence to be injurious to life and safety;";

(d) "consumer" means any person who—

(i) buys any goods for a consideration which has been paid or promised or partly paid and partly promised, or under any system of deferred payment and includes any user of such goods other than the person who buys such goods for consideration paid or promised or partly paid or partly promised, or under any system of deferred payment when such use is made with the approval of such person, but does not include a person who obtains such goods for resale or for any commercial purpose; or

(ii) hires or avails of any services for a consideration which has been paid or promised or partly paid and partly prom-ised, or under any system of deferred payment and includes any beneficiary of such services other than the person who 'hires or avails of the services for consideration paid or promised, or partly paid and partly promised, or under any system of deferred payment, when such services are availed of with the approval of the first mentioned person *but does not include a person who avails of such services for any commercial purposes*;

Explanation.— For the purposes of this clause, "commercial purpose" does not include use by a person of goods bought and used by him and services availed by him exclusively for the purposes of earning his livelihood by means of self-employment;

(e) "consumer dispute" means a dispute where the person against whom a complaint has been made, denies or disputes the allega-tions contained in the complaint.

(f) "defect" means any fault, imperfection or shortcoming in the quality, quantity, potency, purity or standard which is required to be maintained by or under any law for the time being in force under any contract, express or implied or as is claimed by the trader in any manner whatsoever in relation to any goods;

(g) "deficiency" means any fault, imperfection, shortcoming or inade-quacy in the quality, nature and manner of performance which is required to be maintained by or under any law for the time being in force or has been undertaken to be performed by a person in pursuance of a contract or otherwise in relation to any service;

(h) "District Forum" means a Consumer Disputes Redressal Forum established under clause (a) of section 9;

(i) "goods" means goods as defined in the Sale of Goods Act, 1930 (3 of 1930);

(j) "manufacturer" means a person who—

(i) makes or manufactures any goods or part thereof; or

(ii) does not make or manufacture any goods but assembles parts thereof made or manufactured by others; or

(iii) puts or causes to be put his own mark on any goods made or manufactured by any other manufacturer;

Explanation. — Where a manufacturer dispatches any goods or part thereof to any branch office maintained by him, such branch office shall not be deemed to be the manufacturer even though the parts so dispatched to it are assembled at such branch office and are sold or distributed from such branch office;

(jj) "member" includes the President and a member of the National Commission or a State Commission or a District Forum, as the case may be;

(k) "National Commission" means the National Consumer Disputes Redressal Commission established under clause (c) of section 9;

(l) "notification" means a notification published in the Official Gazette;

(m) "person" includes,—

(i) a firm whether registered or not;

(ii) a Hindu undivided family;

(iii) a co-operative society;

(iv) every other association of persons whether registered under the Societies Registration Act, 1860 (21 of 1860) or not;

(n) "prescribed" means prescribed by rules made by the State Gov-ernment, or as the case may be, by the Central Government under this Act;

(nn)"regulation" means the regulations made by the National Commission under this Act;

(nnn) "restrictive trade practice" means a trade practice which tends to bring about manipulation of price or conditions of delivery or to affect flow of supplies in the market relating to goods or services in such a manner as to impose on the consumers unjustified costs or restrictions and shall include—

(a) delay beyond the period agreed to by a trader in supply of such goods or in providing the services which has led or is likely to lead to rise in the price;

(b) any trade practice which requires a consumer to buy, hire or avail of any goods or, as the case may be, services as condition precedent to buying, hiring or availing of other goods or services;

(o) "service" means service of any description which is made avail-able to potential users and includes, but not limited to, the provision of facilities in connection with banking, financing insurance, transport, processing, supply of electrical or other energy, board or lodging or both, housing construction, entertainment, amusement or the purveying of news or other information, but does not include the rendering of any service free of charge or under a contract of personal service;

(oo) "spurious goods and services" mean such goods and services which are claimed to be genuine but they are actually not so;

(p) "State Commission" means a Consumer Disputes Redressal Commission established in a State under clause (b) of section 9;

(q) "trader" in relation to any goods means a person who sells or distributes any goods for sale and includes the manufacturer thereof, and where such goods are sold or distributed in package form, includes the packer thereof;

(r) "unfair trade practice" means a trade practice which, for the purpose of promoting the sale, use or supply of any goods or for the provision of any service, adopts any unfair method or unfair or deceptive practice including any of the following practices, namely;—

(1) the practice of making any statement, whether orally or in writing or by visible representation which,—

(i) falsely represents that the goods are of a particular standard, quality, quantity, grade, composition, style or model;

(ii) falsely represents that the services are of a particular standard, quality or grade;

(iii) falsely represents any re-built, second-hand, reno-vated, reconditioned or old goods as new goods;

(iv) represents that the goods or services have sponsor-ship, approval, performance, characteristics, accesso-ries, uses or benefits which such goods or services do not have;

(v) represents that the seller or the supplier has a spon-sorship or approval or affiliation which such seller or supplier does not have;

(vi) makes a false or misleading representation concern-ing the need for, or the usefulness of, any goods or services;

(vii) gives to the public any warranty or guarantee of the performance, efficacy or length of life of a product or of any goods that is not based on an adequate or proper test thereof;

Provided that where a defence is raised to the effect that such warranty or guarantee is based on adequate or proper test, the burden of proof of such defence shall lie on the person raising such defence;

(viii) makes to the public a representation in a form that purports to be—

(i) a warranty or guarantee of a product or of any goods or services; or

(ii) a promise to replace, maintain or repair an article or any part thereof or to repeat or continue a service until it has achieved a specified result, if such purported warranty or guarantee or prom-ise is materially misleading or if there is no reasonable prospect that such warranty, guaran-tee or promise will be carried out;

(ix) materially misleads the public concerning the price at which a product or like products or goods or services, have been or are, ordinarily sold or provided, and, for this purpose, a representation as to price shall be deemed to refer to the price at which the product or goods or services has or have been sold by sellers or provided by suppliers generally in the relevant market unless it is clearly specified to be the price at which the product has been sold or services have been provided by the person by whom or on whose behalf the representation is made;

(x) gives false or misleading facts disparaging the goods, services or trade of another person.

Explanation. - For the purposes of clause (1), a statement that is—

(a) expressed on an article offered or displayed for sale, or on its wrapper or container; or

(b) expressed on anything attached to, inserted in, or accompanying, an article offered or displayed for sale, or on anything on which the article is mounted for display or sale; or

(c) contained in or on anything that is sold, sent, delivered, transmit-ted or in any other manner whatsoever made available to a member of the public, shall be deemed to be a statement made to the public by, and only by, the person who had caused the statement to be so expressed, made or contained;

(2) permits the publication of any advertisement whether in any news-paper or otherwise, for the sale or supply at a bargain price, of goods or services that are not intended to be offered for sale or supply at the bargain price, or for a period that is, and in quantities that are, reasonable, having regard to the nature of the market in which the business is carried on, the nature and size of business, and the nature of the advertisement.

Explanation .—For the purpose of clause (2), "bargaining price" means—

(a) a price that is stated in any advertisement to be a bargain price, by reference to an ordinary price or otherwise, or

(b) a price that a person who reads, hears or sees the advertisement, would reasonably understand to be a bargain price having regard to the prices at which the product advertised or like products are ordinarily sold;

(3) permits—

(a) the offering of gifts, prizes or other items with the intention of not providing them as offered or creating impression that something is being given or offered free of charge when it is fully or partly covered by the amount charged in the transaction as a whole;

(b) the conduct of any contest, lottery, game of chance or skill, for the purpose of promoting, directly or indirectly, the sale, use or supply of any product or any business interest;

(3A) withholding from the participants of any scheme offering gifts, prizes or other items free of charge, on its closure the information about final results of the scheme.

Explanation. — For the purposes of this sub-clause, the participants of a scheme shall be deemed to have been informed of the final results of the scheme where such results are within a reasonable time, published, prominently in the same newspapers in which the scheme was originally advertised;

(4) permits the sale or supply of goods intended to be used, or are of a kind likely to be used, by consumers, knowing or having reason to believe that the goods do not comply with the standards prescribed by competent authority relating to performance, composition, contents, design, constructions, fin-ishing or packaging as are necessary to prevent or reduce the risk of injury to the person using the goods;

(5) permits the hoarding or destruction of goods, or refuses to sell the goods or to make them available for sale or to provide any service, if such hoarding or destruction or refusal raises or tends to raise or is intended to raise, the cost of those or other similar goods or services.

(6) manufacture of spurious goods or offering such goods for sale or adopts deceptive practices in the provision of services.

(2) Any reference in this Act to any other Act or provision thereof which is not in force in any area to which this Act applies shall be construed to have a reference to the corresponding Act or provision thereof in force in such area.

3. Act not in derogation of any other law.—The provisions of this Act shall be in addition to and not in derogation of the provisions of any other law for the time being in force.

CONSUMER PROTECTION COUNCILS

4. The Central Consumer Protection Council.—

(1) The Central Government *shall*, by notification, establish with effect from such date as it may specify in such notification, a Council to be known as the Central Consumer Protection Council (hereinafter referred to as the Central Council).

(2) The Central Council shall consist of the following members, namely:—

(a) the Minister in charge of the consumer affairs in the Central Government, who shall be its Chairman, and

(b) such number of other official or non-official members represent-ing such interests as may be prescribed.

5. Procedure for meetings of the Central Council.—(1) The Central Council shall meet as and when necessary, but at least one meeting of the Council shall be held every year.

(2) The Central Council shall meet at such time and place as the Chairman may think fit and shall observe such procedure in regard to the transaction of its business as may be prescribed.

6. Objects of the Central Council.—

The objects of the Central Council shall be to promote and protect the rights of the consumers such as,—

(a) the right to be protected against the marketing of goods and services which are hazardous to life and property;

(b) the right to be informed about the quality, quantity, potency, purity, standard and price of goods or services, as the case may be so as to protect the consumer against unfair trade practices;

(c) the right to be assured, wherever possible, access to a variety of goods and services at competitive prices;

(d) the right to be heard and to be assured that consumer's interests will receive due consideration at appropriate forums;

(e) the right to seek redressal against unfair trade practices or restrictive trade practices or unscrupulous exploitation of con-sumers; and

(f) the right to consumer education.

7. The State Consumer Protection Councils.-

(1) The State Government shall, by notification, establish with effect from such date as it may specify in such notification, a Council to be known as the Consumer Protection Council for..................... (hereinafter referred to as the State Council).

(2) The State Council shall consist of the following members, namely:—

(a) the Minister incharge of consumer affairs in the State Government who shall be its Chairman;

(b) such number of other official or non-official members representing such interests as may be prescribed by the State Government.

(c) such number of other official or non-official members, not exceeding ten, as may be nominated by the Central Government.

(3) The State Council shall meet as and when necessary but not less than two meetings shall be held every year.

(4) The State Council shall meet at such time and place as the Chairman may think fit and shall observe such procedure in regard to the transaction of its business as may be prescribed by the State Government.

8. Objects of the State Council. —

The objects of every State Council shall be to promote and protect within the State the rights of the consumers laid down in clauses (a) to (f) of section 6.

8A. (1) The State Government shall establish for every district, by notification, a council to be known as the District Consumer Protection Council with effect from such date as it may specify in such notification.

(2) The District Consumer Protection Council (hereinafter referred to as the District Council) shall consist of the following members, namely:—

(a) the Collector of the district (by whatever name called), who shall be its Chairman; and

(b) such number of other official and non-official members representing such interests as may be prescribed by the State Government.

(3) The District Council shall meet as and when necessary but not less than two meetings shall be held every year.

(4) The District Council shall meet at such time and place within the district as the Chairman may think fit and shall observe such procedure in regard to the transaction of its business as may be prescribed by the State Government.

8B. The objects of every District Council shall be to promote and protect within the district the rights of the consumers laid down in clauses (a) to (f) of section 6.

CONSUMER DISPUTES REDRESSAL AGENCIES

9. Establishment of Consumer Disputes Redressal Agencies. There shall be established for the purposes of this Act, the following agencies, namely:—

(a) a Consumer Disputes Redressal Forum to be known as the "District Forum" established by the State Government in each district of the State by notification: Provided that the State Government may, if it deems fit, establish more than one District Forum in a district.

(b) a Consumer Disputes Redressal Commission to be known as the "State Commission" established by the State Government in the State by notification; and

(c) a National Consumer Disputes Redressal Commission established by the Central Government by notification.

10. Composition of the District Forum. —

(1) Each District Forum shall consist of,—

(a) a person who is, or has been, or is qualified to be a District Judge, who shall be its President;

(b) two other members, one of whom shall be a woman, who shall have the following qualifications, namely:—

(i) be not less than thirty-five years of age,

(ii) possess a bachelor's degree from a recognised university,

(iii) be persons of ability, integrity and standing, and have adequate knowledge and experience of at least ten years in dealing with problems relating to economics, law, commerce, accountancy, industry, public affairs or administration:

Provided that a person shall be disqualified for appointment as a member if he—

(a) has been convicted and sentenced to imprisonment for an offence which, in the opinion of the state Government involves moral turpitude; or

(b) is an undischarged insolvent; or

(c) is of unsound mind and stands so declared by a competent court; or

(d) has been removed or dismissed from the service of the Government or a body corporate owned or controlled by the Government; or

(e) has, in the opinion of the state Government, such financial or other interest as is likely to affect prejudicially the discharge by him of his functions as a member; or

(f) has such other disqualifications as may be prescribed by the State Government;

(1A) Every appointment under sub-section (I) shall be made by the State Government on the recommendation of a selection committee consisting of the following, namely:—

(i)	the President of the State Commission	— Chairman.
(ii)	Secretary, Law Department of the State	— Member.
(iii)	Secretary incharge of the Department dealing with consumer affairs in the State	— Member.

Provided that where the President of the State Commission is, by reason of absence or otherwise, unable to act as Chairman of the Selection Committee, the State Government may refer the matter to the Chief Justice of the High Court for nominating a sitting Judge of that High Court to act as Chairman.

(2) Every member of the District Forum shall hold office for a term of five years or up to the age of sixty-five years, whichever is earlier:

Provided that a member shall be eligible for re-appointment for another term of five years or up to the age of sixty-five years, whichever is earlier, subject to the condition that he fulfills the qualifications and other conditions for appointment mentioned in clause (b) of sub-section (1) and such re-appointment is also made on the basis of the recommendation of the Selection Committee:

Provided further that a member may resign his office in writing under his hand addressed to the State Government and on such resignation being accepted, his office shall become vacant and may be filled by appointment of a person possessing any of the qualifications mentioned in sub-section (1) in relation to the category of the member who is required to be appointed under the provisions of sub-section (1A) in place of the person who has resigned:

Provided also that a person appointed as the President or as a member, before the commencement of the Consumer Protection (Amendment) Act, 2002, shall continue to hold such office as President or member, as the case may be, till the completion of his term.

(3) The salary or honorarium and other allowances payable to, and the other terms and conditions of service of the members of the District Forum shall be such as may be prescribed by the State Government.

Provided that the appointment of a member on whole-time basis shall be made by the State Government on the recommendation of the President of the State Commission taking into consideration such factors as may be prescribed including the work load of the District Forum.

11. Jurisdiction of the District Forum.—

(1) Subject to the other provisions of this Act, the District Forum shall have jurisdiction to entertain complaints where the value of the goods or services and the compensation, if any, claimed "does not exceed rupees twenty lakhs.

(2) A complaint shall be instituted in a District Forum within the local limits of whose jurisdiction,—

(a) the opposite party or each of the opposite parties, where there are more than one, at the time of the institution of the complaint, actually and voluntarily resides or carries on business or has a branch office or personally works for gain, or

(b) any of the opposite parties, where there are more than one, at the time of the institution of the complaint, actually and voluntarily resides, or carries on business or has a branch office, or personally works for gain, provided that in such case either the permission of the District Forum is given, or the opposite parties who do not reside, or carry on business or have a branch office, or personally work for gain, as the case may be, acquiesce in such institution; or

(c) the cause of action, wholly or in part, arises.

12. Manner in which complaint shall be made.—

(1) A complaint in relation to any goods sold or delivered or agreed to be sold or delivered or any service provided or agreed to be provided may be filed with a District Forum by –

(a) the consumer to whom such goods are sold or delivered or agreed to be sold or delivered or such service provided or agreed to be provided;

(b) any recognised consumer association whether the consumer to whom the goods sold or delivered or agreed to be sold or delivered or service provided or agreed to be provided is a member of such association or not;

(c) one or more consumers, where there are numerous consumers having the same interest, with the permission of the District Forum, on behalf of, or for the benefit of, all consumers so interested; or

(d) the Central Government or the State Government, as the case may be, either in its individual capacity or as a representative of interests of the consumers in general.

(2) Every complaint filed under sub-section (1) shall be accompanied with such amount of fee and payable in such manner as may be prescribed.

(3) On receipt of a complaint made under sub-section (1), the District Forum may, by order, allow the complaint to be proceeded with or rejected:

Provided that a complaint shall not be rejected under this section unless an opportunity of being heard has been given to the complainant: Provided further that the admissibility of the complaint shall ordinarily be decided within twenty-one days from the date on which the complaint was received.

(4) Where a complaint is allowed to be proceeded with under sub-section (3), the District Forum may proceed with the complaint in the manner provided under this Act:

Provided that where a complaint has been admitted by the District Forum, it shall not be transferred to any other court or tribunal or any authority set up by or under any other law for the time being in force.

Explanation. - For the purpose of this section "recognised consumer association" means any voluntary consumer association registered under the Companies Act, ***1956*** *or any other law for the time being in force".*

13. Procedure on admission of complaint. —

(1) The District Forum shall, on admission of a complaint, if it relates to any goods,—

(a) refer a copy of the admitted complaint, within twenty-one days from the date of its admission to the opposite party mentioned in the complaint directing him to give his version of the case within a period of thirty days or such extended period not exceeding fifteen days as may be granted by the District Forum;

(b) where the opposite party on receipt of a complaint referred to him under clause *(a)* denies or disputes the allegations contained in the complaint, or omits or fails to take any action to represent his case within the time given by the District Forum, the District Forum shall proceed to settle the consumer dispute in the manner specified in clauses (c) to (g);

(c) where the complaint alleges a defect in the goods which cannot be determined without proper analysis or test of the goods, the District Forum shall obtain a sample of the goods from the complainant, seal it and authenticate it in the manner prescribed and refer the sample so sealed to the appropriate laboratory along with a direction that such laboratory make an analysis or test, whichever may be necessary, with a view to finding out whether such goods suffer from any defect alleged in the complaint or from any other defect and to report its findings thereon to the District Forum within a period of forty-five days of the receipt of the reference or within such extended period as may be granted by the District Forum;

(d) before any sample of the goods is referred to any appropriate laboratory under clause (c), the District Forum may require the complainant to deposit to the credit of the Forum such fees as may be specified, for payment to the appropriate laboratory for carry-ing out the necessary analysis or test in relation to the goods in question;

(e) the District Forum shall remit the amount deposited to its credit under clause (d) to the appropriate laboratory to enable it to carry out the analysis or test mentioned in clause (c) and on receipt of the report from the appropriate laboratory, the District Forum shall forward a copy of the report along with such remarks as the District Forum may feel appropriate to the opposite party;

(f) if any of the parties disputes the correctness of the findings of the appropriate laboratory, or disputes the correctness of the meth-ods of analysis or test adopted by the appropriate laboratory, the District Forum shall require the opposite party or the complain-ant to submit in writing his objections in regard to the report made by the appropriate laboratory;

(g) the District Forum shall thereafter give a reasonable opportunity to the complainant as well as the opposite party of being heard as to the correctness or otherwise of the report made by the appro-priate laboratory and also as to the objection made in relation thereto under clause (*l*) and issue an appropriate order under section 14.

(2) the District Forum shall, if the complaint admitted by it under section 12 relates to goods in respect of which the procedure specified in sub-section (1) cannot be followed, or if the complaint relates to any services,—

(a) refer a copy of such complaint to the opposite party directing him to give his version of the case within a period of

thirty days or such extended period not exceeding fifteen days as may be granted by the District Forum;

(*b*) where the opposite party, on receipt of a copy of the complaint, referred to him under clause (*a*) denies or disputes the allegations contained in the complaint, or omits or fails to take any action to represent his case within the time given by the District Forum, the District Forum shall proceed to settle the consumer dispute,—

(i) on the basis of evidence brought to its notice by the complainant and the opposite party, where the opposite party denies or disputes the allegations contained in the complaint, or

(ii) ex parte on the basis of evidence brought to its notice by the complainant where the opposite party omits or fails to take any action to represent his case within the time given by the Forum.

(c) where the complainant fails to appear on the date of hearing before the District Forum, the District Forum may either dismiss the complaint for default or decide it on merits.

(3) No proceedings complying with the procedure laid down in sub-sections [1] and [2] shall be called in question in any court on the ground that the principles of natural justice have not been complied with.

(3A) Every complaint shall be heard as expeditiously as possible and endeavour shall be made to decide the complaint within a period of three months from the date of receipt of notice by opposite party where the complaint does not require analysis or testing of commodities and within five months if it requires analysis or testing of commodities:

Provided that no adjournment shall be ordinarily granted by the District Forum unless sufficient cause is shown and the reasons for grant of adjournment have been recorded in writing by the Forum:

Provided further that the District Forum shall make such orders as to the costs occasioned by the adjournment as may be provided in the regulations made under this Act.

Provided also that in the event of a complaint being disposed of after the period so specified, the District Forum shall record in writing, the reasons for the same at the time of disposing of the said complaint.

(3B) Where during the pendency of any proceeding before the District Forum, it appears to it necessary, it may pass such interim order as is just and proper in the facts and circumstances of the case.

(4) For the purposes of this section, the District Forum shall have the same powers as are vested in a civil court under Code of Civil Procedure, 1908 while trying a suit in respect of the following matters, namely:—

(i) the summoning and enforcing the attendance of any defendant or witness and examining the witness on oath;

(ii) the discovery and production of any document or other material object producible as evidence;

(iii) the reception of evidence on affidavits;

(iv) the requisitioning of the report of the concerned analysis or test from the appropriate laboratory or from any other relevant source;

(v) issuing of any commission for the examination of any witness, and

(vi) any other matter which may be prescribed.

(5) Every proceeding before the District Forum shall be deemed to be a judicial proceeding within the meaning of sections 193 and 228 of the Indian Code (45 of 1860), and the District Forum shall be deemed to be a civil court for the purposes of section 195, and Chapter XXVI of the Code of Criminal Procedure, 1973 (2 of 1974).

(6) Where the complainant is a consumer referred to in sub-clause (iv) of clause (b) of sub-section (1) of section 2, the provisions of rule 8 of Order I of the First Schedule to the Code of Civil Procedure, 1908 (5 of 1908) shall apply subject to the modification that every reference therein to a suit or decree shall be construed as a reference to a complaint or the order of the District Forum thereon.

(7) In the event of death of a complainant who is a consumer or of the opposite party against whom the complaint has been filed, the provisions of Order XXII of the First Schedule to the Code of Civil Procedure, 1908 (5 of 1908) shall apply subject to the modification that every reference therein to the plaintiff and the defendant shall be construed as reference to a complainant or the opposite party, as the case may be.

14. Finding of the District Forum. — (1) If, after the proceeding conducted under section 13, the District Forum is satisfied that the goods complained against suffer from any of the defects specified in the complaint or that any of the allegations contained in the complaint about the services are proved, it shall issue an order to the opposite party directing him to do one or more of the following things, namely:—

(a) to remove the defect pointed out by the appropriate laboratory from the goods in question;

(b) to replace the goods with new goods of similar description which shall be free from any defect;

(c) to return to the complainant the price, or, as the case may be, the charges paid by the complainant;

(d) to pay such amount as may be awarded by it as compensation to the consumer for any loss or injury suffered by the consumer due to the negligence of the opposite party.

Provided that the District Forum shall have the power to grant punitive damages in such circumstances as it deems fit;

(e) to remove the defects in goods or deficiencies in the services in question;

(f) to discontinue the unfair trade practice or the restrictive trade practice or not to repeat it;

(g) not to offer the hazardous goods for sale;

(h) to withdraw the hazardous goods from being offered for sale;

(ha)to cease manufacture of hazardous goods and to desist from offering services which are hazardous in nature;

(hb)to pay such sum as may be determined by it if it is of the opinion that loss or injury has been suffered by a large

number of consumers who are not identifiable conveniently: Provided that the minimum amount of sum so payable shall not be less than five per cent. of the value of such defective goods sold or service provided, as the case may be, to such consumers:

Provided further that the amount so obtained shall be credited in favour of such person and utilized in such manner as may be prescribed;

(hc)to issue corrective advertisement to neutralize the effect of misleading advertisement at the cost of the opposite party responsible for issuing such misleading advertisement;

(i) to provide for adequate costs to parties.

(2) Every proceeding referred to in sub-section (1) shall be conducted by the President of the District Forum and at least one member thereof sitting together:

Provided that where a member, for any reason, is unable to conduct a proceeding till it is completed, the President and the other member shall continue the proceeding from the stage at which it was last heard by the previous member.

(2A) Every order made by the District Forum under sub-section (1) shall be signed by its President and the member or members who conducted the proceeding:

Provided that where the proceeding is conducted by the President and one member and they differ on any point or points, they shall state the point or points on which they differ and refer the same to the other member for hearing on such point or points and the opinion of the majority shall be the order of the District Forum.

(3) Subject to the foregoing provisions, the procedure relating to the conduct of the meetings of the District Forum, its sittings and other matters shall be such as may be prescribed by the State Government.

15. Appeal. — Any person aggrieved by an order made by the District Forum may prefer an appeal against such order to the State Commission within a period of thirty days from the date of the order, in such form and manner as may be prescribed:

Provided that the State Commission may entertain an appeal after the expiry of the said period of thirty days if it is satisfied that there was sufficient cause for not finding it within that period.

Provided further that no appeal by a person, who is required to pay any amount in terms of an order of the District Forum, shall be entertained by the State Commission unless the appellant has deposited in the prescribed manner fifty per cent. of that amount or twenty-five thousand rupees, whichever is less:

16. Composition of the State Commission. — (1) Each State Com-mission shall consist of—

(a) a person who is or has been a Judge of a High Court, appointed by the State Government, who shall be its President:

Provided that no appointment under this clause shall be made except after consultation with the Chief Justice of the High Court;

(b) not less than two, and not more than such number of members, as may be prescribed, and one of whom shall be a woman, who shall have the following qualifications, namely:—

(i) be not less than thirty-five years of age;

(ii) possess a bachelor's degree from a recognised university; and

(iii) be persons of ability, integrity and standing, and have adequate knowledge and experience of at least ten years in dealing with problems relating to economics, law, commerce, accountancy, industry, public affairs or administration:

Provided that not more than fifty per cent. of the members shall be from amongst persons having a judicial background.

Explanation. — For the purposes of this clause, the expression "persons having judicial background" shall mean persons having knowledge and experience for at least a period of ten years as a presiding officer at the district level court or any tribunal at equivalent level:

Provided further that a person shall be disqualified for appointment as a member if he—

(a) has been convicted and sentenced to imprisonment for an offence which, in the opinion of the State Government, involves moral turpitude; or

(b) is an undischarged insolvent; or

(c) is of unsound mind and stands so declared by a competent court; or

(d) has been removed or dismissed from the service of the Government or a body corporate owned or controlled by the Government; or

(e) has, in the opinion of the State Government, such financial or other interest, as is likely to affect prejudicially the discharge by him of his functions as a member; or

(f) has such other disqualifications as may be prescribed by the State Government.

(1A) Every appointment under sub-section (1) shall be made by the State Government on the recommendation of a Selection Committee consisting of the following members, namely:—

(i) President of the State Commission — Chairman;

(ii) Secretary of the Law Department of the State — Member;

(iii) Secretary incharge of the Department dealing with Consumer Affairs in the State — Member:

Provided that where the President of the State Commission is, by reason of absence or otherwise, unable to act as Chairman of the Selection Committee, the State Government may refer the matter to the Chief Justice of the High Court for nominating a sitting Judge of that High Court to act as Chairman.

(1B)(i) The jurisdiction, powers and authority of the State Commission may be exercised by Benches thereof.

(ii) A Bench may be constituted by the President with one or more members as the President may deem fit.

(iii) If the members of a Bench differ in opinion on any point, the points shall be decided according to the opinion of the majority, if there is a majority, but if the Members are

equally divided, they shall state the point or points on which they differ, and make a reference to the President who shall either hear the point or points himself or refer the case for hearing on such point or points by one or more or the other members and such point or points shall be decided according to the opinion of the majority of the members who have heard the case, including those who first heard it.

(2) The salary or honorarium and other allowances payable to, and the other terms and conditions of service of, the members of the State Commission shall be such as may be prescribed by the State Government.

Provided that the appointment of a member on whole-time basis shall be made by the State Government on the recommendation of the President of the State Commission taking into consideration such factors as may be prescribed including the work load of the State Commission.

(3) Every member of the State Commission shall hold office for a term of five years or up to the age of sixty-seven years, whichever is earlier:

Provided that a member shall be eligible for re-appointment for another term of five years or up to the age of sixty-seven years, whichever is earlier, subject to the condition that he fulfills the qualifications and other conditions for appointment mentioned in clause (b) of sub-section (1) and such re-appointment is made on the basis of the recommendation of the Selection Committee:

Provided further that a person appointed as a President of the State Commission shall also be eligible for re-appointment in the manner provided in clause (a) of sub-section (1) of this section: Provided also that a member may resign his office in writing under his hand addressed to the State Government and on such resignation being accepted, his office shall become vacant and may be filled by appointment of a person possessing any of the qualifications mentioned in sub-section (1) in relation to the category of the member who is required to be appointed under the provisions of sub-section (1A) in place of the person who has resigned.

(4) Notwithstanding anything contained in sub-section (3), a person appointed as the President or as a member, before the commencement of the Consumer Protection (Amendment) Act, 2002, shall continue to hold such office as President or member, as the case may be, till the completion of his term.

17. Jurisdiction of the State Commission. — *(1)* Subject to the other provisions of this Act, the State Commission shall have jurisdiction—

(a) to entertain—

(i) complaints where the value of the goods or services and compensation, if any, claimed exceeds rupees *twenty lakhs* but does not exceed rupees *one crore*; and

(ii) appeals against the orders of any District Forum within the State; and

(b) to call for the records and pass appropriate orders in any con-sumer dispute which is pending before or has been decided by any District Forum within the State, where it appears to the State Commission that such District Forum has exercised a jurisdiction not vested in it by law, or has failed to exercise a jurisdiction so vested or has acted in exercise of its jurisdiction illegally or with material irregularity.

(2) A complaint shall be instituted in a State Commission within the limits of whose jurisdiction,—

(a) the opposite party or each of the opposite parties, where there are more than one, at the time of the institution of the complaint, actually and voluntarily resides or carries on business or has a branch office or personally works for gain; or

(b) any of the opposite parties, where there are more than one, at the time of the institution of the complaint, actually and voluntarily resides, or carries on business or has a branch office or personally works for gain, provided that in such case either the permission of the State Commission is given or the opposite parties who do not reside or carry on business or have a branch office or personally work for gain, as the case may be, acquiesce in such institution; or

(c) the cause of action, wholly or in part, arises.

17A. Transfer of cases. - On the application of the complainant or of its own motion, the State Commission may, at any stage of the proceeding, transfer any complaint pending before the District Forum to another District Forum within the State if the interest of justice so requires.

17B. Circuit Benches.-The State Commission shall ordinarily function in the State Capital but may perform its functions at such other place as the State Government may, in consultation with the State Commission, notify in the Official Gazette, from time to time.

18. Procedure applicable to State Commissions.—The provisions of Sections 12, 13 and 14 and the rules made thereunder for the disposal of complaints by the District Forum shall, with such modifications as may be necessary, be applicable to the disposal of disputes by the State Commission.

(18A. Omitted)

19. Appeals.—Any person aggrieved by an order made by the State Commission in exercise of its powers conferred by sub-clause (i) of clause (a) of section 17 may prefer an appeal against such order to the National Commission within a period of thirty days from the date of the order in such form and manner as may be prescribed:

Provided that the National Commission may entertain an appeal after the expiry of the said period of thirty days if it is satisfied that there was sufficient cause for not filing it within that period.

Provided further that no appeal by a person, who is required to pay any amount in terms of an order of the State Commission, shall be entertained by the National Commission unless the appellant has deposited in the prescribed manner fifty per cent. of the amount or rupees thirty-five thousand, whichever is less:

19A. Hearing of Appeal - An appeal filed before the State Commission or the National Commission shall be heard as expeditiously as possible and an endeavour shall be made to finally dispose of the appeal within a period of ninety days from the date of its admission: Provided that no adjournment shall be ordinarily granted by the State Commission or the National

Commission, as the case may be, unless sufficient cause is shown and the reasons for grant of adjournment have been recorded in writing by such Commission:

Provided further that the State Commission or the National Commission, as the case may be, shall make such orders as to the costs occasioned by the adjournment as may be provided in the regulations made under this Act.

Provided also that in the event of an appeal being disposed of after the period so specified, the State Commission or, the National Commission, as the case may be, shall record in writing the reasons for the same at the time of disposing of the said appeal.

20. Composition of the National Commission.—(1) The National Commission shall consist of—

(a) a person who is or has been a Judge of the Supreme Court, to be appointed by the Central Government, who shall be its President;

Provided that no appointment under this clause shall be made except after consultation with the Chief Justice of India;

(b) not less than four, and not more than such number of members, as may be prescribed, and one of whom shall be a woman, who shall have the following qualifications, namely:—

(i) be not less than thirty-five years of age;

(ii) possess a bachelor's degree from a recognised university; and

(iii) be persons of ability, integrity and standing and have adequate knowledge and experience of at least ten years in dealing with problems relating to economics, law, commerce, accountancy, industry, public affairs or administration:

Provided that not more than fifty per cent. of the members shall be from amongst the persons having a judicial background.

Explanation. — For the purposes of this clause, the expression "persons having judicial background" shall mean persons having knowledge and experience for at least a period of ten years as a presiding officer at the district level court or any tribunal at equivalent level:

Provided further that a person shall be disqualified for appointment if he—

(a) has been convicted and sentenced to imprisonment for an offence which, in the opinion of the Central Government, involves moral turpitude; or

(b) is an undischarged insolvent; or

(c) is of unsound mind and stands so declared by a competent court; or

(d) has been removed or dismissed from the service of the Government or a body corporate owned or controlled by the Government; or

(e) has in the opinion of the Central Government such financial or other interest as is likely to affect prejudicially the discharge by him of his functions as a member; or

(f) has such other disqualifications as may be prescribed by the Central Government :

Provided also that every appointment under this clause shall be made by the Central Government on the recommendation of a selection committee consisting of the following, namely:—

(a) a person who is a Judge of the Supreme Court, to be nominated by the Chief Justice of India — Chairman;

(b) the Secretary in the Department of Legal Affairs in the Government of India — Member;

(c) Secretary of the Department dealing with consumer affairs in the Government of India — Member.;

(1A)(i) The jurisdiction, powers and authority of the National Commission may be exercised by Benches thereof.

(ii) A Bench may be constituted by the President with one or more members as the President may deem fit.

(iii) if the Members of a Bench differ in opinion on any point, the points shall be decided according to the opinion of

the majority, if there is a majority, but if the members are equally divided, they shall state the point or points on which they differ, and make a reference to the President who shall either hear the point or points himself or refer the case for hearing on such point or points by one or more or the other Members and such point or points shall be decided according to the opinion of the majority of the Members who have heard the case, including those who first heard it.

(2) The salary or honorarium and other allowances payable to and the other terms and conditions of service of the members of the National Commission shall be such as may be prescribed by the Central Government.

(3) Every member of the National Commission shall hold office for a term of five years or up to the age of seventy years, whichever is earlier: Provided that a member shall be eligible for re-appointment for another term of five years or up to the age of seventy years, whichever is earlier, subject to the condition that he fulfills the qualifications and other conditions for appointment mentioned in clause (b) of sub-section (1) and such re-appointment is made on the basis of the recommendation of the Selection Committee:

Provided further that a person appointed as a President of the National Commission shall also be eligible for re-appointment in the manner provided in clause (a) of sub-section (1) : Provided also that a member may resign his office in writing under his hand addressed to the Central Government and on such resignation being accepted, his office shall become vacant and may be filled by appointment of a person possessing any of the qualifications mentioned in sub-section (1) in relation to the category of the member who is required to be appointed under the provisions of sub-section (1A) in place of the person who has resigned.

(4) Notwithstanding anything contained in sub-section (3), a person appointed as a President or as a member before the commencement of the Consumer Protection (Amendment) Act, 2002 shall continue to hold such office as President or member, as the case may be, till the completion of his term.

21. Jurisdiction of the National Commission. — Subject to the other provisions of this Act, the National Commission shall have jurisdiction—

(a) to entertain—

(i) complaints where the value of the goods or services and compensation, if any, claimed exceeds rupees *one crore*; and

(ii) appeals against the orders of any State Commission; and

(b) to call for the records and pass appropriate orders in any con-sumer dispute which is pending before or has been decided by any State Commission where it appears to the National Commission that such State Commission has exercised a jurisdiction not vested in it by law, or has failed to exercise a jurisdiction so vested, or has acted in the exercise of its jurisdiction illegally or with material irregularity.

22. Power of and procedure applicable to the National Commission. — *(1) The provisions of sections 12, 13 and 14 and the rules made thereunder for the disposal of complaints by the District Forum shall, with such modifications as may be considered necessary by the Commission, be applicable to the disposal of disputes by the National Commission.*

(2) Without prejudice to the provisions contained in sub-section (1), the National Commission shall have the power to review any order made by it, when there is an error apparent on the face of record.

22A. Power to set aside ex parte orders. - Where an order is passed by the National Commission ex parte against the opposite party or a complainant, as the case may be, the aggrieved party may apply to the Commission to set aside the said order in the interest of justice.

22B. Transfer of cases - On the application of the complainant or of its own motion, the National Commission may, at any stage of the proceeding, in the interest of justice, transfer any complaint pending before the District Forum of one State to a District Forum of another State or before one State Commission to another State Commission.

22C. Circuit Benches - The National Commission shall ordinarily function at New Delhi and perform its functions at such other place as the Central Government may, in consultation with the National Commission, notify in the Official Gazette, from time to time.

22D. Vacancy in the Office of the President - When the office of President of a District Forum, State Commission, or of the National Commission, as the case may be, is vacant or a person occupying such office is, by reason of absence or otherwise, unable to perform the duties of his office, these shall be performed by the senior-most member of the District Forum, the State Commission or of the National Commission, as the case may be:

Provided that where a retired Judge of a High Court is a member of the National Commission, such member or where the number of such members is more than one, the senior-most person among such members, shall preside over the National Commission in the absence of President of that Commission.

23. Appeal. — Any person, aggrieved by an order made by the National Commission in exercise of its powers conferred by sub-clause (i) of clause *(a)* of section 21, may prefer an appeal against such order of the Supreme Court within a period of thirty days from the date of the order: Provided that the Supreme Court may entertain an appeal after the expiry of the said period of thirty days if it is satisfied that there was sufficient cause for not filing it within that period. Provided further that no appeal by a person who is required to pay any amount in terms of an order of the National Commission shall be entertained by the Supreme Court unless that person has deposited in the prescribed manner fifty per cent. of that amount or rupees fifty thousand, whichever is less.

24. Finality of orders. — Every order of a District Forum, the State Commission or the National Commission shall, if no appeal has been preferred against such order under the provisions of this Act, be final.

24A. Limitation period. - (1) The District Forum, the State Commis-sion or the National Commission shall not admit a complaint unless it is filed within two years from the date on which the cause of action has arisen.

(2) Notwithstanding anything contained in sub-section (1), a complaint may be entertained after the period specified in sub-section (l), if the complainant satisfies the District Forum, the State Commission or the National Commission, as the case may be, that he had sufficient cause for not filing the complaint within such period: Provided that no such complaint shall be entertained unless the National Commission, the State Commission or the District Forum, as the case may be, records its reasons for condoning such delay.

24B. Administrative Control.—(1) The National Commission shall have administrative control over all the State Commissions in the following matters, namely:—

(i) calling for periodical return regarding the institution, disposal pendency of cases;

(ii) issuance of instructions regarding adoption of uniform pro-cedure in the hearing of matters, prior service of copies of documents produced by one party to the opposite parties, furnishing of English translation of judgments written in any language, speedy grant of copies of documents;

(iii) generally overseeing the functioning of the State Commis-sions or the District Fora to ensure that the objects and purposes of the Act are best served without in any way interfering with their *quasi-judicial* freedom.

(2) The State Commission shall have administrative control over all the District Fora within its jurisdiction in all matters referred to in sub-section (1).

25. Enforcement of orders of the District Forum, the State Commission or the National Commission. — (1) Where an interim order made under this Act, is not complied with the District Forum or the State Commission or the National Commission, as the case may be, may order the property of the person, not complying with such order to be attached.

(2) No attachment made under sub-section (1) shall remain in force for more than three months at the end of which, if the non-compliance continues, the property attached may be sold

and out of the proceeds thereof, the District Forum or the State Commission or the National Commission may award such damages as it thinks fit to the complainant and shall pay the balance, if any, to the party entitled thereto.

(3) Where any amount is due from any person under an order made by a District Forum, State Commission or the National Commission, as the case may be, the person entitled to the amount may make an application to the District Forum, the State Commission or the National Commission, as the case may be, and such District Forum or the State Commission or the National Commission may issue a certificate for the said amount to the Collector of the district (by whatever name called) and the Collector shall proceed to recover the amount in the same manner as arrears of land revenue.

26. Dismissal of frivolous or vexatious complaints. — Where a complaint instituted before the District Forum, the State Commission or as the case may be, the National Commission, is found to be frivolous or vexatious, it shall, for reasons to be recorded in writing, dismiss the complaint and make an order that the complainant shall pay to the opposite party such cost, not exceeding ten thousand rupees, as may be specified in the order

27. Penalties. — *(1)* Where a trader or a person against whom a complaint is made or the complainant fails or omits to comply with any order made by the District Forum, the State Commission or the National Commission, as the case may be, such trader or person or complainant shall be punishable with imprisonment for a term which shall not be less than one month but which may extend to three years, or with fine which shall not be less than two thousands rupees but which may extend to ten thousand rupees, or with both:

(2) Notwithstanding anything contained in the Code of Criminal Procedure, 1973, (2 of 1974), the District Forum or the State Commission or the National Commission, as the case may be, shall have the power of a Judicial Magistrate of the first class for the trial of offences under this Act, and on such conferment of powers, the District Forum or the State Commission or the National Commission, as the case may be,

on whom the powers are so conferred, shall be deemed to be a Judicial Magistrate of the first class for the purpose of the Code of Criminal Procedure, 1973 (2 of 1974).

(3) All offences under this Act may be tried summarily by the District Forum or the State Commission or the National Commission, as the case may be.

27A. Appeal against order passed under section 27 - (1) Notwithstanding anything contained in the Code of Criminal Procedure, 1973 (2 of 1974), an appeal under section 27, both on facts and on law, shall lie from -

(a) the order made by the District Forum to the State Commission ;

(b) the order made by the State Commission to the National Commission; and

(c) the order made by the National Commission to the Supreme Court.

(2) Except as aforesaid, no appeal shall lie to any court from any order of a District Forum or a State Commission or the National Commission.

(3) Every appeal under this section shall be preferred within a period of thirty days from the date of an order of a District Forum or a State Commission or, as the case may be, the National Commission :

Provided that the State Commission or the National Commission or the Supreme Court, as the case may be, may entertain an appeal after the expiry of the said period of thirty days, if, it is satisfied that the appellant had sufficient cause for not preferring the appeal within the period of thirty days.

MISCELLANEOUS

28. Protection of action taken in good faith. — No suit, prosecution or other legal proceedings shall lie against the members of the District Forum, the State Commission or the National Commission or any officer or person acting under the direction of the District Forum, the State Commission or the National Commission for executing any order made by it or in respect of anything which is in good faith done or intended to

be done by such member, officer or person under this Act or under any rule or order made thereunder.

28A. Service of notice, etc. - (1) All notices required by this Act to be served shall be served in the manner hereinafter mentioned in sub-section (2).

(2) The service of notices may be made by delivering or transmitting a copy thereof by registered post acknowledgment due addressed to opposite party against whom complaint is made or to the complainant by speed post or by such courier service as are approved by the District Forum, the State Commission or the National Commission, as the case may be, or by any other means of transmission of documents (including FAX message).

(3) When an acknowledgment or any other receipt purporting to be signed by the opposite party or his agent or by the complainant is received by the District Forum, the State Commission or the National Commission, as the case may be, or postal article containing the notice is received back by such District Forum, State Commission or the National Commission, with an endorsement purporting to have been made by a postal employee or by any person authorized by the courier service to the effect that the opposite party or his agent or complainant had refused to take delivery of the postal article containing the notice or had refused to accept the notice by any other means specified in sub- section (2) when tendered or transmitted to him, the District Forum or the State Commission or the National Commission, as the case may be, shall declare that the notice had been duly served on the opposite party or to the complainant

Provided that where the notice was properly addressed, pre-paid and duly sent by registered post acknowledgment due, a declaration referred to in this sub-section shall be made notwithstanding the fact that the acknowledgment has been lost or mislaid, or for any other reason, has not been received by the District Forum, the State Commission or the National Commission, as the case may be, within thirty days from the date of issue of notice.

(4) All notices required to be served on an opposite party or to complainant shall be deemed to be sufficiently served, if

addressed in the case of the opposite party to the place where business or profession is carried and in case of complainant, the place where such person actually and voluntarily resides.

29. Power to remove difficulties.—(l) If any difficulty arises in giving effect to the provisions of this Act, the (Central Government may, by order in the official Gazette, make such provisions not inconsistent with the provisions of this Act as appear to it to be necessary or expedient for removing the difficulty : Provided that no such order shall be made after the expiry of a period of two years from the commencement of this Act.

(2) Every order made under this section shall, as soon as may be after it is made be laid before each House of Parliament

(3) If any difficulty arises in giving effect to the provisions of the Consumer Protection (Amendment) Act, 2002, the Central Government may, by order, do anything not inconsistent with such provisions for the purpose of removing the difficulty:

Provided that no such order shall be made after the expiry of a period of two years from the commencement of the Consumer Protection (Amendment) Act, 2002.

(4) Every order made under sub-section (3) shall be laid before each House of Parliament.

29A. Vacancies or defects in appointment not to invalidate orders.—No act or proceeding of the District Forum, the State Commission or the National Commission shall be invalid by reason only of the existence of any vacancy amongst its member or any defect in the constitution thereof.

30. Power to make rules. - (1) The Central Government may, by notification, make rules for carrying out the provisions contained in clause (a) of sub-section (1) of section 2, clause (b) of sub-section (2) of section 4, sub-section (2) of section 5, sub-section (2) of section 12, clause (vi) of sub-section (4) of section 13, clause (hb) of sub-section (1) of section 14, section 19, clause (b) of sub-section (1) and sub-section (2) of section 20, section 22 and section 23 of this Act.

(2) The State Government may, by notification, make rules for carrying out the provisions contained in clause (b) of sub-

section (2) and sub-section (4) of section 7, clause (b) of sub-section (2) and sub-section (4) of section 8A, clause (b) of sub-section (1) and sub-section (3) of section 10, clause (c) of sub-section (1) of section 13 clause (hb) of sub-section (1) and sub-section (3) of section 14, section 15 and clause (b) of sub-section (1) and sub-section (2) of section 16 of this Act.

30A. Power of the National Commission to make regulations - (1) The National Commission may, with the previous approval of the Central Government, by notification, make regulations not inconsistent with this Act to provide for all matters for which provision is necessary or expedient for the purpose of giving effect to the provisions of this Act.

(2) In particular and without prejudice to the generality of the foregoing power, such regulations may make provisions for the cost of adjournment of any proceeding before the District Forum, the State Commission or the National Commission, as the case may be, which a party may be ordered to pay.

31. Rules and regulations to be laid before each House of Parliament - (1) Every rule and every regulation made under this Act shall be laid, as soon as may be after it is made, before each House of Parliament, while it is in session, for a total period of thirty days which may be comprised in one session or in two or more successive sessions, and if, before the expiry of the session immediately following the session or the successive sessions aforesaid, both Houses agree in making any modification in the rule or regulation or both Houses agree that the rule or regulation should not be made, the rule or regulation shall thereafter have effect only in such modified form or be of no effect, as the case may be; so, however, that any such modification or annulment shall be without prejudice to the validity of anything previously done under that rule or regulation.

(2) Every rule made by a State Government under this Act shall be laid as soon as may be after it is made, before the State Legislature.

3

Consumer Protection and National Consumer Disputes Redressal Commission

The Consumer Protection Act, 1986 (here in after to be referred to as the 'Act') is one of the benevolent social legislation intended to protect the large body of consumers from exploitation. The Act has come as a panacea for consumers all over the country and has assumed the shape of practically the most important legislation enacted in the country during the last few years. It has become the vehicle for enabling people to secure speedy and in-expensive redressal of their grievances. With the enactment of this law, consumers now feel that they are in a position to declare "sellers beware" whereas previously the consumers were at the receiving end and generally told "buyers beware".

The Act postulates establishment of Central Consumer Protection Council and the State Consumer Protection Councils for the purpose of spreading consumer awareness. Central Council is headed by Minster, incharge of the Consumer Affairs in the Central Government and in the State it is the Minister incharge of the Consumer Affairs in the State Government who heads State Council.

To provide cheap, speedy and simple redressal to consumer disputes, quasi-judicial machinery is set up at each District, State and National levels called District Forums, State Consumer Disputes Redressal Commission and National Consumer Disputes Redressal Commission respectively. At present, there are 604 District Forums, 35 State Commissions with apex body as a National Consumer Disputes Redressal Commission (NCDRC) having its office at Janpath Bhawan, A Wing, 5th Floor, Janpath, New Delhi.

The District Forums are headed by the person who is or has been or is eligible to be appointed as a District Judge and the State Commissions are headed by a person who is or has been a Judge of High Court.

National Commission was constituted in the year, 1988. It is headed by a sitting or retired Judge of the Supreme Court of India. National Commission is presently headed by Hon'ble Mr. Justice M.B. Shah, former Judge of the Supreme Court of India as President and having eight Members, viz. Mrs. Rajyalakshmi Rao, Mr. B.K. Taimni, Hon'ble Mr. Justice K. S. Gupta, Hon'ble Mr. Justice S.N. Kapoor, Dr. P. D. Shenoy, Mr. Anupam Dasgupta, Mr. S. K. Naik & Hon'ble Justice R.C. Jain. .

The provisions of this Act cover 'Products' as well as 'Services'. The products are those which are manufactured or produced and sold to consumers through wholesalers and retailers. The services are of the nature of transport, telephones, electricity, constructions, banking, insurance, medical treatment etc. etc. The services are, by and large, include those provided by professionals such as Doctors, Engineers, Architects, Lawyers etc.

A written complaint, as amended by Consumer Protection (Amendment) Act, 2002, can be filed before the District Consumer Forum (upto Rupees twenty lakhs), State Commission (upto Rupees One crore), National Commission (above Rrupees One crore) in relation to a product or in respect of a service, but does not include rendering of any service free of cost or under a contract of personal service. The service can be of any description, the illustrations given above are only indicative and not exhaustive.

The Consumer Protection Act is an alternative and cheapest remedy already available to the aggrieved persons/consumers by way of civil suit. In the complaint/appeal/petition submitted under the Act, a consumer is not required to pay any court fees or even process fee.

Proceedings are summary in nature and endeavour is made to grant relief to the parties in the quickest possible time keeping in mind the spirit of the Act which provides for disposal of the cases within possible time schedule prescribed under the Act.

If a consumer is not satisfied by the decision of the District Forum, he can challenge the same before the State Commission and against the order of the State Commission a consumer can come to the National Commission.

In order to attain the objects of the Consumer Protection Act, the National Commission has also been conferred with the powers of administrative control over all the State Commissions by calling for periodical returns regarding the institution, disposal and pendency of cases.

National Commission is empowered to issue instructions regarding, (1) adoption of uniform procedure in the hearing of the matters; (2) prior service of copies of documents produced by one party to the opposite parties; (3) speedy grant of copies of documents; and (4) generally over-seeing the functioning of the State Commissions or the District Forums to ensure that the objects and purposes of the Act are best served without in any way interfering with their quasi-judicial freedom.

The Registry of the National Commission, is on 7th Floor, 'B' Wing, Janpath Bhawan, Janpath, New Delhi which remains open on all working days except Sundays, Saturdays and Central Govt. holidays. For any enquiry from the Registry of the National Commission, one can contact on Telephone Nos. 011-23712109, 23712459, 23389248 and Fax No. 23712456. The filing timings are from 10.00 A.M. to 5.00 P.M. Every matter filed with the Registry in person is listed on 7th day of its filing for admission before the National Commission. Functioning of District Forum, State Commission and National Commission is consumer friendly, and thus consumer can file complaint and can address arguments in person. In genuine cases where the parties are unable to engage the services of an advocate Bar Association of NCDRC also provides legal aid to needy.

COMMENTARY ON CONSUMER PROTECTION ACT

1.1 The moment a person comes into this would, he starts consum-ing. He needs clothes, milk, oil, soap, water, and many more things and these needs keep taking one form or the other all along his life. Thus we all are consumers in the literal sense of the term. When we approach the market as a consumer, we expect value for money, *i.e.,* right quality, right quantity, right prices, information about the mode of use, etc. But there may be instances where a consumer is harassed or cheated.

The Government understood the need to protect consumers from unscrupulous suppliers, and several laws have been made for this purpose. We have the Indian Contract Act, the Sale of Goods Act, the Dangerous Drugs Act, the Agricultural Produce (Grading and Marketing) Act, the Indian Standards Institution (Certification Marks) Act, the Prevention of Food Adulteration Act, the Stand-ards of Weights and Measures Act, etc. which to some extent protect consumer interests. However, these laws require the con-sumer to initiate action by way of a civil suit involving lengthy legal process which is very expensive and time consuming.

The Consumer Protection Act, 1986 was enacted to provide a sim-pler and quicker access to redressal of consumer grievances. The Act for the first time introduced the concept of 'consumer' and conferred express additional rights on him. It is interesting to note that the Act doesn't seek to protect every consumer within the literal meaning of the term. The protection is meant for the person who fits in the definition of 'consumer' given by the Act.

Now we understand that the Consumer Protection Act provides means to protect consumers from getting cheated or harassed by suppli-ers. The question arises how a consumer will seek protection ? The answer is the Act has provided a machinery whereby consumers can file their complaints which will be entertained by the Con-sumer Forums with special powers so that action can be taken against erring suppliers and the possible compensation may be awarded to consumer for the hardships he has undergone. No court fee is required to be paid to these forums and there is no need to engage a lawyer to present the case.

Following chapter entails a discussion on who is a consumer under the Act, what are the things which can be complained against, when and by whom a complaint can be made and what are the relief available to consumers.

Who is a Consumer

1.2 Section 2(*d*) of the Consumer Protection Act says that consum-er means any person who—

(*i*) buys any goods for a consideration which has been paid or promised or partly paid and partly promised, or under any system of deferred payment, and includes any user of such goods other than the person who buys such goods for consideration paid or promised or partly paid or partly promised, or under any system of deferred payment when such use is made with the approv-al of such person, but does not include a person who obtains such goods for resale or for any commercial purpose; or

(*ii*) hires or avails of any services for a consideration which has been paid or promised or partly paid and partly prom-ised, or under any system of deferred payment, and includes any beneficiary of such services other than the person who hires or avails of the services for consideration paid or promised, or partly paid and partly promised, or under any system of deferred pay-ment, when such services are availed of with the approval of the first mentioned person;

Explanation.—For the purposes of the sub-clause (*i*), "commercial purpose" does not include use by a consumer of goods bought and used by him exclusively for the purpose of earning his liveli-hood, by means of self-employment.

1.2-1 *Consumer of goods* - The provision reveals that a person claiming himself as a consumer of goods should satisfy that—

1-2-1a THE GOODS ARE BOUGHT FOR CONSIDERATION - *There must be a sale transaction between a seller and a buyer; the sale must be of goods; the buying of goods must be for consideration.* The terms sale, goods, and consideration have not been defined in the Consumer Protection Act. The meaning of the terms 'sale', and 'goods' is to be construed according to the Sale of Goods Act, and the meaning of the term 'consideration' is to be construed according to the Indian Contract Act.

1-2-1b ANY PERSON WHO USE THE GOODS WITH THE APPROVAL OF THE BUYER IS A CONSUMER - When a person buys goods, they may be used by his family members, relatives and friends. Any person who is making actual use of the goods may come across the defects in goods. Thus the law construe users of the goods as consumers although they may not be buyers at the same time. The words "....with the approval of the buyer" in the definition denotes that the user of the goods should be a rightful user.

Example : A purchased a scooter which was in B's possession from the date of purchase. B was using it and taking it to the seller for repairs and service from time to time. Later on B had a complaint regarding the scooter. He sued the seller. The seller pleaded that since B did not buy the scooter, he was not a con-sumer under the Act. The Delhi State Commission held that B, the complainant was using it with the approval of A, the buyer, and therefore he was consumer under the Act. [*Dinesh Bhagat* v. *Bajaj Auto Ltd.* (1992) III CPJ 272]

Note : This is an exception to the general rule of law that a stranger to a contract cannot sue.

1-2-1c ANY PERSON WHO OBTAINS THE GOODS FOR 'RESALE' OR COMMER-CIAL PURPOSES' IS NOT A CONSUMER - The term 'for resale' implies that the goods are brought for the purpose of selling them, and the expression 'for commercial purpose' is intended to cover cases other than those of resale of goods. When goods are bought to resell or commercially exploit them, such buyer or user is not a consumer under the Act.

Examples :

1. A jeep was purchased to run it as a taxi. The question was whether the buyer of the jeep was a consumer under the Act. The Rajasthan State Commission held that to use the jeep as a taxi with the object to earn profits was a commercial purpose, and therefore, the buyer/user was not a consumer within the meaning of the Act. [*Smt. Pushpa Meena* v. *Shah Enterprises (Rajasthan) Ltd.* (1991) 1 CPR 229].
2. L Ltd. purchased a computer system from Z. The computer system was giving constant trouble and Z was not attending it properly. L Ltd. filed a complaint against Z with the National Commission. Z contended that L Ltd. was not a consumer under the Act because computer system was used for commercial purposes. L Ltd. argued that computer system was not directly used of commer-cial purposes rather it was used to facilitate the work of the company. The Commission rejected the argument on the grounds that the system made part of the assets of the company, and its ex-penses were met by it out of business income. Thus the said purchase was a purchase for commercial purposes and L Ltd. was held not to be a consumer under the Act.

One thing is plain and clear from the decided cases that what is important to decide is - Whether a particular good is used for commercial purposes. If it is the buyer/user is not a consumer, and if it is not - the buyer/user is a consumer.

1.2-1d PERSON BUYING GOODS FOR SELF EMPLOYMENT IS A CONSUMER - When goods are bought for commercial purposes and such purchase satisfy the following criteria :

- the goods are used by the buyer himself;
- exclusively for the purpose of earning his livelihood;
- by means of self-employment,then such use would not be termed as use for commercial purposes under the Act, and the user is recognised as a consumer.

Examples :

1. A buys a truck for plying it as a public carrier by himself, A is a consumer.
2. A buys a truck and hires a driver to ply it, A is not a consumer.
3. A has one cloth shop. He starts another business of a photocopier and buys a photocopy machine therefor. He hasn't bought this machine exclusively for the purpose of earning live-lihood. He is not a consumer under the Act.

Note : That this is an exception to the rule that a buyer of commercial goods is not a consumer under the Act.

The intention of the legislature is to exclude big business houses carrying on business with profit motive from the purview of the Act. At the same time it is pertinent to save the inter-ests of small consumers who buy goods for self employment to earn their livelihood, like a rickshaw puller buying rickshaw for self employment, or a farmer purchasing fertilizer for his crops, or a taxi driver buying a car to run it as a taxi, etc.

Example : A was running a small type institute to earn his live-lihood. He purchased a photocopy machine-canon NP 150. It proved defective. He sued the seller who contended that A is not a consumer under the Act as he purchased the photocopier for com-mercial use. The Commission held that by no stretch of imagina-tion it can be said that the photocopier would bring large scale profits to A. It was a part of his small scale enterprise. He was construed as consumer under the Act.

However, if such a buyer takes assistance of two or more persons to help him in operating the vehicle or machine, etc., he does not cease to be a consumer.

Examples :

1. A buys a truck, ply it himself and hires a cleaner who accompany him all the time and at times drives also when A is busy otherwise, A is a consumer.
2. P, an eye surgeon, purchased a machine from R for the hospital run by him. The machine was found to be a

defective one. R contended that P was not a consumer under the Act as the ma-chine was bought for commercial purposes. The National Commis-sion rejected this contention and held that P is a medical prac-titioner, a professional working by way of self employment by using his knowledge and skill to earn his livelihood. It was not proved by any evidence that P is running a huge hospital. Thus the purchase of machinery is in the nature of self employment. [*Rampion Pharmaceuticals* v. *Dr. Preetam Shah* (1997) I CPJ 23 (NCDRC)].

1.2-2 *Consumer of services* - A person is a consumer of services if he satisfy the following criteria :

1.2-2a SERVICES ARE HIRED OR AVAILED OF - The term 'hired' has not been defined under the Act. Its Dictionary meaning is - to procure the use of services at a price. Thus the term 'hire' has also been used in the sense of 'avail' or 'use'. Accordingly it may be understood that consumer means any person who avails or uses any service.

Example : A goes to a doctor to get himself treated for a frac-ture. Here A is hiring the services of the doctor. Thus he is a consumer.

What constitutes hiring has been an issue to be dealt with in many consumer disputes. If it is established that a particular act constitutes hiring of service, the transaction falls within the net of the Consumer Protection Act, and *vice-versa.*

Examples :

1. A passenger getting railway reservation after payment is hiring service for consideration.
2. A landlord neglected and refused to provide the agreed amenities to his tenant. He filed a complaint against the land-lord under the Consumer Protection Act. The National Commission dismissed the complaint saying that it was a case of lease of immovable property and not of hiring services of the landlord. [*Smt. Laxmiben Laxmichand Shah* v. *Smt. Sakerben Kanji Chandan* [1992] 1 Comp. LJ 177 (NCDRC)].

3. A presented before the Sub-Registrar a document claim-ing it to be a will for registration who sent it to the Collec-tor of Stamps for action. The matter remain pending for about six years. In the meantime A filed a complaint under the Consumer Protection Act alleging harrassment by the Sub-Registrar and Collector and prayed for compensation. The National Commission held the view that A was not a "consumer" under the CPA. Because there was no hiring of services by the complainant for considera-tion and because a Government official doing his duty as func-tionary of the State under law could not be said to be rendering a service to the complainant. [*S.P. Goel* v. *Collector of Stamps* (1995) III CPR 684 (SC)].

1.2-2b CONSIDERATION MUST BE PAID OR PAYABLE - Consideration is regarded necessary for hiring or availing of services. However, its payment need not necessarily be immediate. It can be in instal-ments. For the services provided without charging anything in return, the person availing the services is not a consumer under the Act.

Examples :

1. A hires an advocate to file a suit for recovery of money from his employer. He promises to pay fee to the advocate after settlement of the suit. A is a consumer under the Act.
2. A goes to a Doctor to get himself treated for a frac-ture. The Doctor being his friend charged him nothing for the treatment. A is not a consumer under the Act.
3. B issued an advertisement that a person could enter the contest by booking a Premier Padmini car. S purchased the car and thus entered the contest. He was declared as winner of the draw and was thus entitled to the two tickets from New Delhi to New York and back. S filed a complaint alleging that the ticket was not delivered to him. The National Commission held that S was not a consumer in this context. He paid for the car and got it. B was not liable so far as the contract of winning a

lottery was con-cerned. [*Byford* v. *S.S. Srivastava* (1993) II CPR 83 (NCDRC)].

The Direct and Indirect taxes paid to the State by a citizen is not payment for the services rendered.

Example : T was paying property tax for his house to the local corporation. This corporation was responsible for proper water supply to the premises under its work area. T raised a consumer dispute over the inadequacy of water supply by the corporation. The National Commission held that it was not a consumer dispute as water supply was made by the corporation out of its statutory duty and not by virtue of payment of taxes by T. - *Mayor, Calcut-ta Municipal Corporation* v. *Tarapada Chatterjee* (1994) 1 CPR 87 (NCDRC).

1.2-2c BENEFICIARY OF SERVICES IS ALSO A CONSUMER - When a person hires services, he may hire it for himself or for any other person. In such cases the beneficiary (or user) of these services is also a consumer.

Example : A takes his son B to a doctor for his treatment. Here A is hirer of services of the doctor and B is beneficiary of these services. For the purpose of the Act, both A and B are consumers.

Note : This is an exception to the rule of privity to the con-tract.

Note that in case of goods, buyer of goods for commercial purpose ceases to be a consumer under the Act. On the other hand, a consumer of service for commercial purpose remains a consumer under the Act.

Example : S applied to Electricity Board for electricity connec-tion for a flour mill. There was a delay in releasing the connec-tion. S made a complaint for deficiency in service. He was held a consumer under the Act. - *Shamsher Khan* v. *Rajasthan State Elec-tricity Board* (1993) II CPR 6 (Raj.).

Complaint

1.3 An aggrieved consumer seeks redressal under the Act through the instrumentality of complaint. It does not mean that the consumer can complain against his each and every problem. The Act has provided certain grounds on which complaint can be made. Similarly, relief against these complaints can be granted within the set pattern.

1.3-1 *What constitutes a complaint [Section 2(1)(c)]* - Complaint is a statement made in writing to the National Commission, the State Commission or the District Forum by a person competent to file it, containing the allegations in detail, and with a view to obtain relief provided under the Act.

1.3-2 *Who can file a complaint [Sections 2(b) & 12]* - At the outset it is clear that a person who can be termed as a consumer under the Act can make a complaint. To be specific on this ac-count, following are the persons who can file a complaint under the Act :

(*a*) a consumer; or

(*b*) any voluntary consumer association registered under the Companies Act, 1956 or under any other law for the time being in force, or

(*c*) the Central Government or any State Government,

(*d*) one or more consumers, where there are numerious con-sumers having the same interest.

In addition to the above following are also considered as a consumer and hence they may file a complaint :

Beneficiary of the goods/services : The definition of consumer itself includes beneficiary of goods and services - *K.B. Jayalax-mi* v. *Government of Tamil Nadu* 1994(1) CPR 114.

Where a young child is taken to the hospital by his parents and the child is treated by the doctor, the parents of such a minor child can file a complaint under the Act - *Spring Meadows Hospi-tal* v. *Harjot Ahluwalia JT* 1998(2) SC 620.

Legal representative of the deceased consumer : The Act does not expressly indicate that the LR of a consumer are also included in its scope. But by operation of law, the legal representatives get clothed with the rights, status and personality of the deceased. Thus the expression consumer would include legal representative of the deceased consumer and he can exercise his right for the purpose of enforcing the cause of action which has devolved on him - *Cosmopolitan Hospital* v. *Smt. Vasantha P. Nair* (1) 1992 CPJ NC 302.

Legal heirs of the deceased consumer : A legal heir of the de-ceased consumer can well maintain a complaint under the Act - *Joseph Alias Animon* v. *Dr. Elizabeth Zachariah* (1) 1997 CPJ 96.

Husband of the consumer : In the Indian conditions, women may be illiterate, educated women may be unaware of their legal rights, thus a husband can file and prosecute complaint under the Consum-er Protection Act on behalf of his spouse - *Punjab National Bank, Bombay* v. *K.B. Shetty* 1991 (2) CPR 633.

A relative of consumer : When a consumer signs the original complaint, it can be initiated by his/her relative - *Motibai Dalvi Hospital* v. *M.I. Govilkar* 1992 (1) CPR 408.

Insurance company : Where Insurance company pays and settles the claim of the insured and the insured person transfers his rights in the insured goods to the company, it can file a complaint for the loss caused to the insured goods by negligence of goods/service providers. For example, when loss is caused to such goods because of negligence of transport company, the insurance company can file a claim against the transport company - *New India Assurance Company Ltd.* v. *Green Transport Co.* II 1991 CPJ (1) Delhi.

1.3-3 *What a complaint must contain [Section 2(1)(c)]* - A com-plaint must contain any of the following allegations :

(*a*) An unfair trade practice or a restrictive trade prac-tice has been adopted by any trader;

Example : A sold a six months old car to B representing it to be a new one. Here B can make a complaint against A for following an unfair trade practice.

(*b*) The goods bought by him or agreed to be bought by him suffer from one or more defects;

Example : A bought a computer from B. It was not work-ing properly since day one. A can make a complaint against B for supplying him a defective computer.

(*c*) The services hired or availed of or agreed to be hired or availed of by him suffer from deficiency in any respect.

Example : A hired services of an advocate to defend himself against his landlord. The advocate did not appear every time the case was scheduled. A can make a complaint against the advocate.

(*d*) A trader has charged for the goods mentioned in the complaint a price in excess of the price fixed by or under any law for the time being in force or displayed on the goods or any package containing such goods.

Example : A bought a sack of cement from B who charged him Rs. 100 over and above the reserve price of the cement de-clared by the Government. Here A can make a complaint against B.

(*e*) Goods which will be hazardous to life and safety when used, are being offered for sale to the public in contravention of the provisions of any law for the time being in force requir-ing traders to display information in regard to the contents, manner and effect of use of such goods.

Example : A bought a tin of disinfectant powder. It had lid which was to be opened in a specific manner. Trader did not inform. A about this. While opening the lid in ordinary way, some powder flew in the eyes of A which affected his vision. Here A can make a complaint against the trader.

Note : The terms 'unfair trade practice', 'restrictive trade practice', 'Goods', 'Defect', 'service', 'Deficiency', 'trader', 'Excess price', and 'Hazardous goods' have been discussed in detail in the chapter separately.

1.3-4 *Time frame within which a complaint can be filed* - Section 24A of the Act provides that a consumer dispute can be filed within two years from the date on which the cause of action arises.

Since this provision was inserted in the Act in 1993, before that the Consumer Forums were following the Limitation Act, 1963, which says that a suit can be filed within three years after the cause of action arises. The point of time when cause of action arises is an important factor in determining the time period available to file a com-plaint. There are no set rules to decide such time. It depends on the facts and circumstances of each case.

Examples :

1. A got his eye operated by B in 1989. He got a certifi-cate of blindness on 18th December, 1989. He was still in hope of gaining his sight and went from second operation in 1992 and was discharged on 21-1-1992. He filed a complaint against B on 11-1-1994. B opposed on the ground that more than 2 years were over after 18-12-1989, thus the complaint is not maintainable. The Commission held that here the cause of action for filing the complaint would arose after the second operation when A lost entire hope of recovery. Thus the suit is maintainable - *Mukund Lal Ganguly* v. *Dr. Abhijit Ghosh* III 1995 CPJ 64.
2. A house was allotted on 1-1-1999. Defects appeared in the house on 10-1-1999. Here the cause of action will arise on 10-1-1999.

It may be noted that these time frames are not absolute limita-tions. If the Consumer Forum is satisfied that there was suffi-cient cause for not filing the complaint within the prescribed period, it can entertain a complaint beyond limitation time. However the Forum must record the reasons for condonation of delay.

Example : A deposited some jewellery with a bank. Bank lost it. Bank kept giving her false sense of hope to retrieve the jewel-lery, and thus A was put in a state of inaction. Later on when A filed a suit on the Bank, it claimed that the suit was not main-tainable as the limitation time after the cause of action arose has lapsed. The Commission reprimanded the bank and admitted the case - *Agnes D'Mello* v. *Canara Bank* [1992] I CPJ 335 (NCDRC).

1.3-5 *Relief available against complaint [Sections 14 and 22]* - A complainant can seek any one or more of the following relief under the Act:

(*a*) to remove the defect pointed out by the appropriate laboratory from the goods in question;

(*b*) to replace the goods with new goods of similar descrip-tion which shall be free from any defect;

(*c*) to return to the complainant the price, or, as the case may be, the charges paid by the complainant;

(*d*) to pay such amount as may be awarded by it as compensa-tion to the consumer for any loss or injury suffered by the consumer due to the negligence of the opposite party;

(*e*) to remove the defects or deficiencies in the services in question;

(*f*) to discontinue the unfair trade practice or the re-strictive trade practice or not to repeat it;

(*g*) not to offer the hazardous goods for sale;

(*h*) to withdraw the hazardous goods from being offered for sale;

(*i*) to provide from adequate costs to complainant.

1.3-6 *When a complaint cannot be filed* - A complaint on behalf of the public which consists of unidentifiable consumers cannot be filed under the Act.

Example : A complaint was filed on the basis of a newspaper report that passengers travelling by flight No. 1C-401 from Cal-cutta to Delhi on May 13, 1989 were made to stay at the airport and the flight was delayed by 90 minutes causing great inconven-ience to the passengers. It was held that such a general com-plaint cannot be entertained. No passenger who boarded that plane came forward or authorised the complainant to make the complaint - *Consumer Education and Research Society, Ahmedabad* v. *Indian Airlines Corporation,* New Delhi (1992) 1 CPJ 38 NC.

A complaint by an individual on behalf of general public is not permitted - *Commissioner of Transport* v. *Y.R. Grover* 1994 (1) CPJ 199 NC.

An unregistered association cannot file a complaint under the Act.

Example : The complainant was an association formed in the Gulf and was unregistered in India. It was held that since the peti-tioner was not a voluntary organization registered under any law in force in India, cannot come within clause (*d*) of section 2(1) of the Act and hence can't file a complaint - *Gulf Trivendrum air Fare Forum* v. *Chairman & Managing Director, Air India* 1991 (2) CPR 129.

A complaint after expiry of limitation period is not permitted. A complaint cannot be filed after the lapse of two years from the date on which the cause of action arise unless the Forum is satisfied about the genuineness of the reason for not filing complaint within the prescribed time.

Example : A supplied defective machinery to B on 12-1-1998. B filed a suit against A on 10-3-2001. It was not admitted before the Forum for the reason that the time available to make complaint lapsed.

1.3-7 *Dismissal of frivolous and vexatious complaints* - Since the Act provides for an inexpensive procedure (Court fees is not charged in consumer complaints under the Act) for filing com-plaints, there is a possibility that the Act is misused by people for filing vexations claims. To discourage frivolous and vexa-tious claims, the Act has provided that such complaints will be dismissed and the complainant can be charged with the costs not exceeding Rs. 10,000.

Example : A filed a complaint against B to recover compensation of Rs. 55,99,000 with the motive of indulging in speculative litigation taking undue advantage of the fact that no court fee was payable under the Consumer Protection Act. The National Commission held that the complainant has totally failed to make a case against B, and dismissed the complaint as frivolous and vexatious imposing Rs. 10,000 as costs to A- *Brij Mohan Kher* v. *Dr. N.H. Banka* I 1995 CPJ 99 NC.

Unfair Trade Practice and Restrictive Trade Practice [Section 2(1)(r) and (nn)].

1.4 We have discussed that a consumer can make a complaint when an unfair or a restrictive trade practice is followed by a trad-er. What can be termed as an unfair or a restrictive trade prac-tice is another question of law.

1.4-1 *What is an Unfair Trade Practice* - The Act says that, "unfair trade practice" means a trade practice which, for the purpose of promoting the sale, use or supply of any goods or for the provison of any service, adopts any unfair method or unfair or deceptive practice including any of the following practices, namely—

(1) The practice of making any statement, whether orally or in writing or by visible representation which—

(*i*) falsely represents that the goods are of particular standard, quality, quantity, grade, composition, style or model;

(*ii*) falsely represents that the services are of a particu-lar standard, quality or grade;

(*iii*) falsely represents any re-built, second-hand, renovated, reconditioned or old goods as new goods;

(*iv*) represents that the goods or services have sponsor-ship, approval performance, characteristics, accessories, uses or benefits which such goods or services do not have;

(*v*) represents that the seller or the supplier has a sponsorship or approval or affiliation which such seller or supplier does not have;

(*vi*) makes false or misleading statement concerning the need for, or the usefulness of, any goods or services;

(*vii*) gives to the public any warranty or guarantee of the performance, efficacy or length of life of a product or of any goods that is not based on an adequate or proper test thereof;

(*viii*) makes to the public a representation in a form that purports to be a warranty or guarantee of a product or of any goods or services; or a promise to replace, maintain or repair an article or any part thereof or to repeat or continue a service until it has achieved a specified result, if such perported war-ranty or guarantee or promise is materially misleading or if there is no reasonable prospect that such warranty, guarantee or promise will be carried out;

(*ix*) materially misleads the public concerning the price at which a product or like products or goods or services, have been or are, ordinarily sold or provided, and, for this purpose, a representation as to price shall be deemed to refer to the price at which the product or goods or services has or have been sold by sellers or provided by suppliers generally in the rele-vant market unless it is clearly specified to be the price at which the product has been sold or services have been provided by the person by whom or on whose behalf other representation is made;

(*x*) gives false or misleading facts disparaging the goods, services or trade of another person.

Note : A statement is said to be made to public when it is—

(*a*) expressed on an article offered or displayed for sale, or on its wrapper or container; or

(*b*) expressed on anything attached to, inserted in, or accompanying, an article offered or displayed for sale, or on anything on which the article is mounted for display or sale; or

(*c*) contained in or on anything that is sold, sent, deliv-ered, transmitted or in any other manner whatsoever made avail-able to a member of the public, by the person who had caused the statement to be so expressed, made or contained.

(2) Permits the publication of any advertisement whether in any newspaper or otherwise, for the sale or supply at a *bargain price,* of goods or services that are not intended to be offered for sale or supply at the bargain price, or for a period that is, and in quantities that are, reasonable, having regard to the nature of the market in which the business is carried on, the nature and size of business, and the nature of the advertisement.

Note : "Bargain price" means—

(*a*) a price that is stated in any advertisement to be a bargain price, by reference to an ordinary price or otherwise, or

(*b*) a price that a person who reads, hears or sees the advertisement, would reasonably understand to be bargain price having regard to the prices at which the product advertised or like products are ordinarily sold.

(3) Permits the offering of gifts, prizes or other items with the intention of not providing them as offered or creating impression that something is being given or offered free of charge when it is fully or partly covered by the amount charged in the transac-tion as a whole; or the conduct of any contest, lottery, game of chance or skill, for the purpose of promoting, directly or indi-rectly, the sale, use or supply of any product or any business interest;

(4) Permits the sale or supply of goods intended to be used, or are of a kind likely to be used, by consumers, knowing or having reason to believe that the goods do not comply with the standards prescribed by competent authority relating to performance, compo-sition, contents, design, constructions, finishing or packaging as are necessary to prevent or reduce the risk of injury to the person using the goods;

(5) Permits the hoarding or destruction of goods, or refuses to sell the goods or to make them available for sale or to provide any service, if such hoarding or destruction or refusal raises or tends to raise or is intended to raise, the cost of those or other similar goods or services.

1.4-2 *What is a Restrictive Trade Practice* - Section 2(1)(*nn*) of the Act provides that, "restrictive trade practice" means "any trade practice which requires a consumer to buy, hire or avail of any goods or, as the case may be, services as a condition prece-dent for buying, hiring or availing of other goods or services".

An analysis of above definition reveals that where sale or pur-chase of a product or service is made conditional on the sale or purchase of one or more other products and services, it amounts to restrictive trade practice.

Technically, this type of arrangement is called 'tie-up sales' or 'tying arrangement'. The effect of such an arrangement is that a purchaser is forced to buy some goods or services which he may not require alongwith the goods or services which he wants to buy. Thus where a buyer agrees to purchase product 'X' upon a condition that he will also purchase product 'Y' from the seller, the sale of product 'Y' (tied product) is tied to the sale of product 'X' (tying product).

The buyer has to forego his free choice between competing products. This results in neutralizing healthy competition in the 'tied' market.

Example : A, a gas distributor instead his customers to buy gas stove as a condition to give gas connection. It was held that it was a restrictive trade practice - *Re. Anand Gas* RTPE 43/ 1983 (MRTPC).

However, where there is no such precondition and the buyer is free to take either product, no tying arrangement could be alleged even though the seller may offer both the products as a single unit at a composite price.

Example : A is a furniture dealer. He is selling Sofa at Rs. 20,000 and Bed at

Rs. 15,000. He has an offer that whoever will buy Sofa and Bed both, he will charge Rs. 30,000 only. Here the choice is open to the customer to buy the products single or composite. This is not a restrictive trade practice.

Note : The term 'restrictive trade practice' has a very wide meaning when read in context of the MRTP Act, 1969. However under Consumer Protection Act, 1986, it has been used in a narrower sense.

Goods and Defect [Section 2(1)(i) and (f)]

1.5 A consumer can make complaint when he come across defective goods. Here it is required to understand what are the items which can be considered as 'goods' and what constitutes 'defect' under the Act.

1.5-1 *Goods* - The Consumer Protection Act does not define the term 'Goods' It says that - "goods" means goods as defined in the Sale of Goods Act, 1930.

Section 2(7) of the Sale of Goods Act, 1930, defines 'goods' as - "Goods means every kind of movable property other than actionable claims and money; and includes stock and shares, growing crops, grass, and things attached to or forming part of the land which are agreed to be severed before sale or under the contract of sale."

The definition reveals that—

(*a*) Goods must be movable;

(*b*) Things attached to or forming part of land which can be severed satisfy the movability criteria;

(*c*) Actionable claim and Money have been specifically excluded from definition of goods.

Note : For elaboration on the term 'goods', refer para 15-2-1d.

1.5-2 *Defect* - Section 2(1)(*f*) of the Act provides that, "de-fect" means any fault, imperfection or shortcoming in the quali-ty, quantity, potency, purity or standard *which is required to be maintained* by or under any law of the time being in force under any contract, express or implied or as is claimed by the trader in any manner whatsoever *in relation to any goods.*

This is an exhaustive definition. It means that the Act recognises only those defects which are covered by the definition. Any type of defect not mentioned here will not be entertained by Consumer Forums. Moreover the defect has to be in relation to goods only, *i.e.,* if an item does not fall within the definition of 'Goods', no defect can be complained therein. However, the coverage of this definition is very wide.

Examples:

1. A Pressure Cooker burst and caused injury to the user. It was held to be a manufacturing defect - *T.T. (P.) Ltd.* v. *Akhil Bhartiya Grahak Panchayat II* [1996] CPJ 239 NC.
2. Failure to handover registration book along with jeep purchased by complainant is a defect. [*Ramesh Chandra* v. *Commer-cial Tax Officer* [1993] 3 CPR 182 (Ori.).

3. Where laboratory test report showed that soft drink was not fit for human consumption, it was held defective- *Narayanan Vyankatkrishnan Iyengar* v. *Shakti Foods* [1994] 2 CPJ 652 (Mah.).
4. Rape seed oil adulterated with toxic substances, which led to paralysis of limbs and other disabilities, has been con-sidered as defective - *Barsad Ali* v. *MD West Bengal Essential Commodities Supply Corporation Ltd.* (1993) 1 CPR 217 WB.
5. Electric household appliances which are not in accord-ance with the standards prescribed by ISI, being unsafe are defective - *Farooq Hazi Ismail Saya* v. *Gavabhai Bhesania* (1991) 2 CPJ 452 (Guj.).
6. Gas Cylinder with excessive gas is defective goods - *Dayanand A Avasare* v. *Bharat Petroleum Corporation Ltd.* (1993) 1 CPR 278 (Mah.).
7. Development of cracks of half inch to three and a half inch in walls and mosaic floor in a flat after taking possession from a Housing Board - *R. Shanmugasundaram* v. *Tamil Nadu Housing Board* (1998) 1 CPJ 96 NC.
8. A supplied white marble to B. Later on the colour of the marble changed. B sued a alleging supply of defective marble. It was held that A should have expressly told B that the marble would not retain its colour when polished. In the absence of such assertion, it is deemed that A made B to understand that the marble would retain its white colour and when the colour changed, it comes within the scope of 'defect' in goods under the Act- *Chitranjan Sahu* v. *N.C. Jain II* (1993) CPJ 1127 (Ori.).
9. A sold a stolen car to B. B wanted to sue A for defect in the title of the car. Here B cannot sue A under the Consumer Protection Act as the defect in title of goods would not consti-tute defective goods as defined under the Act.

Service and Deficiency [Section 2(1)(*o*) and (*g*)]

1.6 When a service is found deficient by a consumer, he can make a complaint under the Act. Thus the prime requirement is that the matter must fall within the definition of service, and it must entail a deficiency as per the norms given by the Act.

1.6-1 *What can be termed as a service* - Section 2(1)(*o*) of the Act provides that "service" means service of any description which is made available to potential users and includes the provision of facilities in connection with *banking, financing, insurance, transport, processing, supply of electrical or other energy, board or loading or both, housing construction, entertainment, amusement or the purveying of news or other information,* but does not include the rendering of any service free of charge or under a contract of personal service.

The definition provides a list of eleven sectors to which service may pertain in order to come under the purview of the Act. The list of these sectors is not an exhaustive one. Service may be of any description and pertain to any sector if it satisfy the following criteria:

1. service is made *available to the potential users, i.e.,* service not only to the actual users but also to those who are capable of using it.
2. it *should not be free of charge, e.g.,* the medical service rendered free of charge in Government hospital is not a service under the Act;
3. it should not be under a *contract of personal service.*

When we talk about 'service' under the Consumer Protection Act, we take it as a regular commercial transaction. Thus the services rendered under the contract of personal service are specifically excluded from the definition.

The expression 'contract of personal service' is not defined under the Act. In common parlance, it means - a contract to render service in a private capacity to an individual. For example, where a servant enters into an agreement with a master for em-ployment, or where a landlord agrees to supply water to his tenant, these are the contracts of personal service. The idea is that under a personal service relationship, a person can discon-tinue the service at any time according to his will, he need not approach Consumer Forum to complaint about deficiency in service.

There is a difference between 'contract of personal service' and 'contract for personal service'. In case of 'contract of personal service', the service seeker can order or require what is to be done and how it should be done. Like a master can tell his serv-ant to bring goods from a particular place. But in a 'contract for personal service', the service seeker can tell only what is to be done. How the work will be done is at the wish of the performer. Like when a person gives a suit to the tailor for stitching, he does not tell him which method he should use to stitch it.

Note : That it is 'contract of personal service' is excluded from the definition of service, 'contract for personal service' is recognised as service under the Act.

It does not make a difference whether the service provider is a Government body or a Private body. Thus even if a statutory corporation provides a deficient service, it can be made liable under the Act.

Example : A applied for electricity connection for his flour mill to Rajasthan State Electricity Board. The Board delayed in re-leasing the connection. It was held deficient in performing serv-ice.

Some other sectors/professionals/services which are not specified in the definition of service but which have been considered by the Consumer Forums as service sectors from time to time are listed below:

Advocates, Airlines, Chartered Accountants, Courier, Chit Fund, Education, Gas Cylinder/LPG, Medical services, Postal services, Railways, Investment related services, and Telephone services.

Thus, the test is - whether the person against whom the complaint is made performs a service for consideration which is sought by a potential user.

1.6-2 *What is meant by "deficiency" in service* - Section 2(1)(g) of the Act provides that, "deficiency" means any fault, imperfection, shortcoming or inadequacy in the quality, nature and manner of performance which is required to be maintained by or under any law for the time being in force or has been under-taken to be performed by a person in pursuance of a contract or otherwise in relation to any service.

Reading the above definition by breaking it into elements, we get—

(*a*) "deficiency" means any fault, imperfection, shortcoming or *inadequacy in the quality, nature and manner of performance*

Examples :

1. A boarded a train. The compartment in which he and his wife travelled was in a bad shape-fans not working, shutters of windows were not working, rexin of the upper berth was badly torn and there were rusty nails which caused some injuries to the wife of A. A made a complaint against the railway department. It was held that the complaint constituted 'deficiency in service' and the compensation of Rs. 1500 was awarded to A - *General Manager, South Eastern Railway* v. *Anand Prasad Sinha I* [1991] CPJ 10 (12) NC.
2. Dr. A treated P under Allopathic system, though he himself was a Homoeopathic practitioner. Later on P allegated A for wrong treatment. The Commission held it as deficiency in service - *Poonam Verma* v. *Ashwin Patel* [1996] II CPJ 1 SC.
3. A booked a car for B and promised to deliver it within one month of booking. The car was not delivered even after four months. Here A could be held liable for deficiency in service.

   One interesting aspect is that deficiency in service should occur during the happening of performance. Thus it is crucial to determine when the performance of a service commenced.

   Example : A contracted with B to supply, erect and commission cold rolling mill. A supplied the mill, but failed to erect and commission the mill. B filed a suit alleging deficiency of service on A's failure to elect and commission the mill. The National Commission observed that the deficiency must pertain to performance of service. Since A never started erecting and com-missioning the mill, the question of performance did not arise. Thus the case is not that of deficiency of service - *Jaipur Metals & Electricals Ltd.* v. *Laxmi Inds.* [1991] II CPJ 602 (NC).

(*b*) Such quality and manner of performance of service should have been required to be maintained by or under any law for the time being in force or undertaken to be performed by a person in pursuance of a contract or otherwise.

Example : A, the builder, promised under written agree-ment to provide a flat to B. Subsequently he expressed his inability to give possession of the flat and entered into a fresh agreement to pay Rs. 9,51,000 to B in place of flat. A didn't even pay this money. B sued A. The Commission held that since A had not even paid the money as per subsequent contract, the rights of earlier contract can be involved by B. And that there was a deficiency of service on the part of builders - *Lata Con-struction* v. *Dr. Rameshchandra Ramniklal Shah* AIR 2000 SC 380 (384).

(*c*) *The deficiency must be in relation to a service* - The words '....in relation to any service' in the definition signifies that the deficiency is always in terms of service. Thus if the grievance pertains to a matter which does not fall in the definition of service, the concept of deficiency would not apply.

Example : A deposited Rs. 100 with B as application fee and executed bond for the purpose of drilling tubewell. B did not drill the tubewell because it was not feasible. A alleged defi-ciency in service. It was held that depositing Rs. 100 as appli-cation fee and executing a bond does not amount to hiring of services, thus the deficiency of service cannot be complained of in the matter - *Mangilal* v. *Chairman District Rural Development Agency* [1991] 1 CPJ 474 (Raj.).

Deficiency in Service Due to Circumstances beyond Control

In normal course, if the service is found deficient as per the above criteria, it is held deficient and the compensation is awarded. However there may be abnormal circumstances beyond the control of the person performing service. If such circumstances prevent a person from rendering service of the desired quality, nature and the manner, such person should not be penalised for the same.

Example : A undertook to supply water to B for irrigation of crops. Due to power grid failure of the State, A could not get sufficient power to perform the service. Here A cannot be held liable for deficiency in service.

However, negligence on the part of performer may not be excused under the cover of circumstances beyond control.

Example : A agreed to supply water to B for irrigation of crops. He failed to do so because of a power breakdown due to burning of transformer. As a result crops damaged. B sued A for providing deficient service. The National Commission held that it was duty of A to get the transformer repaired immediately. Since he was negligent in doing so, he is liable for the deficiency in service - *Orissa Lift Irrigation Corpn. Ltd.* v. *Birakishore Raut* [1991] 2 CPJ 213 (NC).

Trader and Manufacturer [Section 2(1)(q) and (j)]

1.7 When a person finds any defect in the goods, be it manufacturing defect, or excessive price, or lack of information about hazardous nature, or restrictive or unfair trade practice, he can make a complaint against the trader. Thus it is very important to know who can be termed as a trader under the Act.

1.7-1 *Trader* - Section 2(1)(*q*) of the Act says that 'trader' means any person who

sells or distributes any goods for sale and

includes the manufacturer thereof, and

where such goods are sold or distributed in package form, in-cludes the packer thereof.

Generally speaking 'trader' means any person who carries on a trade. Under the Consumer Protection Act, even a packer has been included in the definition of trader. Packer means one who packs the goods.

Examples :

1. A got an agency of 'Indana' products. He sells and distributes these products in North India. He is a trader under the Act.
2. A manufactures combs. He is a trader under the Act.
3. A provide bottles to pack the perfume manufactured by B. Here A is also a trader under the Act.

Note : "Trader" is a wider term which includes a manufacturer also.

1.7-2 *Manufacturer* - In terms if clause (*j*) of section 2(1) of the Act, "manufacturer" means a person who—

(*i*) makes or *manufactures* any goods or parts thereof; or

(*ii*) does not make or manufacture any goods but *assembles* parts thereof made or manufactured by others and claims the end-product to be goods manufactured by himself; or

(*iii*) puts or causes to be *put his own mark* on any goods made or manufactured by any other manufacturer and claims such goods to be goods made or manufactured by himself.

Thus manufacturer is a person who either himself manufactures goods, or assemble any goods manufactured by others, or puts his own mark or trade mark on the goods manufactured by others.

Examples :

1. A Ltd. were into manufacturing of Pressure Cookers. B bought a Cooker which burst out while using. B sued A Ltd. for compensation. Here A Ltd. being manufacturer of the Cooker is liable for the loss.

2. A Ltd. used to buy components and assemble computers therefrom. They were selling them under the brand name 'Rotal'. B bought a Rotal computer which turned out to be defective. Here B can hold A Ltd. Liable for the loss as they will be considered manufacturer of Rotal computer under the Act.
3. N bought H-4 Cotton seeds from the market which were labelled as produced and marketed by the Hindustan Levers Ltd. N established that the seeds were defective. He sued HLL. HLL contended that it did not manufactured the seeds but had only marketed them, and that some company based in Gujarat produced the same. The Commission held that in this case HLL comes under the third limb of the definition of manufacturer under the Act. Thus it is liable for the loss suffered by N - *Namdeo Baijrao Raut* v. *Hindustan Lever Ltd.* [1993] 3 CPR 346 (Mah. CDRC).

It may be noted that where a manufacturer despatches any goods or part thereof to any branch office maintained by him, such branch office shall not be deemed to be the manufacturer even though the parts so despatched to it are assembled at such branch office and are sold or distributed from such branch office.

Example : A Ltd. based in Delhi was having a branch office in Chennai. It used to sent components of computers to its Chennai branch which was assembling and selling them. B purchased a computer from Chennai branch which turned out to be defective. Here A Ltd. is responsible for the loss, and not the Chennai branch.

1.7-3 *Who should be sued by a consumer - manufacturer or seller* - Generally when a consumer finds defect in the goods, he sues the person from whom he bought the goods. Reason being privity of contract.

If the defect is a manufacturing defect, the consumer may sue the manufacturer also along with the seller. This is an option with the consumer. Thus the manufacturer is a possible party, and not a necessary party.

Example : A was manufacturer of "X" brand cars and B was a dealer for them. C bought a car from B and found it defective. Here he may sue B alone, or A and B both.

Charging Excessive Price

1.8 A complaint may be made against a trader who has charged a price in excess of the price :

(*a*) fixed by or under any law for the time being in force, or

(*b*) displayed on the goods, or

(*c*) displayed on any package containing the goods.

Examples :

1. Government fixed control rate of milk at Rs. 15 per litre in the month of June 2001. A sold it at the rate of Rs. 18 per litre in the same period. Price charged by A are excessive.
2. The price displayed on a one Kg. packet ot salt was Rs. 4. Suddenly there was paucity of salt in the market. A started selling the same @ Rs. 6 per kg. The price charged by A is exces-sive.

It may be noted that when price of an article is not fixed by law, or when the same is not displayed on goods or on the package containing goods, no complaint can be made under the Act for excess pricing.

Example : Mahaboobnagar Milk Chilling Centre charged 15 paise extra per half litre of milk supplied in sachets in comparison to the other varieties of milk. The National Commission held that in the absence of any law requiring an article to be sold at or below a particular price fixed thereunder, and when there was no declaration of the price on the packet containing the goods, a case for excessive pricing may not be construed.

Hazardous Goods

1.9 The term "Hazardous goods' has not been defined in the Act. The dictionary meaning of the term is - dangerous or risky. However, the term is used in context of 'goods' only, *i.e.*, a person can make a complaint if he is not informed about the hazardous nature of the goods but the same is not true in case of hazardous services.

The rationale behind this provision is to ensure physical safety of the consumers. The law seeks to ensure that those responsible for bringing goods to the market, in particular, suppliers, exporters, importers, retailers and the like should ensure that while in their care these goods are not rendered unsafe through improper handling or storage.

Consumers should be instructed in the proper use of goods and should be informed of the risks involved in intended or normally foreseeable use. Vital safety information should be conveyed to consumers.

Example : A bought an insecticide from B. B did not inform A that touching this insecticide with bare hands can create skin prob-lem. A, while using the insecticide came in contact with it and suffered from skin problem consequently. Here B can be held liable under the Act.

Consumer Protection Councils

2.1 Ram, an engineer by profession shifted to Delhi. He bought a computer from Shyam, a dealer who gave him all guarantees and warranties. The moment he plugged in the computer, some noise came and the computer was shut down. He called up Shyam, but got no response from him. After making many calls to him, he under-stood that he was cheated of his money.

Ram could have gone to courts, but knowing the lengthy and expensive procedures involved, he preferred not to initiate any action against Shyam. One day while watching television he came across a programme on consumer protection. Ram got interested in it and noted the address of consumer council which was sponsoring the programme. Thereafter he contacted the Council and talked about his computer affair. The Council made him aware that there is a speedy and inexpensive way to assert his right as a consum-er, and that where and how a complaint can be filed for that, and that he need not hire an advocate for the suit, and assured him of any assistance he may need for the same. The Consumer Councils are created to advise and assist the con-sumers in seeking and enforcing their rights. We have Consumer Protection Councils both at Centre level and State level, that is one Central Council and many State Councils.

These councils work towards the promotion and protection of consumers. They make investigations and give publicity to the matters concerning consumer interests, take steps towards furthering consumer education and protecting consumer from exploitation, advice the Government in the matter of policy formulation keeping consumer interest as pivotal concern, etc. Although their suggestions are recommendatory in nature, but they have significant impact in policy making.

While deciding about the composition of these councils, the State keeps in mind that it should have proper representation from all the possible areas affecting consumer interests. Again the rules as to when should these councils meet, what should they aim at, how they conduct their business are framed by the Government with a view to balance the efficacy and practicability of its busi-ness.

Objects of the Councils [Sections 6 and 8]

2.2 There is one basic thought that 'consumer need to be protect-ed'. Another thought is - how he can be protected ? Definitely, there has to be some agency to work towards this protection. The Act has provided for constitution of Consumer Councils for this purpose.

Now, when we say that these councils are there to protect the consumers, a question arises - consumers are protected against what ? Thus the Act has detailed some rights of consumers which need to be protected by the councils. These are :

Right to safety - It is right to be protected against the marketing of goods and services which are hazardous to life and property.

Unsafe goods may cause death or serious injury to the user due to defective ingredients, defective design, poor workmanship, or any other reason. At times safety hazards are found due to absence of proper instructions to use the product. Thus it is to be ensured that—

Manufacturers and traders ensure that the goods are safe for the users, in case of hazardous goods, they give clear instructions as to mode of use, consumer is informed of the risk involved in improper use of goods, vital safety information is conveyed to consumers.

Manufacturers or distributors who become aware of the unforeseen hazards after the goods are supplied must inform the authorities and the public in order to forewarn consumers about such hazards.

Where a product is found such as is likely to be hazardous even when properly used, traders should either recall it and modify the same, or replace it with a new product, or adequately compen-sate for it.

Right to information - It is right to be informed about the quality, quantity, potency, purity, standard and price of goods or services, with a view to protect the consumer against unfair trade practices.

Adequate information is very important in order to make a right choice. In our country, however, consumers do not get adequate comparative information about the quality, quantity, potency, purity, standard and price of different kinds of goods or services which are available. As a result buying decisions become difficult. Therefore consumers need to be given maximum information about the wide variety of competing goods available in the market.

Right to choose - The right to choose can be made meaningful by ensuring access to a variety of goods and services at competitive prices.

Fair and effective competition must be encouraged so as to provide consumers with the widest range of products and services at the lowest cost.

Right to represent - It is right to be heard and to be assured that consumer's interests will receive due consideration at appropriate forums.

The Consumer Protection Act, 1986 has well taken care of this right by making available the instrumentality of Redressal Forums. Every consumer has a right to file complaint and be heard in that context.

Right to redressal - It is a right to seek redressal against unfair trade practices or restrictive trade practices or unserpu-lous exploitation of consumers.

When consumers are wronged in a market place transaction, appropriate and adequate redress must be available. The Act has ensured this right by establishing Consumer Forums and recognising restrictive and unfair trade practices as a ground to make a complaint.

Right to education - The right to consumer education is a right which ensures that consumers are informed about the practices prevalent in the market and the remedies available to them.

For spreading this education, media, or school curriculum, or cultural activities, etc. may be used as a medium.

Note that the Central Council's object is to ensure these rights of the consumers throughout the country while the State Councils look to ensure these rights to consumers within their territo-ries.

Central Council

2.3-1 *Composition [Section 2 and rule 3]* Members of the councils are selected from various areas of consumer interest, who are, when possible, leading members of statewide organisations repre-senting segments of the consumer public so as to establish a broadly based and representative consumer council. The Consumer Protection Act has authorised the Central Government to make rules as to the composition of the Central Council. Accordingly, the Central Government has provided that the Central Council shall consist of the following members not exceeding 150, namely :—

1. the Minister in-charge of Consumer Affairs in the Central Government who shall be the Chairman of the Central Council;

2. the Minister of State (where he is not holding inde-pendent charge) or Deputy Minister in-charge of Consumer Affairs in the Central Government who shall be the Vice-Chairman of the Central Council;
3. the Secretary in-charge of Consumer Affairs in the Central Government who shall be the member-secretary of the Central Council;
4. the Minister in-charge of Consumer Affairs in States;
5. eight Members of Parliament—five from the Lok Sabha and three from the Rajya Sabha;
6. the Secretary of the National Commission for Scheduled Castes and Scheduled Tribes;
7. representatives of the Central Government Departments and autonomous organisations concerned with consumer interests—not exceeding twenty;
8. representatives of the Consumer Organisations or con-sumers—not less than thirty-five;
9. representatives of women—not less than ten;
10. representatives of farmers, trade and industries—not exceeding twenty;
11. persons capable of representing consumer interest not specified above—not exceeding fifteen;

2.3-2 *Vacancy* - Any member may, by writing under his hand to the Chairman of the Central Council, resign from the Council. The vacancies, so caused or otherwise, are filled from the same category by the Central Government and such person shall hold office so long as the member whose place he fills would have been entitled to hold office, if the vacancy had not occurred.

2.3-3 *Term* - The term of the Council is three years.

2.3-4 *Meatings of the Central Council [Section 5 and rule 4]* - Central Council is required to organise at least one meeting every year. In addition, it may meet as and when necessary. Time and place of the meeting is decided by the Chairman of the council.

Each meeting of the Central Council shall be called by giving, not less than ten days from the date of issue, notice in writing to every member.

Every notice of a meeting of the Central Council shall specify the place and the day and hour of the meeting and shall contain statement of business to be transacted thereat.

The meeting of the Central Council shall be presided over by the Chairman. In the absence of the Chairman, the Vice-Chairman shall preside over the meeting of the Central Council. In the absence of the Chairman and the Vice-Chairman, the Central Council shall elect a member to preside over that meeting of the Council.

The resolutions passed by the Central Council are recommendatory in nature.

No proceedings of the Central Council shall be invalid merely by reasons of existence of any vacancy in or any defect in the constitution of the Council.

State Consumer Protection Councils (State Councils) [Section 7]

2.4-1 *Composition* - The power to establish State Councils is with the States. The Act provides that the Minister incharge of con-sumer affairs in the State Government shall be the Chairman of the State Council. About the number and qualifications of the rest of the members, State is the deciding authority.

2.4-2 *Meetings* - The State Council meet at least twice a year. In addition, it may meet as and when necessary. The council may meet at such time and place as the Chairman may think fit.

Procedure in regard to the transaction of its business is pre-scribed by the State Government.

Working Groups [Rule 3]

2.5 For the purpose of monitoring the implementation of the recommendations of the Central Council and to suggest the working of the Council, the Central Government may constitute from amongst the members of the Council, a Standing Working

Group, under the chairmanship of the Member Secretary of the Council. The Standing Working Group shall consist of not exceeding 30 members and shall meet as and when considered necessary by the Central Government.

Consumer Forums

3.1 Ram, a resident of Panipat district, took his son Shyam to a doctor for eye treatment. Due to negligence of the doctor, Shyam lost sight of his left eye. Ram filed a suit against the doctor in District Forum claiming Rs. 4 lakh as compensation. The Dis-trict Forum dismissed his complaint on the ground that negligence of the doctor could not be proved.

Ram appealed to Haryana State Commission against this order. State Commission also upheld the decision of District Forum. Now Ram approached the National Commission and made an appeal there-in. Ram knew that after National Commission also, he is still left with an option to approach the Supreme Court against the order of the Commission. However, the National Commission decided in favour of Ram.

The Consumer Protection Act provides for a 3 tier approach in resolving consumer disputes. There are three levels of consumer courts —

First, there is the district court, called District Consumer Disputes Rederessal Forum (*District Forum*),

Next comes the State Consumer Disputes Redressal Commission (*State Commission*),

At the national level, there is National Consumer Disputes Re-dressal Commission (National Commission).

District Forum and State Commission are formed by States with the permission of the Central Government while the National Commis-sion is formed by the Central Government. These forums have not taken away the jurisdiction of the civil courts but have provided an alternative remedy.

The Consumer Protection Act, 1986 has given powers to the Central and State Governments to make rules with regard to various as-pects of the consumer protection machinery. In our discussion, we have included the Consumer Protection

Rules, 1987 made by the Central Government, wherever required.

Constitution of the Forums

3.2 The composition of the District Forum and the State Commis-sion has been detailed out by the Consumer Protection Act, 1986. As for the National Commission, the Consumer Protection Rules, 1987, elaborates upon its composition.

3.2-1 *District Forum [Section 10]*

3.2-1a COMPOSITION - District Forum consist of one president and two other members (one of whom is to be a woman).

The president of the Forum is a person who is, or has been quali-fied to be a District Judge, and other members are persons of ability, integrity and standing, and have adequate knowledge or experience of, or have shown capacity in dealing with, problems relating to economics, law, commerce, accountancy, industry, public affairs or administration.

The object underlying the inclusion of non-judicial members appears to be to impart a balance to the functioning of the District Forum by ensuring that the members are able to understand the economic and social impact of the matters. Further inclusion of one female members ensures that the matters are viewed from a woman's angle also.

3.2-1b APPOINTING AUTHORITY - Every appointment of the president and members of the District Forum is made by the State Government on the recommendation of a selection committee consisting of the following, namely—

(*i*) the President of the State Commission — Chairman.

(*ii*) Secretary, Law Department of the State — Member.

(*iii*) Secretary incharge of the Department dealing with consumer affairs in the State — Member.

3.2-1c TERM OF OFFICE [SECTION 10(2)] - Every member of the District Forum is to hold office for a term of five years or up to the age of 65 years, whichever is earlier. However, he/she shall not be eligible for re-appointment.

3.2-1d VACANCY - A vacancy in the office of president or a member may occur after the expiry of his term, or by his death, resigna-tion, or removal.

In terms of proviso to section 10(2), a member may resign his office in writing under his hand addressed to the State Govern-ment and on such resignation being accepted, his office shall become vacant and may be filled by the appointment of a person possessing the requisite qualifications in relation to the category of the member who has resigned.

The Consumer Protection Act does not have any specific provision for removal of the president and members of the District Forum. But the consumer protection rules made by various States provide for such removal. Accordingly, a president or member of a Dis-trict Forum may be removed by the State Government, who—

(*a*) has been adjudged an insolvent, or

(*b*) has been convicted of an offence involving moral turpi-tude, or

(*c*) has become physically or mentally incapable of perform-ing his duties, or

(*d*) has acquired such financial interest in the matter as would prejudicially affect his functions as president or member, or

(*e*) has abused his position so as to render his continuance to office prejudicial to public interest.

3.2-1e TERMS AND CONDITIONS OF SERVICE [SECTION 10(3)] - The salary or honorarium and other allowances payable to, and the other terms and conditions of service of the members of the District Forum shall be such as may be prescribed by the State Government. Different States have made different rules in this regard.

3.2-2 *State Commission [Section 16]* - After the District Forum, State Commission is next in the hierarchy of Consumer Rederessal Forums under the Act.

3.2-2a COMPOSITION - State Commission consists of a president and two members one of whom is to be a woman.

President is a person who is or has been a Judge of a High Court, and the members, are persons of ability, integrity and standing and have adequate knowledge or experience of, or have shown capacity in dealing with, problems relating to economics, law, commerce, accountancy, industry, public affairs or administra-tion.

3.2-2b APPOINTING AUTHORITY - President of a State Commission is appointed by the State Government after consultation with the Chief Justice of the High Court.

Other members of the Commission are made by the State Government on the recommendation of a selection committee consisting of the following, namely—

(*i*) President of the State Commission — Chairman.

(*ii*) Secretary of the Law Department of the State — Member.

(*iii*) Secretary, incharge of Department dealing with consumer affairs in the State — Member.

3.2-2c TERM OF OFFICE [SECTION 16(3)] - Every member of the State Commission shall hold office for five years or upto the age of 67 years whichever is earlier and he shall not be eligible for re-appointment.

3.2-2d VACANCY - Rules as to the vacancy related in the office of the president or any member are similar to those discussed in context of the members of the District Forum. Refer para 33.2-1d for the details.

3.2-1e TERMS AND CONDITIONS OF SERVICE [SECTION 16(2)] - The salary or honorarium and other allowances payable to, and the other terms and conditions of service of, the members of the State Commission shall be such as may be prescribed by the State Gov-ernment.

3.2-3 *National Commission [Section 20]* - The National Commission is the top most layer in the three level hierarchy of the Consum-er Forums.

3.2-3a COMPOSITION - The National Commission consists of a presi-dent, and four other members (one of whom is to be a woman).

The president should be the one who is or has been a Judge of the Supreme Court, and the members should be the persons of ability, integrity and standing and have adequate knowledge or experience of, or have shown capacity in dealing with, problems relating to economics, law, commerce, accountancy, industry, public affairs or administration.

3.2-3b APPOINTING AUTHORITY - The President is appointed by the Central Government after consultation with the Chief Justice of India;

The appointment of other members of the Commission is made by the Central Government on the recommendation of a *selection commit-tee.*

This selection committee consists of, namely:—

(*a*) a person who is a Judge of the Supreme Court, to be nominated by the Chief Justice of India—Chairman.

(*b*) the Secretary in the Department of Legal Affairs in the Government of India—Member.

(*c*) Secretary of the Department dealing with consumer affairs in the Government of India — Member.

Note that before appointment, the president and member(s) of the National Commission have to take an undertaking that he does not and will not have any such financial or other interest as is likely to affect prejudicially his functions as such member.

3.2-3c TERM OF OFFICE [SECTION 20(3)] - Every member of the National Commission is to hold office for a term of five years or upto the age of seventy years, whichever is earlier and is not eligible for re-appointment.

3.2-3d VACANCY - A vacancy in the office of president or a member may occur after the expiry of his term, or by his death, resigna-tion, or removal.

In terms of proviso to rule 12(3), the president or a member may resign his office in writing under his hand addressed to the Central Government, or he can be removed from his office in accordance with the provisions of rule 13.

Removal of the president and members in certain circumstances: In terms of Rule 13 of the Consumer Protection Rules, 1987, the Central Government may remove from office, the President or any member, who —

(*a*) has been adjudged as an insolvent; or

(*b*) has been convicted of an offence which, in the opinion of the Central Government, involves moral turpitude; or

(*c*) has become physically or mentally incapable of acting as the President or the member; or

(*d*) has acquired such financial or other interest as is likely to affect prejudicially his functions as the President or a member; or

(*e*) has so abused his position as to render his continuance in office prejudicial to the public interest; or

(*f*) remain absent in three consecutive sittings except for reasons beyond his control.

Note that the President or any member shall not be removed from his office on the grounds specified in clauses (*d*), (*e*) and (*f*) above except on an inquiry held by Central Government in accord-ance with such procedure as it may specify in this behalf and finds the President or a member to be guilty of such ground.

Note : 1. A casual vacancy caused by resignation or removal of the President or any other member of the National Commission is filled by fresh appointment.

2. When the President of the National Commission is unable to discharge the functions owing to absence, illness or any other cause, the senior most member of the National Commission with judicial background, if authorised so to do by the President in writing, shall discharge the functions of the President until the day on which the President resumes the charge of his functions.

3.2-3e TERMS AND CONDITIONS OF SERVICE [SECTION 20(2)] - In terms of the rules 11 and 12 made by the Central Government in pursu-ance of the powers given under the Act, the terms and conditions of service of the president and the members of the Commission are as follows:

(*a*) The President of the National Commission is entitled to salary, allowances and other perquisites as are available to a sitting Judge of the Supreme Court.

(*b*) The members, if sitting on whole-time basis, are enti-tled to a consolidated honorarium of ten thousand rupees per month or if sitting on part-time basis, a consolidated honorarium of five hundred rupees per day of sitting.

(*c*) The President and the members are entitled to travel-ling and daily allowances on official tours at the same rates as are admissible to group 'A' Officers of the Central Government.

(*d*) The President and the members of the National Commis-sion are entitled to conveyance allowance of one hundred fifty rupees per day of its sitting or a sum of one thousand and five hundred rupees per month, as may be opted by them.

Notes : 1. The terms and conditions of service of the President and the members should not be varied to their disadvantage during their tenure of office.

2. The money payable to these members and the president shall be defrayed out of the Consolidated Fund of India.

Further it is worth noting that in case any defect lies in the constitution of the District Forum, or State Commission or National Commission, or any vacancy remains therein while proceedings are made for any dispute, such defect or vacancy shall not affect the validity of the order of the Forum. [Section 29A].

Jurisdiction

3.3 The term jurisdiction may be defined as authority or legal power to hear and decide the cases. Thus a court may adjudicate only those matters which fall under its jurisdiction. The ques-tion of jurisdiction has to be considered with reference to the value, place, and nature of the subject matter.

Example : A and B reside in Bombay. They have some dispute. Here the dispute may be subjected to the jurisdiction of the Bombay courts (except matters pertaining to Supreme Court). Courts of Delhi, or Chennai, or any other place for that matter cannot adjudicate the issue.

The general rule is that if the court rendering the judgment suffers from want of jurisdiction, its judgment is nullity and may be ignored.

Jurisdiction of Consumer Forums (*i.e.,* consumer courts) differ in terms of monetary value of claims, geographical area, and appel-late powers.

District Forum

3.3-1a PECUNIARY JURISDICTION - District Forum entertains the cases where the value of claim is upto Rs. 5 Lakh. Where a claim exceed this limit, the matter is beyond the jurisdiction of the Forum.

This limit of Rs. 5 lakh is as to the value of claim filed by the party. Value of goods or services in question or value of relief granted is not relevant for this purpose.

Example : A purchased machinery for Rs. 7 lakhs. After working for some time, the machine broke down due to some manufacturing defect. A filed a claim for compensation worth Rs. 4.5 lakh. Since the value of claim is less than Rs. 5 Lakh, it will fall under the jurisdiction of District Forum.

The complainant has a right to reduce value of his claim in order to bring his claim within the jurisdiction of a junior forum.

Example : A filed a complaint with a District Forum claiming Rs. 6,00,000 as against a supplier of machinery. The complaint was rejected on the ground that it was beyond the jurisdiction of the District Forum. A revised his claim to

Rs. 4,99,999 and filed the plaint again with the same District Forum. The plaint was accept-ed and tried.

3.3-1b TERRITORIAL JURISDICTION - Every District Forum has defi-nite geographical limits within which it can exercise its juris-diction. A case is supposed to fall within such territory when at the time of the institution of the complaint—

(*a*) The party against whom the claim is made actually and voluntarily resides or carries on business or has a branch office or personally works for gain in that area, or

(*b*) Where there are more than one opposite party, each such party actually and voluntarily resides or carries on business or has a branch office or personally works for gain in that area, or

(*c*) Where there are more than one opposite party, and any such party actually and voluntarily resides or carries on busi-ness or has a branch office or personally works for gain in that area, provided the other parties not so residing or working agrees, or the District Forum gives permission in this regard,

(*d*) The cause of action, wholly or in part, arises in that area.

3.3-1c APPELLATE JURISDICTION - District Forum is the lowest rung of the ladder of the consumer courts. Thus this is not an appel-late court, *i.e.,* no appeal lies in this court.

State Commission

3.3-2a PECUNIARY JURISDICTION - State Commission entertains the cases where the value of claim exceeds Rs. 5 lakh. But where value of a claim exceed Rs. 20 lakh, the matter is beyond the jurisdiction of the Commission.

Example : A of Delhi bought a house from housing board for Rs. 4 lakh. Due to defect in the house, its wall fell down on the daughter of A and she dies. A sue the Housing Board claiming Rs. 15 lakh as compensation. This matter will lie with the State Commission of Delhi.

Note : That although the value of house is less than 5 lakh, the decisive factor regarding jurisdiction is the value of claim.

3.3-2b TERRITORIAL JURISDICTION - The Consumer Protection Act does not specifically provides for the territorial jurisdiction of the State Commission. Thus it is governed by the general principle of the law which are contained in section

20 of the Civil Procedure Code. Broadly these principles are on the similar lines on which the territorial jurisdiction of District Forum is based. Thus a suit can be instituted in the State Commission *within whose local limits*—

(*a*) the party against whom the claim is made actually and voluntarily resides or carries on business or personally works for gain, or

(*b*) where there are more than one opposite party, each such party actually and voluntarily resides or carries on business or personally works for gain, or

(*c*) where there are more than one opposite party, and any such party actually and voluntarily resides or carries on busi-ness or has a branch office or personally works for gain, provid-ed the other parties not so residing or working agrees, or the State Commission gives permission in this regard, or

(*d*) the cause of action, wholly or in part, arises.

3.3-2c APPELLATE JURISDICTION [SECTION 17(*a*)(*ii*)] - State Commission has power to adjudicate upon the appeals made against the order of the District Forums. Any person aggrieved by an order made by the District Forum may prefer an appeal against such order within 30 days from the date of order. However, the State Commission may entertain an appeal after the expiry of 30 days if it is satisfied that there was sufficient cause for delay.

Note : 30 days are counted not from the date of order but from the date when the order is communicated to the appellant.

3.3-2d REVISIONAL JURISDICTION [SECTION 17(*b*)] - State Commission may call for the records and pass appropriate orders in any consumer dispute which is pending before or has been decided by any District Forum within the State, where State Commission is of the view that the District Forum—

- has exercised jurisdiction which it was not entitled to, or
- has failed to exercise such jurisdiction which it was entitled to, or

- has exercised its jurisdiction illegally or with mate-rial irregularity.

Such revisional jurisdiction may be exercised by the Commission on its own or on the application of a party.

3.3-3 *National Commission*

3.3-3a PECUNIARY JURISDICTION - Since National Commission is the highest level of Consumer Forums, it may entertain all the mat-ters where the value of claim exceeds Rs. 20 lakh.

3.3-3b TERRITORIAL JURISDICTION - The territorial jurisdiction of the National Commission is whole of India except the State of Jammu & Kashmir.

However, the Consumer Protection Act is applicable only if the cause of action arise in India. If the cause of action arises out of India, National Commission has no jurisdiction over the matter as it cannot be tried in India under the Act.

Example: The complainant alleged that they were not properly treated by the Egyptian Airlines authorities at Barcelona. It was held that the cause of action arose at Barcelona, so the com-plaint under the Act is not maintainable in India - *Gulab Hot-chand Bhagchandaney* v. *Egyptian Airlines* III 1994 CPJ 172 (NC).

3.3-3c APPELLATE JURISDICTION - The National Commission has jurisdiction to entertain appeals against the order of any State Commission. The appeal may be made within 30 days from the date of the order of the State Commission. However the National Com-mission may entertain an appeal filed after the expiry of 30 days if it is satisfied that there was sufficient cause for not filing the appeal within the given time.

3.3-3d REVISIONAL JURISDICTION [SECTION 21(*b*)] - National Commis-sion can call for the records and pass the appropriate orders in any consumer dispute which is pending before or has been decided by any State Commission it is of the view that the State Commis-sion—

- has exercised jurisdiction which it was not entitled to, or

- has failed to exercise such jurisdiction which it was entitled to, or
- has exercised its jurisdiction illegally or with mate-rial irregularity.

Note that the revisional jurisdiction is available to the Nation-al Commission only in the cases where there has been wrongful, illegal, and improper exercise of jurisdiction or failure to exercise jurisdiction on the part of State Commission.

Example: K made an appeal to the National Commission against the order of the State Commission whereby the State Commission had made an order against him although he was not a made a party to the dispute by the complainant. The National Commission observed that the order of the State Commission was vitiated by illegal exercise of jurisdiction resulting immaterial irregularity and accordingly, the same was liable to be set aside - *Kinetic Engi-neering Ltd.* v. *Samasi Saunand* [1993] II CPR 409 (NC).

Procedures

3.4 We understand that the Consumer Forums are the bodies who function like courts in order to settle the consumer disputes. Their composition is so made as to best represent the interests of the consumers, and they have specified jurisdictions. The next question is - what procedure these Forums adopt in order to deal with the consumer disputes.

Section 13 of the Act has detailed the procedure in context of District Forum only. For State Commission, section 18 says that it will follow the same procedure as followed by District Forum with such modifications as necessary, and for the National Commission, section 22 gives power to the Central Government to make rules in this regard. These rules in turn have included therein the procedure given by section 13. In addition, these rules have prescribed some procedures to be followed by the par-ties to the complaint.

A complaint may be made with respect to the goods or services. When complaint relates to goods, the criteria for the decision is - whether the goods are defective or not. Now the question is - how to hold that the goods are defective. The most logical way is to get the goods tested to determine the defect. However, in certain cases defect can be determined without technical support or it may happen that the test is not feasible. These are—

- The opposite party admits the defect.
- The defect is obvious and is visible to naked eyes, like in a complaint about contamination of water, the sample of water given was so dirty that the Forum did not consider it necessary to send it for test.
- When the complainant is not in possession of the sub-ject matter of the complaint, *e.g.*, in a matter the complainant had given to the dealer the tyre and tube which had burst, the dealer sent the same to the manufacturer. Thus the complainant was not in possession of the same.
- When subject matter of the complaint gets destroyed, like in case a pressure cooker burst, its remains can't be send to the laboratory for testing.
- In case of complaint regarding deficiency in service there is no question of testing or analysis.

Thus the procedure to be followed by the Forums can be discussed under the two heads—

1. where laboratory test is required to determine the defect in goods.
2. where no laboratory test is required to determine the defect in goods or the complaint relates to services.

3.4-1 *Procedure to be followed by the District Forum [Section 13]* - The following procedure is equally applicable to the District Forum, State Commission with required modifications, and National Commission with additional procedures required by the rules.

3.4-1a WHERE LABORATORY TEST IS REQUIRED TO DETERMINE THE DEFECT IN GOODS - A consumer is supposed to file as many copies of the complaint as there are number of judges, with all essential information, supporting papers like correspondence, and specify-ing the compensation demanded.

On receipt of such complaint—

(*a*) The District Forum should refer a copy of the complaint to the opposite party directing him to give his version of the case within a period of thirty days which can be extended to forty five days.

Where the opposite party on receipt of a complaint referred to him denies or disputes the allegations contained in the complaint, or omits or fails to take any action to represent his case within the time given by the District Forum, the District Forum would take the following steps to settle the dispute :

(*b*) The District Forum may require the complainant to deposit specified fees for payment to the appropriate laboratory for carrying out the necessary analysis or test in relation to the goods in question.

(*c*) The District Forum will obtain a sample of the goods, seal it, authenticate it and refer the sample so sealed to the **appropriate laboratory* for an analysis or test, whichever may be necessary, with a view to finding out whether such goods suffer from any defect.

The District Forum will remit the fees to the appropriate labora-tory to enable it to carry out required analysis or test.

The laboratories supposed to report its findings to the District Forum within a period of fifty-five days. This period is extendi-ble by the District Forum.

(*d*) Upon receiving laboratory's report, its copy will be forwarded by the District Forum to the opposite party alongwith its own remarks.

(*e*) In the event of any party disputing the correctness of the findings, or the methods of analysis or test adopted by the appropriate laboratory, the District Forum shall require the objecting party to submit his objections in writing.

(*f*) The District Forum will give an opportunity of hearing to the objecting party.

(*g*) The District Forum shall issue appropriate order after hearing the parties.

3.4-1b WHERE NO LABORATORY TEST IS REQUIRED TO DETERMINE THE DEFECT IN GOODS OR THE COMPLAINT RELATES TO SERVICES

(*a*) On receiving the complaint, the District Forum should refer a copy of the complaint to the opposite party directing him to give his version of the case within a period of thirty days which can be extended to forty five days.

(*b*) The opposite party on receipt of a complaint referred to him may—

(*i*) admit the complaint

(*ii*) deny or dispute the allegations contained in the com-plaint, or

(*iii*) omits or fails to respond within the time given by the District Forum.

(*c*) Where the opposite party admits the allegation, the District Forum should decide the matter on the basis of the merits of the case and the documents before it.

Where the opposite party denies or disputes the allega-tions made in the complaint, the District Forum will proceed to settle the dispute on the basis of evidence brought to its notice by both the parties.

Where the opposite party omits or fails to respond within the time given by the Forum, the District Forum will proceed to settle the dispute on the basis of evidence brought to its notice by the complainant.

(*d*) The District Forum shall issue an appropriate order after hearing the parties and taking into account available evidence.

Note : Although this procedure may be followed by all - the District Forum, State Commission, and National Commission, we have used the name of 'District Forum' while describing the procedure.

**What is an appropriate laboratory under the Act*

Section 2(1)(*a*) of the Act defines an "appropriate laboratory" as a laboratory or organisation—

(*i*) recognised by the Central Government;

(*ii*) recognised by a State Government, subject to such guidelines as may be prescribed by the Central Government in this behalf; or

(*iii*) any such laboratory or organisation established by or under any law for the time being in force, which is main-tained, financed or aided by the Central Government or a State Government for carrying out analysis or test of any goods with a view to determining whether such goods suffer from any defect.

Note : Rule 2A of the Consumer Protection Rules, 1987 provides the procedure to be followed by the laboratories in order to get recognition from the States. We have not discussed this procedure here since it is beyond purview of our study.

3.4-2 *Procedure to be followed by the National Commission [Sec-tion 22]* - Section 22 of the Act provides that the National Commission shall follow such procedure as prescribed by the Central Government. The Consumer Protection Rules, 1987 framed by the Central Government lay down the procedure which is as follows :

(1) A complaint containing the following particulars shall be presented by the complainant in person or by his agent to the National Commission or be sent by registered post, addressed to the National Commission :

(*a*) the name, description and the address of the complain-ant;

(*b*) the name, description and address of the opposite party or parties, as the case may be, so far as they can be ascer-tained;

(*c*) the facts relating to the complaint and when and where it arose;

(*d*) documents in support of the allegations contained in the complaint;

(*e*) the relief which the complainant claims.

(2) The National Commission shall, in disposal of any complaint before it, as far as possible, follow the procedures laid down section 13 of the Act. (discussed in para 33.4-1)

(3) On the date of hearing, it shall be obligatory on the parties or their agents to appear before the National Commission. Where the complainant or his agent fails to appear, the National Commission may either dismiss the complaint for default or decide it on merits. Where the opposite party or its agent fails to appear on the date of hearing the National Commission may decide the complaint *ex parte*.

(4) The complaint shall be decided as far as possible within a period of three months from the date of notice received by oppo-site party where complaint does not require analysis or testing of commodities and within five months if it requires analysis or testing of commodities.

(5) After the proceedings, the National Commission shall issue the orders accordingly. (Refer para 33.5-3)

Powers of the Consumer Forums [Sections 13(4), 14(1) and Rule 10]

3.5 For the purpose of adjudicating a consumer dispute, section 13(4) has vested the Consumer Forums with certain powers of a civil court. Apart from these powers, the Central Government has provided some additional powers to them under Rule 10 of the Consumer Protection Rules, 1987. Finally section 14 of the Act has provided them with the power to issues orders.

3.5-1 *Powers akin to those of civil court [Section 13(4)]* - The Forums are vested with the Civil Court powers with respect to the following :

(*a*) summoning and enforcing the attendance of any defendant or witness and examining the witness on oath;

(*b*) discovery and production of any document or other mate-rial object producible as evidence;

(*c*) receiving of evidence on affidavits;

(*d*) requisitioning of the report of the concerned analysis or test from the appropriate laboratory or from any other rele-vant source;

(*e*) issuing of any commission for the examination of any witness; and

(*f*) any other matter which may be prescribed.

3.5-2 *Additional powers of the consumer forums [Rule 10]* - The National Commission, the State Commission and the District Forum have following additional powers :

(*a*) Requiring production of any books, accounts, documents, or commodities from any person, examining and retaining them.

(*b*) Obtaining information required for the purpose of the proceedings from any person.

(*c*) enter and search any premises and seize from such premises books, papers, documents, commodities required for the purpose of proceedings under the Act.

3.5-3 *Power to issue order [Section 14(1)]* - If, after the pro-ceedings, the Forum is satisfied that the complainant suffer from any defect in goods or deficiency in service, it may issue an order to the opposite party directing him to do one or more of the following things, namely :—

(*a*) to remove the defect pointed out by the appropriate laboratory from the goods in question;

(*b*) to replace the goods with new goods of similar descrip-tion which shall be free from any defect;

(*c*) to return to the complainant the price, or, as the case may be, the charges paid by the complainant;

(*d*) to pay such amount as may be awarded by it as compensa-tion to the consumer for any loss or injury suffered by the consumer due to the negligence of the opposite party;

(*e*) to remove the defects or deficiencies in the services in question;

(*f*) to discontinue the unfair trade practice or the re-strictive trade practice or not to repeat it;

(*g*) not to offer the hazardous goods for sale;

(*h*) to withdraw the hazardous goods from being offered for sale;

(*i*) to provide for adequate costs to complainant.

Sitting of the Forums

3.6 The law has provided certain norms as to the number of judges who will handle a dispute. The rationale must have been to make the decisive body as broad as possible.

3.6-1 *Sitting of the District Forum* - For conducting any proceedings to resolve a consumer dispute, at least two members of the Forum must be there one of whom should be the president.

Where the member, for any reason, is unable to conduct the pro-ceeding till it is completed, the President and the other member shall conduct such proceeding *de novo i.e.* from the beginning.

Example - A District Forum has three members, P the president, and X and Y, the other two members. P and X started dealing with a particular case. In the meantime, X fell ill and dropped out. Now the proceedings in the given case will be started afresh by P and Y (or any other member appointed in place of X).

3.6-2 *Sitting of the State Commission* - Every proceeding is required to be conducted by the president of the State Commission and at least one member thereof sitting together.

However, if for any reason the member is unable to conduct the proceeding till it is completed, the president and the other member shall conduct such proceeding afresh.

3.6-3 *Sitting of the National Commission* - The disputes must be disposed of by at least three members of the National Commission, one of whom must be the president (or the senior most member authorised to work as president).

Where the member(s) for any reason are unable to conduct the proceeding till it is completed, the president (or the senior most member acting as president) shall conduct the proceeding afresh.

Note *that the rules regarding sitting are mandatory. Any failure to comply with the same may invalidate the order.*

Orders of the Forums

3.7 The orders of the Consumers Forums are like orders of the Civil Court and are enforceable like a decree of the court. The order of a junior Forum is appealable with the senior Forum, and when no appeal is instituted, the order is final. However, the law has prescribed certain norms as to the signing of orders without complying which the orders cannot be made.

3.7-1 *District Forum - Signing requirement* - Section 14(2A) provides that every order made by the District Forum shall be signed by its President and the member or members who conducted the proceeding.

Example : A complaint was dismissed by the President of a Dis-trict Forum where other members of the Forum were not parties to it. On appeal, the State Commission held that section 14(2) of the Act makes it abundantly clear that for the decision on a complaint, one member of the Forum is must besides the President. Thus in the present case, the President of the Forum alone is not competent to dismiss the claim - *Pankaj* v. *Chairman Central Secondary Education Board* [1991] 1 CPR 711 Delhi (CDRC).

If there is difference of opinion between any two members, matter should be referred to the third member for a decision. And the decision of the majority would be final. Thus any order passed by a single member of the District Forum is not warranted.

3.7-2 *State Commission - Signing requirement* - Every order made by the State Commission shall be signed by its President and the member or members who conducted the proceeding.

If there is difference of opinion between any two members, matter should be referred to the third member for a decision. And the decision of the majority would be final.

3.7-3 *National Commission - Signing requirement* - Every order made by the National Commission must be signed by the president (or the senior most member acting as president), and at least two members who conducted the proceeding, and in case of any difference of opinion, the opinion of the majority shall be the order of the Commission.

3.7-4 *Appeals against orders* - 'Appeal' is a legal instrumentali-ty whereby a person not satisfied with the findings of a court has an option to go to a higher court to present his case and seek justice. In the context of Consumer Forums -

1. An appeal can be made with the State Commission against the order of the District Forum within 30 days of the order which is extendable for further 15 days. [Section 15]
2. An appeal can be made with the National Commission against the order of the State Commission within 30 days of the order or within such time as the National Commission allows. [Section 19]
3. An appeal can be made with the Supreme Court against the order of the National Commission within 30 days of the order or within such time as the Supreme Court allows. [Section 23]

3.7-5 *Finality of orders* - Where no appeal has been preferred against the order made by the District Forum, or State Commission, or the National Commission, such order shall be final. [Section 24]

3.7-6 *Penalties for non-compliance* - Every order made by the District Forum or State Commission, or the National Commission may be enforced in the same manner as if it were a decree of the court. [Section 25]

All the persons- the trader, or complainant, or the opposite party, are supposed to comply with the orders. When any such person fails or omits to comply with the order, the District Forum, or State Commission, or the National Commission, as the case may be, may punish him with—

- imprisonment for a term ranging between one month and three years, or
- with fine ranging between Rs. 2,000 and Rs. 10,000, or
- with both.

THE CONSUMER PROTECTION RULES 1987

(Amended up to 13.10.2006)

In exercise of the powers conferred by sub-section (1) of section 30 of the Consumer Protection Act, 1986 (68 of 1986), the Central Government hereby makes the following rules, namely:-

1. Short title, extent and commencement. -

(1) These rules may be called the Consumer Protection (Second Amendment) Rules, 2006.

(2) They shall come into force on the date of their publication in the Official Gazette.

2. Definitions. - In these rules, unless the context otherwise requires—

(a) "Act' means the Consumer Protection Act 1986 (68 of 1986);

(b) "agent" means a person duly authorised by a party to present any complaint, appeal or reply on its behalf before the National Commission;

(c) "appellant" means a party which makes an appeal against the order of the State Commission;

(d) "chairman" means a chairman of the Central Consumer Protection Council established under sub-section (1) of the section 4 of the Act;

(e) "memorandum" means any memorandum of appeal filed by the appellant;

(f) "opposite party" means a person who answers complaint or claim;

(g) "president" means the President of the National Commission;

(h) "respondent" means the person who answers any memorandum of appeal;

(i) "section" means section of the Act;

(j) "state" includes Union territories also;

(k) words and expressions used in the rules and not defined but defined in the Act shall have the meanings respectively assigned to them in the Act.

2A. State Governments to recognise a laboratory as an appropriate Laboratory. -

(1) For the purpose of obtaining recognition as an appropriate laboratory, the applicant shall send application, in triplicate, in the proforma prescribed by the Bureau of Indian Standards with the relevant details to the Department concerned with the consumer protection work in the State Government.

(2) The State Government on receiving the application from the applicant, shall forward its two copies to the Bureau of Indian Standards to assess the suitability of the laboratory from the standards prescribed by them (Bureau of Indian Standards). The fee charged by the Bureau of Indian Standards, for this purpose, shall be paid by the applicant.

(3) The State Government on receiving the recommendations and approval of the Bureau of Indian Standards, shall notify that laboratory as an "appropriate laboratory" for the purpose of Consumer Protection Act, 1986 for a period of three years.

3. The Constitution of the Central Consumer Protection Council and the Working Groups. -

(1) The Central Government shall, by notification in the Official Gazette constitute the Central Consumer Protection Council (herein after referred to as the Central Council) which shall consist of the following members, not exceeding 35, namely:—

(a) the Minister in-charge of Consumer Affairs in the Central Government who shall be the Chairman of the Central Council;

(b) the Minister of State (where he is not holding independent charge) or Deputy Minister in charge of Consumer Affairs in the Central Government who shall be the Vice-Chairman of the Central Council;

(c) the Minister in-charge of Consumer Affairs of two of the States from each region as mentioned in Schedule I to be changed by rotation on expiration of the term of the Council on each occasion;

(ca) an administrator (whether designated as administrator or Lieutenant Governor), of a Union Territory, to represent a Union Territory, as mentioned in Schedule II, to be changed by rotation on expiration of the term of the Council on each occasion;

(d) two Members of Parliament — one from the Lok Sabha and one from the Rajya Sabha;

(f) representatives of the Central Government Departments and autonomous orginisations concerned with consumer interests—not exceeding five;

(f(a)The Registrar, National Consumer Disputes Redressal Commission, New Delhi.

(g) representatives of the Consumer Organisations from amongst the Indian members of the International Organisation, namely, Consumer International – not exceeding six, to be nominated by the Central Government;

(ga) representatives with proven expertise and experience who are capable of representing consumer interests, drawn from amongst consumer organizations, consumer activists, women, farmers trade and industry – not exceeding five, one from each of the regions specified in Schedule annexed to these rules;

(j) the Secretary in-charge of Consumer Affairs in the State to be nominated by the Central Government – not exceeding three;

(k) the Secretary in-charge of Consumer Affairs in the Central Government shall be the member – secretary of the Central Council.

(2) The term of the Council shall be three years.

(3) Any member may, by writing under his hand to the Chairman of the Central Council, resign from the Council. The vacancies, so caused or otherwise, shall be filled from the same

category by the Central Government and such person shall hold office so long as the member whose place he fills would have been entitled to hold office, if the vacancy had not occurred.

4. Procedure of the Central Council.—Under sub-section (2) of section 5, the Central Council shall observe the following procedure in regard to the transaction of its business,—

(1) The meeting of the Central Council shall be presided over by the Chairman. In the absence of the Chairman, the Vice-Chairman shall preside over the meeting of the Central Council. In the absence of the Chairman and the Vice-Chairman, the Central Council shall elect a member to preside over that meeting of the Council.

(2) Each meeting of the Central Council shall be called by giving, not less than ten days from the date of issue, notice in writing to every member.

(3) Every notice of a meeting of the Central Council shall specify the place and the day and hour of the meeting and shall contain statement of business to be transacted thereat.

(4) No proceedings of the Central Council shall be invalid merely by reasons of existence of any vacancy in or any defect in the constitution of the Council.

(5) For the purpose of performing its functions under the Act, the Central Council may constitute from amongst its members, such working groups as it may deem necessary and every working group so constituted shall perform such functions as are assigned to it by the Central Council. The findings of such working groups shall be placed before the Central Council for its consideration.

(6) In connection with the journey undertaken to and fro by the non-official members for attending the meeting of the Central Consumer Protection Council or its working group, they shall be entitled to avail first class or two-tier air-conditioned class of railway accommodation by all trains (including Rajdhani Express) and claim such fare or cost of actual mode of travel, whichever is less. The non-official members from Island territories shall be entitled to, to and fro air journey (economy class) in domestic airlines from the Islands

to the nearest main-land airport and thereafter rail fare by entitled class. The non-official members who are senior citizens shall be entitled to, to and fro air-journey (economy class) in domestic airlines on availing senior citizen concessional air fare for their journeys provided the distance being travelled is 1000 kms or above. The non-official members shall be entitled to a sum of Rs.1000 per day as incidental charges to cover the expenditure towards their daily allowance, lodging, local conveyance from residence to the station/airport and from station/airport to the venue of meeting and vice-versa. Every claim made under this sub-rule shall be subject to certifying that the member will not claim any benefit from any other Central Government Ministry, Department or Organization during his visit for attending the meeting of the Central Consumer Protection Councilor any of its Working Group. Local non-official members residing at the place of the venue of the meeting, shall be paid consolidated conveyance, hire charges and incidental charges to cover the daily allowances, to the tune of Rs.200 per diem irrespective of the classification of the city'. Members of Parliament attending meetings of the Councilor its Working Group shall be entitled to travelling and daily allowances at such rates as are admissible to such members".

(7) The resolution passed by the Central Council shall be recommendatory in nature.

5. Place of the National Commission.—The office of the National Commission shall be located in the Union Territory of Delhi.

6. Working days and office hours of the National Commission.—The working days and office hours of the National Commission shall be the same as that of the Central Government.

7. Seal and emblem.—The official seal and emblem of the National Commission shall be such as the Central Government may specify.

8. Sitting of the National Commission.—The sitting of the National Commission as and when necessary, shall be convened by the President.

9. Staff of the National Commission.—The Central Government shall appoint such staff as may be necessary to assist the National Commission in its day to day work and to perform such other functions as are provided under the Act and these rules or assigned to it by the President. The salary payable to such staff shall be defrayed out of the Consolidated Fund of India.

9A. Fee for making complaints before District Forum -

(1) Every complaint filed under sub-section (1) of section 12, sub-section (1) of section 17 and clause (a) in sub-clause (i) of section 21 of the Act shall be accompanied by a fee as specified in the table given below in the form of crossed Demand Draft drawn on a nationalised bank or through a crossed Indian Postal Order drawn in favour of the Registrar of the State Commission and payable at the respective place where the State Commission or the National Commission is situated.

(2) The concerned authority referred to in sub-rule (1) shall credit the amount of fee received by it into the Consumer Welfare Fund of the respective State and where such fund is not established into the Receipt Account of the State Government and in the case of the National Commission, to the Consumer Welfare Fund of the Central Government.

TABLE

Sl. No.	Total Value of goods or services and the compensation claimed	Amount of fee payable
(1)	(2)	(3)
	District Forum	
(1)	Upto one lakh rupees – For complainants who are under the Below Poverty Line holding Antyodaya Anna Yojana Cards	Nil
(2)	Upto one lakh rupees – For complainants other than Antyodaya Anna Yojana card holders.	Rs.100
(3)	Above one lakh and upto five lakh rupees	Rs.200
(4)	Above five lakh and upto ten lakh rupees	Rs.400
(5)	Above ten lakh and upto twenty lakh rupees	Rs.500
	State Commission	
(6)	Above twenty lakh and upto fifty lakh rupees	Rs.2000
(7)	Above fifty lakh and upto one crore rupees	Rs.4000
	National Commission	
(8)	Above one crore rupees	Rs.5000

TABLE

Sl. No.	Value of goods or services and the compensation claimed	Amount of fee payable
(1)	(2)	(3)
	District Forum	
(1)	(1) Upto one lakh rupees	Rs.100
(2)	One lakh rupees and above but less than five lakh rupees	Rs.200
(3)	Five lakh rupees and above but less than Rs.10 lakh	Rs.400
(4)	Ten lakh rupees and above but not exceeding twenty lakh rupees	Rs.500

(3) The complainants who are under the Below Poverty Line shall be entitled for the exemption of payment of fee only on production of an attested copy of the Antyodaya Anna Yojana cards.

10. Additional powers of the National Commission, State Commission and District Forum. - (1) The National Commission, the State Commission and the District Forum shall have power to require any person,—

(a) to produce before, and allow to be examined and kept by an officer of the National Commission, the State Commission or the District Forum, as the case may be, specified in this behalf, such books, accounts, documents or commodities in the custody or under the control of the person so required as may be specified or described in the requisition, if the examination of such books, accounts, documents or commodities are required for the purpose of this Act;

(b) to furnish to an officer so specified, such information as may be required for the purpose of this Act.

(2)(a) Where during any proceedings under this Act, the National Commission, the State Commission or the District Forum, as the case may be, has any ground to believe that any book, paper, commodity or document which may be required to be produced in such proceedings, are being or may be, destroyed, mutilated, altered, falsified or secreted, it may, by written order, authorise any officer to exercise the power of entry and search of any premises. Such authorised officer may also seize such books, papers, documents or commodities as are required for the purpose of this Act:

Provided that such seizure shall be communicated to the National Commission, the State Commission or the District Forum, as the case may be, as soon as it is made or within a period not exceeding 72 hours of making such seizure after specifying the reasons in writing for making such seizure.

(b) The National Commission, the State Commission or the District Forum, as the case may be, on examination of such seized documents or commodities, as the case may be, may order the retention thereof or may return it to the party concerned.

10A. Credit of the fine into the Consumer Welfare Fund when consumers are not identified conveniently.

(1) Where an order is passed by the National Commission in exercise of the powers vested under clause (hb) of sub-section (1) of section 14 directing the opposite party to pay such amount as determined by it on account of loss or injury suffered due to defects in goods complained ~gains~ or alleged deficiency of service to a large number of consumers, who are not identifiable conveniently;

Such sum shall be credited by the National Commission in the Consumer Welfare Fund established by the Central Government under section 12 (C) of the Central Excise Act, 1944 (1 of 1944).

(2) Any amount credited to the said Fund shall be utilized in accordance with the provisions of the Consumer Welfare Fund Rules, 1992.

10B. Number of Members in the National Commission: - The National Commission shall consist of not less than four members and not more than nine members and at least one of them shall be a woman.

11. Salaries, honorarium and other allowances of the President and Members of the National Commission.—(1) The President of the National Commission shall be entitled to salary, allowances and other perquisites as are available to a sitting Judge of the Supreme Court.

(1A) The other members of the National Commission appointed on whole time basis shall be entitled to the following honorarium and other allowances with effect from the 1st day of April, 2006, namely :-

(a) the members shall be paid twenty-three thousand rupees per month by way of honorarium:

Provided that the members, who are retired Judges of High Courts or retired Secretaries to the Government of India shall have the option to either receive consolidated honorarium of twenty-three thousand rupees per month or receive remuneration of last pay drawn less pension;

(b) a woman who has not held an office of profit earlier, on appointment as a member shall be entitled to a pay in the scale of Rs.24050-26000 per month along with other benefits;

(c) the members shall be provided with Government accommodation or receive house rent allowance of eight thousand rupees per month in lieu thereof;

(d) the members shall be paid conveyance allowance at the rate of ten thousand rupees per month, if no chauffeur driven government vehicle is provided in which event one hundred fifty liters of petrol shall be supplied or the price thereof shall be paid;

(e) the members shall be entitled to one thousand free calls for the telephone installed at their residence, with STD and ISD facilities; and

(f) the members shall be entitled to fifteen days casual leave in a year.

(2) The members shall be entitled to traveling and daily allowances on official tours at the same rates as are admissible to group 'A' Officers of the Central Government.

(3) The honorarium or the salary, as the case may be, and other allowances shall be defrayed out of the Consolidated Fund of India.

12. Terms and conditions of service of the President and mem-bers of the National Commission.—(1) Before appointment, the Presi-dent and a member of the National Commission shall

have to take an undertaking that he does not and will not have any such financial or other interest as is likely to affect prejudicially his functions as such member.

(3) Notwithstanding anything contained in sub-rule (2) the President or a member may.—

(a) by writing under his hand and addressed to the Central Government resign his office at any time but his office shall become vacant only when such resignation is accepted by the Central Government,

(b) be removed from his office in accordance with the provisions of rule 13.

(4) The terms and conditions of service of the President and the members shall not be varied to their disadvantage during their tenure of office.

(5) A casual vacancy caused by resignation or removal of the President or any other member of the National Commission under sub-rule (3) or otherwise shall be filled by fresh appointment.

(6) when the office of the President of the National Commission is vacant or a person occupying such office is by reason of absence or otherwise, unable to perform the duties of his office, the same shall, save as otherwise provided in the proviso to section 22 D be performed by the senior most member of the National Commission.

(7) The President or any member ceasing to hold office as such shall not hold any appointment in or be connected with the management or administrations of an organisation which have been the subject of any proceeding under the Act during his tenure for a period of 5 years from the date on which he ceases to hold such office.

12A. Procedure for selection of members. - (1) Save as otherwise provided in sub-rule (2), the process of appointment of a member shall be initiated at least three months before the vacancy arises.

(2) If a post falls vacant due to resignation or death of a member or creation of a new post, the process for filling the

post shall be initiated immediately after the post has fallen vacant or its created, as the case may be.

(3) An advertisement of a vacancy inviting applications from eligible candidates may be published in leading newspapers in India or by vacancy circulars or both, as may be decided by the Central Government.

(4) After scrutiny of the applications received till the last date specified for receipt of applications, a list of eligible candidates alongwith their applications shall be placed before the Selection Committee constituted under the third proviso to sub-section (1) of section 20.

(5) The Selection Committee shall consider all the applications of eligible applicants referred to it.

(6) The Selection Committee shall, subject to the provisions of sub-rule (6A), assess the suitability of the candidates for the post of Member.

Provided that the Selection Committee may, if it considers necessary, depending on the number of candidates, short list them on the basis of comparative merit and experience of such candidates for selection.

(6A) The Selection Committee shall assess the suitability of the candidates and where short listing is done, from among the short-listed candidates, for the post of Member in the Following manner, namely:-

(a) in the case of candidates having judicial background, by assessing them on the basis of the judgments and other judicial orders passed by such candidates;

(b) in the case of candidates having experience of working under the Central Government or any State Government or an undertaking under the Central Government or a State Government, by assessing such candidates on the basis of their Annual Confidential Reports and their experience relevant to the post applied for;

(c) in other cases, the suitability of the short listed candidates shall be assessed by the Selection Committee on the basis of personal interview conducted by it:

Provided that notwithstanding anything contained in this sub-rule, the Selection Committee may, for assessing the suitability of a class or category of candidates, if it considers necessary, call such class or category of candidates for interview for assessing their suitability for the post of Member.

(7) The Selection Committee may, on the basis of its assessment made by it, recommend a panel of names of candidates for appointment as members from amongst the applicants referred to in sub-rule (5) in order of merit for the consideration of the Central Government.

(8) The Central Government shall, before seeking approval of the Appointments Committee of the Cabinet, verify or cause to be verified the credentials and antecedents of the candidates selected by the Central Government from the panel recommended by the Selection Committee and satisfy the suitability of such candidates for appointment as members,

(9) Every appointment of a member shall be subject to his medical fitness.

13. Removal of President or members from office in certain circumstances. - (1) The Central Government may remove from office, the President or any member, who,—

(a) has been adjudged as an insolvent; or

(b) has been convicted of an offence which, in the opinion of the Central Government, involves moral turpitude; or

(c) has become physically or mentally incapable of acting as the President or the member; or

(d) has acquired such financial or other interest as is likely to affect prejudicially his functions as the President or a member; or

(e) has so abused his position as to render his continuance in office prejudicial to the public interest ;or

(f) remain absent in three consecutive sittings except for reasons beyond his control.

(2) Notwithstanding anything contained in sub rule (1), the President or any member of the National Commission shall not be removed from his office except by an order made by the

Central Government on the grounds specified in clauses (d), (e) and (f) of that sub-rule and after an inquiry held by a sitting Judge of the Supreme Court nominated by the Chief Justice of India in which the President or member of the National Commission, as the case may be, has been informed of the charges against him and given a reasonable opportunity of being heard in respect of those charges and found guilty.

14. Procedure to be followed by the National Commission.—(1) A complaint containing the following particulars shall be presented by the complainant in person or by his agent to the National Commission or be sent by registered post, addressed to the National Commission:

(a) the name, description and the address of the complainant;

(b) the name, description and address of the opposite party or parties, as the case may be, so far as they can be ascertained;

(c) the facts relating to the complaint and when and where it arose;

(d) documents in support of the allegations contained in the complaint;

(e) the relief which the complainant claims.

(1A) Every complaint under sub-rule (1) shall be accompanied by the relevant fee as is specified in rule 9A.

(1B) Every complaint under sub-rule (1) shall be filed in quadruplicate or with such number of copies as may be required by the National Commission.

(2) The National Commission shall, in disposal of any complaint before it, as far as possible, follow the procedure and conditions including the provisions governing adjournments as laid down in sections 12 and 13 in relation to the complaints received by the District Forum, with such modification as may be considered necessary by the Commission.

(3) On the date of hearing or any other date to which hearing could be adjourned, it shall be obligatory on the parties or their agents to appear before the National Commission. Where the complainant or his agent fails to appear before the

National Commission on such days, the National Commission may in its discretion either dismiss the complaint for default or decide it on merits . Where the opposite party or its agent fails to appear on the date of hearing the National Commission may decide the complaint *ex-parte*.

(4) The National Commission may, on such terms as it deems fit and at any stage of the proceedings, adjourn the hearing of the complaint but the complaint shall be decided as far as possible within a period of three months from the date of notice received by opposite party where complaint does not require analysis or testing of commodities and within five months if it requires analysis or testing of commodities.

(4A) In the event of a complaint being disposed of after the period specified in sub-rule (4), the National Commission shall record in writing, the reasons for the delay in such disposal.

(5) If after the proceedings conducted under sub-rule (3), the National Commission is satisfied with the allegations contained in the complaint, it shall issue orders to the opposite party or parties, as the case may be, directing him or them to take one or more of the things as mentioned in sub-section (1) of section 14. The National Commission shall also have the power to direct that any order passed by it, where no appeal has been preferred under section 23 or where the order of the National Commission has been affirmed by the Supreme Court under that section, be published in the Official Gazette or through any other media and no legal proceedings shall lie against the National Commission or any media for such publication.

14A. Appeals before National Commission.- Every appeal filed in terms of section 19 shall be accompanied by such amount as specified in the second proviso to the said section and such amount may be remitted in the form of a crossed Demand Draft drawn on a nationalized bank in favour of the Registrar, National Commission, payable at Delhi. The National Commission dealing with the appeals filed before them shall follow the provisions of section 19 and 19A as may be required to hear the appeals filed before the Commission.

Explanafion.- In this rule, "nationalized bank" means a corresponding new bank specified in the First Schedule to the Banking Companies (Acquisition and Transfer of Undertakings) Act, 1970 (5 of 1970) or a corresponding new bank specified in the First Schedule to the Banking Companies (Acquisition and Transfer of Undertakings) Act, 1980 (40 of 1980).

15. Procedure for hearing the appeal.— (1) Memorandum shall be presented by the appellant or his agent to the National Commission in person or be sent by registered post addressed to the Commission.

(2) Every memorandum filed under sub-rule (I) shall be in legible handwriting preferably typed and shall set forth concisely under distinct heads, the grounds of appeal without any argument or narrative and such grounds shall be numbered consecutively.

(3) Each memorandum shall be accompanied by a crossed demand draft as referred to in rule 14A and by a certified copy of the order of the State Commission appealed against and such of the documents as may be required to support grounds of objection mentioned in the memorandum.

(4) When the appeal is presented after the expiry of the period of limitation as specified in the Act, the memorandum shall be accompanied by an application supported by an affidavit setting forth the facts on which the appellant relies to satisfy the National Commission that he has sufficient cause for not preferring the appeal within the period of limitation.

(5) The appellant shall submit four copies or such number of copies of the memorandum to the Commission for official purpose.

(6) On the date of hearing or on any other day to which hearing may be adjourned, it shall be obligatory for the parties or their agents to appear before the National Commission . If appellant or his agent fails to appear on such date, the National Commission may in its discretion either dismiss the appeal or decide *ex-parte* on merits. If the respondent or his agent fails to appear on such date, the National Commission shall proceed *ex-parte* and shall decide the appeal on merits of the case.

(7) The appellant shall not, except by leave of the National Commission, urge or be heard in support of any ground of objection not set forth in the memorandum but the National Commission, in deciding the appeal, may not confine to the grounds of objection set forth in the memorandum:

Provided that the Commission shall not rest its decision on any other ground other than those specified in the memorandum unless the party who may be affected thereby, has been given, an opportunity of being heard by the National Commission.

(8) No adjournment shall ordinarily be granted by the National Commission, unless sufficient cause is shown and the reasons for grant of adjournment have been recorded in writing by the Commission. The National Commission may also adjourn the hearing of the appeal suo motu, on such terms as it may think fit and at any stage of the proceedings for reasons to be recorded in writing. The appeal shall be decided, as far as possible, within ninety days from the date of its admission. In the event of an appeal being disposed of after the period so specified, the National Commission shall record in writing the reasons of the same at the time of disposal of the said appeal.

(9) The order of the National Commission shall be communicated to the parties concerned free of cost.

15A. Sitting of the National Commission and signing of orders. - (1) Every proceeding of the National Commission shall be conducted by the President or the seniormost member authorised and at least two members thereof sitting together except when a bench is constituted by the President of the National Commission with one or more members as he may deem fit.

Provided that where the member or members for any reason are unable to conduct the proceeding till it is completed, the President or the senior most member, as provided in section 22D of the Act, shall conduct such proceedings from the state at which it was last heard by the previous member.

(2) Every order made by the National Commission shall be signed by the President or the seniormost member as provided

in section 22D and at least two members who conducted the proceeding and if there is any difference of opinion among themselves, the opinion of majority shall be the order of the National Commission:

Provided that where the proceeding is conducted by the President or the seniormost member as provided in section 22D and three members thereof and they differ on any point or points, they shall state the point or points on which they differ and refer the same to the other member for hearing on such point or points and such point or points shall be decided accordingly to the opinion of the majority of the National Commission.

16. Manner of deposit of amount in appeals before Supreme Court - Every appeal filed before the Supreme Court in terms of section 23 shall be accompanied by an amount as provided in the second proviso to that section and such amount may be remitted in the form of a crossed Demand Draft drawn on a nationalized bank in favour of Registrar, Supreme Court, payable at Delhi.

Explanation.- In this rule, "nationalized bank" means a corresponding new bank specified in the First Schedule to the Banking Companies (Acquisition and Transfer of Undertakings) Act, 1970 (5 of 1970) or a corresponding new bank specified in the First Schedule to the Banking Companies (Acquisition and Transfer of Undertakings) Act, 1980 (40 of 1980)

4

Consumer Welfare Fund Rules, 1992

GSR 895(E), Dated 25-11-1992

In exercise of the powers conferred by sub-section (2) of section 37, read with section 12D of the Central Excises and Salt Act, 1944 (1 of 1994), the Central Government hereby makes the follow-ing rules, namely :—

Short title and commencement.

1. (1) These rules may be called the Consumer Welfare Fund Rules, 1992.

(2) They shall come into force on the date of their publication in the Official Gazette.

Definitions.

2. In these rules, unless the context otherwise requires,—

(*a*) "Act" means the Central Excises and Salt Act, 1944 (1 of 1944), or, as the case may be, the Customs Act, 1962 (52 of 1962);

[1][(*b*) "Applicant" means any agency/organisation engaged in consumer welfare activities for a period of three years regis-tered under the Companies Act, 1956 (1 of 1956) or under any other law for the time being in force, including village/mandal/Samiti level cooperatives of consumers especially Women, Scheduled Castes and Scheduled Tribes, or any industry as defined in the Industrial Disputes Act, 1947 (14 of 1947) recom-mended by the Bureau to be engaged for a period of five years

in viable and useful research activity which has made, or is likely to make, significant contribution in formulation of standard mark of the products of mass consumption, or State Government, and includes a consumer for the purpose of reimbursing legal ex-penses as referred to in clause (*d*) of rule 8 of these rules;]

(*c*) "Application" means an application in Form A-I, append-ed to these rules;

(*d*) "Bureau" means the Bureau of Indian Standards consti-tuted under the Bureau of Indian Standards Act, 1986 (63 of 1986);

(*e*) "Central Consumer Protection Council" means the Central Consumer Protection Council established under sub-section (1) of section 4 of the Consumer Protection Act, 1986 (68 of 1986), for promotion and protection of rights of consumers;

(*f*) "Committee" means the Committee constituted under rule 5;

(*g*) "Consumer" has the same meaning as assigned to it in clause (*d*) of sub-section (1) of section 2 of the Consumer Pro-tection Act, 1986 (68 of 1986), and includes consumer of goods on which duty has been paid.

(*h*) "Consumer Welfare Fund" means the fund established by the Central Government under sub-section (1) of section 12C of the Central Excises and Salt Act, 1944 (1 of 1944);

(*i*) "Duty" means the duty paid under the Act ;

[2][(*i-a*) "Proper Officer" means the officer having the power under the Act to make an order that the whole or any part of the duty is refundable;]

(*j*) "Standard mark" shall have the same meaning as assigned to it in clause (*t*) of section 2 of the Bureau of Indian Stand-ards Act, 1986 (63 of 1986);

(*k*) "Welfare of the Consumers" includes promotion and protection of rights of consumers;

(*l*) Words and expressions used in the rules and not defined but defined in the Consumer Protection Act, 1986 (68 of 1986) shall have the meanings respectively assigned to them in that Act.

Establishment of Consumer Welfare Fund

3. There shall be established a Consumer Welfare Fund with the Central Government into which credits of amounts of duty and income from investment along with other monies specified in sub-section (2) of section 12C of the Central Excises and Salt Act, 1944 (1 of 1944) shall be accredited :

Provided that any amount having been credited to the Fund is ordered or directed as payable to any claimant by orders of proper officer, appellate authority or court, shall be paid from the Fund.

Maintenance of Accounts and Records of Consumer Welfare Fund.

4. Proper and separate accounts in relation to the Consumer Welfare Fund shall be maintained by the Central Government and shall be subject to audit by the Comptroller and Auditor General of India.

Constitution of the Committee.

5. (1) The Committee constituted by the Central Government under sub-rule

(2), shall make recommendations for proper utilisation of the money credited to the Consumer Welfare Fund for the wel-fare of the consumers, to carry out the purposes of these rules.

(2) The Committee shall consist of the following Members, namely:—

[2a][(*a*) The Secretary, Ministry of Civil Supplies, Consum-er Affairs and Public Distribution, who shall be the Chairman of the Committee;]

(*b*) Secretary, Department of Expenditure in the Ministry of Finance who shall be the Vice-Chairman of the Committee;

(*c*) Chairman, Central Board of Excise and Customs in the Department of Revenue of the Ministry of Finance ;

(*d*) Member (Central Excise) of the Central Board of Excise and Customs in the Department of Revenue of the Ministry of Finance ;

[3][(*e*) Secretary/Additional Secretary of Department of Rural Development;

(*f*) Director General/Additional Director General, Bureau of Indian Standards;]

[3a][(*g*) The Joint Secretary of Consumer Welfare Fund in the Ministry of Civil Supplies, Consumer Affairs and Public Distribution, who shall be the member Secretary of the Committee:]

[4][Provided that the Chairman or Vice-Chairman, as the case may be, may invite representatives of the State Governments concerned and a nominee of the Consumer co-ordination Council to the meet-ings as and when necessary.]

(3) The Committee shall be a Standing Committee.

[5][Procedure for conduct of business.]

6. (1) The Committee shall meet as and when necessary, but not more than three months shall intervene between any two meetings.

(2) The Committee shall meet at such time and place as the Chair-man, or in his absence the Vice-Chairman of the Committee may deem fit.

(3) The meeting of the Committee shall be presided over by the Chairman, and in the absence of the Chairman, the Vice-Chairman shall preside over the meetings of the Committee.

(4) Each meeting of the Committee shall be called, by giving notice in writing to every member of not less than ten days from the date of issue of such notice.

(5) Every notice of the meeting of the Committee shall specify the place and the day and hour of the meeting and shall contain statement of business to be transacted thereat.

(6) No proceeding of the Committee shall be valid, unless it is presided over by the Chairman or Vice-Chairman and a minimum of [5a][three] other members are present.

Powers and Functions of the Committee

7. (1) The Committee shall have power :—

(*a*) to require any applicant to produce before it, or before a duly authorised Officer of the Central Government, or as the case may be, the State Government, such books, accounts, documents, instruments, or commodities in custody and control of the applicant, as may be necessary for proper evaluation of the application;

(*b*) to require any applicant to allow entry and inspection of any premises, from which activities claimed to be for the welfare of consumers, are stated to be carried on, to a duly authorised officer of Central Government or, as the case may be, State Government;

(*c*) to get the accounts of the applicants audited, for ensuring proper utilization of the grant;

(*d*) to require any applicant, in case of any default, or suppression of material information on his part, to refund in lump sum, the sanctioned grant to the Committee, and to be sub-ject to prosecution under the Act;

(*e*) to recover any sum due from any applicant in accordance with the provisions of the Act.

(*f*) to require any applicant, or class of applicants to submit a periodical report, indicating proper utilization of the grant;

(*g*) to reject an application placed before it on the basis of involvement of factual inconsistency, or inaccuracy in the material particulars;

(*h*) to recommend minimum financial assistance, by way of grant to an applicant, having regard to his financial status, and importance and utility of nature of activity under pursuit, after ensuring that the financial assistance provided shall not be misutilised;

(*i*) to require Central Consumer Protection Council or the Bureau, to formulate broad guidelines for considering the projects/proposals for the purpose of incurring expenditure from the Consumer Welfare Fund;

(*j*) to identify beneficial and safe sectors, where investments out of Consumer Welfare Fund may be made and make recommendations, accordingly.

(2) The Committee shall not consider an application, unless it has been inquired into, in material details and recommended for consideration accordingly, by the Member-Secretary.

Specification of Purposes for Utilization of credits available in Consumer Welfare Fund

8. The Committee shall make recommendations :—

(*a*) for making available grants to any applicant;

(*b*) for making available grants recommended by the Bureau for activities relating to standard marks, which may be considered essential by the Central Government, for the welfare of the consumers;

(*c*) for investment of the money available in the Consumer Welfare Fund;

(*d*) for making available grants [6][on a selective basis], for reimbursing legal expenses incurred by a complainant, or class of complaints in a consumer dispute, after its final adjudication;

(*e*) for making available grants for any other purpose recommended by the Central Consumer Protection Council [7][as may be considered appropriate by the Committee.]

[8]FORM AI

(*See* Rule 8 of the Consumer Welfare Fund Rules, 1992)

Important : Please fill up this form, furnishing correct details sought for, based on verifiable true state of affairs without causing suppression of any material information which, if resorted to, shall entail prosecution under the Act.

1. Name and full postal address of the applicant :
2. Status of the applicant under clause (*b*) of rule 2 :
3. Date of establishment :
4. Whether registered under the Societies Registra-tion Act, 1860 (21 of 1860) or any other relevant Act :

5. If yes, number and year of registration (Attested copy of registration certificate to be enclosed):
6. Whether the organisation is of national/State level :
7. Number of Managing Committee members together with list of names, addresses and occupation of the office bearers:
8. Brief details of the organization, objectives and activities during the last three years :
9. Purpose for which the amount is required (Please state the details of the project and its proposed implementation) :
10. Amount of grant required, itemwise details under non-recurring/recurring to be enclosed :
11. Time schedule of the activities arranged:
12. The total amount incurred/invested by the applicant, or likely to be incurred by the applicant :
13. Sources of funding of balance amount whether the organ-isation is getting financial assistance from any other official/non-official source. If yes,give details :
14. Details of prosecution, if any, in a court of law launched against the applicant, during the last five years

NOTIFICATION

G.S.R. 342(E). - In exercise of the powers conferred by section 30A of the Consumer Protection Act, 1986 (68 of 1986), the National Consumer Disputes Redressal Commission with the previous approval of the Central Government, hereby makes the following regulations, namely:-

1. Short title and commencement.-

(1) These regulations may be called the Consumer Protection Regulations, 2005.

(2) They shall come into force on the date of their publication in the Official Gazette.

2. Definitions.- In these regulations unless the context otherwise requires,-

(a) "Act" means the Consumer Protection Act, 1986 (68 of 1986);

(b) "Consumer Forum" means a District Forum. a Consumer Disputes Redressal Commission established in a State under clause (b) of section 9 (hereafter called the State Commission) or the National Consumer Disputes Redressal Commission;

(c) "Registrar" means the head of the ministerial establishment of the Consumer Forum and exercising such powers and functions as are conferred upon him by the President of the Consumer Forum:

(d) "rules" means the rules made under the Act;

(e) "section" means a section of the Act:

(f) words and expressions used in these regulations and not defined herein but defined either in the Act or in the rules shall have the same meaning respectively assigned to them either in the Act or in the rules, as the case may be.

3. Arrangements in Consumer Forum,—

(1) A Consumer Forum, being not a regular court, shall have the arrangements as to depict it distinct from a court.

(2) In the hall in which the Consumer Forum shall hear the parties, the dais may not be kept more than 30c.m. in height than the place earmarked for the parties to occupy.

(3) At the dais of the hall, the President and the members of the Consumer Forum shall use the same type of chairs at the same level and these chairs need not have high backs.

4. Dress code.-

(1) The President and members of every Consumer Forum while presiding over the Benches,-

(a) shall wear simple and sober dress;

(b) shall not wear-

(i) flashy dress or dress display any affluence;

(ii) Jeans or T-shirts.

(iii) as if they are holding Courts as Judges of a High Court or a District Court.

(2) The advocates shall be allowed to appear in the usual dress as prescribed by the High Court but without the gown.

5. Hearing hours.-Subject to the provisions of the rules, the normal working hours of the Consumer Forum for hearing matters shall be from 10.30 am to 1.00 p.m and 2.00 p.m to 4.00 p.m on all working days of the Central Government in the case of the National Commission and on all working days of the State Government in the case of the State Commission and the District Forum

6. Cause List.-

(1) Cause list of the Consumer forum for the following entire week shall be made ready before the close of the working hours of the preceding week and displayed on the notice board. The cause list in respect of a Consumer Forum having a website shall also be hosted on the website.

(2) Cause list shall be split into three different parts, namely:-

(i) Admission and after notice matters;

(ii) Matters where evidence is to be recorded;

(iii) Final disposal matters.

(3) Every cause list shall contain the following particulars, namely:-

(1) Sl. No.	(2) No. of the matter	(3) Names of the parties appearing	(4) Name of the party or Counsel or agent

(4) If a date of hearing is given in the presence of parties or their agents, it shall not be a ground for non-appearance for the reason that the cause list for the concerned date does not show the matter or contains incorrect entry or there is omission of the particulars of the matter.

7. Institution of complaints, appeals and revision petitions.-

(1) Where a complaint is filed in District Forum or State Commission it shall be filed in three sets and where it is filed in the National Commission it shall be filed in four sets with additional sets equal to the number of opposite party(ies)/respondent(s).

(2) Every complaint shall clearly contain particulars of dispute and the relief claimed and shall also be accompanied by copies of such documents as are necessary to prove the claim made in the complaint.

8. Nomenclature to be given to the complaints, appeals and revisions petitions. -

(1) A complaint shall hereinafter be referred to as Consumer Complaint (C.C.) instead of O.P., e.g., C.C. No.2 of 2005.

(2) An appeal shall be referred to as F.A., Revision Petition as R.P., Execution .Application as E.A, Transfer Application T.A. and Review as RA containing the number and the year of filing.

9. Scrutiny of complaint, appeal, petition and revision petition.-

(1) Every complaint, appeal, or revision petition shall after it is filed be numbered by the Registrar.

(2) If there is any defect in the filing of the complaint, appeal or revision petition, the particulars of such defects shall be recorded and the party or his agents shall be informed of the defects asking them for removing the defects within 15 days.

(3) In case the party disputes in the correctness of the defects pointed out the matter shall be placed before the Consumer Forum for appropriate orders.

(4) After the expiry of the time given, the matter shall, irrespective of the fact as to whether the defects have been removed or not, be placed before the Consumer Forum for appropriate orders.

(5) If the objections raised by the Registrar are substantial and are not removed within the time allowed for the

purpose, those days shall not be excluded for counting the period of limitation.

(6) As required by the second proviso to sub-section (3) of section 12, the admissibility of the complaint shall ordinarily be decided within twenty-one days from the date on which the complaint was received.

(7) In case any defect is pointed out by the Registrar, twenty-one days from the date on which such defect was removed shall be reckoned for the purpose of sub-regulation (5).

(8) All pending complaints, appeals and revision petitions which have not come up for admission till the date of commencement of these regulations and are pending for admission for more than 21 days shall be listed immediately by the Consumer Forum for admission and not later than 21 days from the date of commencement of these regulations.

10. Issue of notice.-

(1) Whenever the Consumer Forum directs the issuance of a notice in respect of a complaint, appeal or revision petition, as the case may be, to the opposite party(ies)/ respondent(s), ordinarily such notice shall be issued for a period of 30 days and depending upon the circumstances of each case even for less than 30 days.

(2) When there is a question of raising presumption of service, 30 days notice shall be required.

(3) Whenever notices are sought to be effected by a courier service, it shall be ascertained that the courier is of repute.

(4) While appointing the courier for the purpose of effecting service, security deposit may also be taken.

(5) Along with the notice, copies of the complaint, memorandum of grounds of appeal, petitions as the case may be and other documents filed shall be served upon the opposite party(ies)/respondent(s).

(6) After the opposite party or respondent has put in appearance, no application or document shall be received

by the Registrar unless it bears an endorsement that a copy thereof has been served upon the other side.

11. Adjournment.-

(1) Every proceeding before a Consumer Forum shall be conducted as expeditiously as possible and as per the requirements of the Act.

(2) The Consumer Forum shall record the reasons for any adjournment made by it.

(3) The cost of adjournment, if asked by the opposite party or parties, shall not be less than five hundred rupees per adjournment and could be more depending upon the value and nature of the complaint as may be decided by the Consumer Forum.

(4). The complainant, appellant or petitioner, as the case may be, may also be burdened with cost unless sufficient cause is shown for seeking adjournment:

Provided that in the circumstances of a particular case, the amount of cost imposed may be less than five hundred rupees but in no case less than one hundred rupees.

(5) The cost imposed may be given to the other party or parties to defray his or their expenses or be deposited in the Consumer Legal Aid Account to be maintained by the respective Consumer Forum, as the Consumer Forum may order.

(6) If any adjournment is granted without awarding cost, the order sheet shall mention the reasons thereof.

(7) All orders adjourning the matter shall be signed by the President and members constituting the Bench and not by the Court Master or Bench Clerk.

(8) Non-availability of a lawyer who is representing the party shall not be a ground for seeking adjournment of the matter unless absence is beyond the control of the lawyer such as his sudden illness or bereavement in the family.

12. Hearing by Benches.-Where a Bench, constituted by the President of the State Commission or the National

Commission as provided under section 16 or section 20, as the case may be, does not have a member with judicial background and any complex question of law arises and there is no precedent to decide the law point, the Bench so constituted may refer the matter to the President of the State Commission or the National Commission as the case may be to constitute another Bench of which the President shall be a member.

13. Arguments.-

(1) Arguments should be as brief as possible and to the point at issue.

(2) Where a party is represented by a counsel, it shall be mandatory to file a brief of written arguments two days before the matter is fixed for arguments.

(3) In case of default to file briefs, the cost shall be imposed at the same rates as laid down for grant of adjournments.

14. Limitation.-

(1) Subject to the provisions of sections 15, 19 and 24A, the period of limitation in the following matters shall be as follows:-

(i) Revision Petition shall be filed within 90 days from the date of the order or the date of receipt of the order as the case may be;

(ii) Application for setting aside the *ex-parte* order under section 22A or dismissal of the complaint in default shall be maintainable if filed within thirty days from the date of the order or date of receipt of the order, as the case may be;

(iii) An application for review under sub-section (2) of section 22 shall be filed to the National Commission within 30 days from the date of the order or receipt of the order, as the case may be;

(iv) The period of limitation for filing any application for which no period of limitation has been specified in the Act, the rules of these regulations shall be thirty days from the date of the cause of action or the date of knowledge.

(2) Subject to the provisions of the Act, the Consumer Forum may condone the delay in filing an application or a petition referred to in sub-regulation (1) if valid and sufficient reasons to its satisfaction are given.

15. Review.-

(1) It shall set out clearly the grounds for review.

(2) Unless otherwise ordered by the National Commission, an application for review shall be disposed of by circulation without oral arguments, as far as practicable between the same members who had delivered the order sought to be reviewed.

16. Appearance of Voluntary Consumer Organisations.-

(1) Recognised Consumer Organisations have a right of audience before the Consumer Forum

(2) An authorisation of a Voluntary Consumer Organisation may be by way of special power of attorney executed on a non-judicial paper or even on plain paper duly attested by a Gazetted Officer or a Notary Public.

(3) The Power of Attorney holder shall be entitled to engage a counsel, if authorised to do so.

(4) A Voluntary Consumer Organisation can engage a counsel or an advocate of its choice or it can itself represent through one of its office bearers as per the rules governing it.

(5) In case of a complaint where the Voluntary Consumer Organisation is a complainant along with the consumer himself and the dispute affects the complainant individually, he can withdraw the complaint:

Provided that if the issue involves unfair trade practice or restrictive trade practice a Voluntary Consumer Organisation may continue to proceed with the complaint even if the complainant wishes to withdraw the same.

(6) A Consumer Forum has to guard itself from touts and busybodies in the garb of power of attorney holders or authorised agents in the proceedings before it.

(7) While a Consumer Forum may permit an authorised agent to appear before it, but authorised agent shall not be one who has used this as a profession:

Provided that this sub-regulation shall not apply in case of advocates.

(8) An authorised agent may be debarred from appearing before a Consumer Forum if he is found guilty of misconduct or any other malpractice at any time.

17. *Ex-parte* interim order.-Any *ex-parte* interim order issued by the Consumer Forum shall stand vacated after 45 days if in the meanwhile the objections to the interim order are not heard and disposed of.

18. Final order.-

(1) An order on the top right hand comer shall show as to when the complaint was filed and the date of the order.

(2) The cause title of the order shall contain the names of all the parties with their addresses.

(3) In the body of the order it is desirable that after mentioning the complainant or the opposite party, their names as shown in the title be mentioned and parties thereafter may not be mentioned as complainant or opposite party No.1 or opposite party No.2, etc.

(4) The cause title shall also clearly show if the appellant or respondent was the complainant or opposite party.

(5) The order of a Consumer Forum disposing of a matter shall be as short and precise as practicable and unnecessary long quotations from the judgments of the higher courts or otherwise shall be avoided.

(6) When a copy of the order is sent to a party, the mode by which it is sent and the date on which it is sent shall be stamped on the last page of the order.

(7) The Consumer Forum shall pass final order invariably within fifteen days of the conclusion of the arguments.

19. Return on institution and disposal of cases.-

(1) A Consumer Forum is expected to dispose of at least 75 to 100 matters every month.

(2) A periodic monthly return of institution and disposal of cases shall be sent by the District Forums to the State Commission.

(3) The State Commission shall submit a periodic monthly return of institution and disposal of cases to the National Commission.

(4) Notwithstanding anything contained in this regulation, the President of the National Commission may, at any time, call for any return or information relating to its functioning from a State Commission or District Forums.

20. Preservation of records. -

(1) In the case of complaint, the record containing main files with original order sheet shall be preserved for a period five years.

(2) In the case of records of first appeal and revision petitions, it shall be preserved for three years from the date of disposal of the appeal or revision as the case may be.

(3) Immediately after the consumer complaint, first appeal or revision petition, as the case may be, is disposed of, extra sets shall be given to the parties who may use the same for filing of appeal or revision petition and in that case the necessity to summon the record from the forums below can be dispensed with.

(4) The Registrar shall inform the parties while forwarding the certified copy of the final order, where they do not appear in person at the time of finally disposing of the matter to arrange to collect the extra sets.

(5) A period of at least one month shall be given for the purpose of collection of records by the party and in case of default the ex1ra sets shall be weeded out.

21. Certified copy.-

(1) A copy of the order is to be given to the parties free of cost as required under the Act and the rules made thereunder.

(2) In case a party requires an extra copy, it shall be issued to him duly certified by the Registry on a payment of Rs.20/- irrespective of number of pages.

(3) A certified copy of an order shall clearly specify the date when free copy was issued, date of application, date when the copy was made ready and the date when it was so delivered to him.

(4) A fee of Rs.20/- shall be paid for obtaining another certified copy.

(5) Any party desiring to get a certified copy of any document on the file of the Consumer Forum, may get the same on payment of certification fee of twenty rupees per copy. Provided that if any such document of which certified copy is sought, is over and above 5 pages, an extra amount of one rupee per page shall be charged over and above the fee of twenty rupees.

(6) Certified copy of any miscellaneous order passed by the Consumer Forum shall be supplied on payment of Rs.5 per copy.

22. Inspection of records.-Parties or their agents can inspect the records of any matter by filing an application on payment often rupees as fee.

23. Filing of criminal complaint.-Wherever a complaint is required to be filed by the Consumer Forum under sub-section (5) of section 13, the Consumer Forum may authorise its Registrar to file the complaint.

24. Practice Directions.- The National Commission shall be entitled to issue practice directions from time to time as may be necessary for the proper conduct of the cases before Consumer Forum including prescribing forms for complaints, notices, returns, certificate to be issued to the collector and the like.

25. Parcsha Yad-dast.- Where a party appears in person and is illiterate, the Court Master or Bench Clerk shall give to that party the next date of hearing in writing.

26. Miscellaneous.-

(1) In all proceedings before the Consumer Forum, endeavour shall be made by the parties and their counsel to avoid the use of provisions of Code of Civil Procedure, 1908 (5 of 1908):

Provided that the provisions of the Code of Civil Procedure, 1908 may be applied which have been referred to in the Act or in the rules made thereunder.

(2) Every State Commission and every District Forum shall take steps for its computerisation and networking.

(3) The Consumer Forum shall give proper respect and courtesy to the parties who appear in person and shall provide separate accommodation in the Hall for the convenience of the parties.

(4) The Consumer Forum shall not insist upon the parties to engage advocates.

(5) The Fees collected for inspection of the documents and supply of certified copies shall be deposited in the account maintained for the purpose of depositing fee for filing a complaint as prescribed by the Central Government by rules.

(6) The cases filed by or against the senior citizens, physically challenged, widows and persons suffering from serious ailments shall be listed and disposed of on a priority basis.

5

Bureau of Indian Standards (Recognition of Consumers' Associations) Rules, 1991

GSR 619(E) DATED 9-10-1991

In exercise of the powers conferred by section 37 of the Bureau of Indian Standards Act, 1986 (63 of 1986), the Central Govern-ment hereby makes the following rules, namely:—

Short title and commencement.

1. (1) These rules may be called the Bureau of Indian Standards (Recognition of Consumers Associations) Rules, 1991.

(2) They shall come into force on the date of their publication in the Official Gazette.

Definitions.

2. In these rules, unless the context otherwise requires—

(*a*) "Act" means the Bureau of Indian Standards Act, 1986 (63 of 1986);

(*b*) "Form" means a Form appended to the Schedule to these rules;

(*c*) "Ministry" means the Ministry of Civil Supplies, Con-sumer Affairs and Public Distribution; and

(*d*) "Principal Officer" in relation to a consumer associa-tion means any individual who is specifically authorised in writing or by means of a resolution adopted by such consumers' association in that behalf.

Application for recognition of consumers' association.

3. (1) Every consumers' association which is desirous of being recognised as a registered Consumers' Association — (*a*) shall have not less than fifty consumers as its members; and (*b*) shall make an application for such recognition in triplicate to the Bureau of Indian Standards in Form I. (2) Every application made under sub-rule (1) shall be accompa-nied by a bank draft of rupees one thousand. (3) On receipt of an application made under sub-rule (1), the Bureau of Indian Standards shall note thereon the date of its receipt and shall forthwith communicate such date to the appli-cant.

Form I

(4) The Bureau of Indian Standards may, before issue of a certif-icate of recognition, require the applicant to furnish, within such period as may be specified by it, such additional informa-tion as may be considered necessary within a period of 30 days of a receipt of that letter by the applicant.

(5) On receipt of an application and such other additional infor-mation as may be sought under sub-rule (4), the Bureau of Indian Standards shall process the application and forward documents to the Ministry of Civil Supplies. Government of India with its recommendations for their consideration.

(6) On receipt of the recommendations of the Bureau under sub-rule (5), the Ministry shall consider those recommendations and after satisfying itself that the applicants' association is fit to be recognised, may recognise the association in this behalf.

(7) The certificate of recognition to be issued by the Ministry under sub-rule (6) shall be in Form II.

(8) Where a certificate of recognition issued under these rules is lost, destroyed or mutilated, a duplicate may be issued on an application made in this behalf and on payment of a fee of rupees one hundred.

Payment of fees.

4. The fees payable under those rules shall be paid in the form of a bank draft in favour of the Bureau of Indian Standards, New Delhi.

Refusal to grant certificate of recognition to consumers' associ-ation.

5. Where a certificate of recognition of a consumers' association has been refused, the applicant shall be informed of the reasons for such refusal by the Bureau. Copies of certificate of recognition to be furnished to certain authorities.

6. Every consumers' association which has been recognised as a 'registered consumers' association under these rules shall fur-nish a copy of the certificate of recognition issued to it while filing a complaint under section 35(1) of the Act.

Verification of application.

7. Every application made under these rules shall be duly veri-fied by the Principal Officer.

Schedule

Form I

[*See* sub-rule (1) of rule 3]

Form of application to be submitted to the Bureau of Indian Standards for recognition of consumers' association.

(to be submitted in triplicate)

(1) Name of the Consumers' Association:

(2) Address:

(*a*) Registered Office:

(*b*) For correspondence:

(*c*) Branches:

(3) If registered under any other law the Act under which regis-tered and date of registration (certified copy of the certificate of registration to be enclosed):

(4) Total number of members of the association (as on date of application):

(5) Objects of the association (certified copy of Memorandum of Association to be enclosed along with copy of the rules and regulations of the Association):

(6) Names, addresses and occupations of persons on the Board of Directors, Governing body, Council/Committee (by

whatever name called), to whom the management of the affairs of the association is entrusted:

(7) Number of employees:

(*a*) Whole-time:

(*b*) Part-time:

(8) Year-wise details of the work done by the association during the last three years in the filed of protection of consumers' interest:

(9) Copies of published annual report and audited accounts of the association of the last three years:

(10) Details of Laboratory organisation, if any, owned, run or operated by the association for purposes of protection of consum-er's interest:

Place :............ Signature :...................................

Date :............. Name & designation :.............

Verification

I, ... do hereby solemnly state that what is stated in terms 1 to 11 above is true to the best of my knowledge and behalf.

Place :............ Signature :...................................

Date :............. Name & designation :.............

Form II

Form II

[*See* sub-rule (7) of rule 3]

Certificate of recognition

(Government of India)

Ministry of Civil Supplies, consumer affairs and Public distribution Certified that the consumers' Association whose particulars are given below has this day been recognised as a "registered Con-sumers' Association" in terms of section 34 of the Bureau of Indian Standards Act, 1986 (63 of 1986).

Particulars

(1) Name of the Consumers' Association:

(2) Address:

(3) Name of persons on the governing board/body/council to whom management of the Association is entrusted:

(4) Number of members:

(5) Registration Number:

Signature : ....

Date : ....

File No : ....

Seal of the Ministry of Civil Supplies,

Consumer Affairs and Public Distribution

SUPREME COURT RULES RELEVANT TO CONSUMER PROTECTION ACT

GSR 409, DATED 3-7-1990

In exercise of the powers conferred by Article 145 of the Constitution and all other powers enabling it in this behalf, the Supreme Court hereby makes, with the approval of the President, the following rules further to amend the Su-preme Court Rules, 1966, namely:—

1. (1) These rules may be called the Supreme Court (First Amend-ment) Rules, 1990.

(2) They shall come into force on the date of their publication in the Official Gazette.*

In the Supreme Court Rules, 1966.

2. (*a*) Order XX(F) with the title "Appeals under section 23 of the Consumer

Protection Act, 1986 (68 of 1986)" shall be inserted after Order XX(E).

XX(F).—The petition of appeal from an order made by tne National Disputes Redressal Commission (hereinafter referred to as "The National Commission") under sub-clause (*i*) of clause (*a*) of section 21 of the Consumer Protection Act, 1986 (69 of 1986) shall, subject to the provisions of sections 4, 5 and 12 of the Limitation Act, 1963 (36 of 1963) be presented by an aggrieved person within thirty days from the date of the order sought to be appealed against:

Provided that computing the said period, the time requisite for obtaining a copy of such order shall be excluded.

2A. The petition of appeal shall recite succinctly and clearly all the relevant facts leading up to the order appealed from, and shall set forth in brief the objections to the order appealed from and the ground relied on in support of the appeal. The petition shall also state the date of the order appealed from as well as the date on which it was received by the appellant.

3. The petition of appeal shall be accompanied by:—

(*i*) an authenticated copy of the order appealed from; and

(*ii*) at least seven spare sets of the petition and the papers filed with it.

*Supreme Court of India, Notification No. GSR 409 dated July 3, 1990, published in the Gazette of India, Part II. Section 3(*i*), dated 7-7-1990, pp. 1541-1544. (F.No. 548/RS/SCI/90).

4. After the appeal is registered, it shall be put up for hearing *ex parte* before the court which may either dismiss it summarily or direct issue of notice to all necessary parties or may make such orders as the circumstances of the case may require.

5. A fixed court fee of Rs. 250 shall be payable on the petition of appeal under this order.

6. Save as otherwise provided by the rules contained in this order, the provisions of other orders shall apply so far as may be, to appeals under section 23 of the Consumer Protection Act,1986 (68 of 1986).

The table of contents (page vi) of the Supreme Court Rules, 1966 and Third Schedule—Part II with regard to fees will be amended as under:—

Order	*Table of Contents*	*Rules*	*Page*
XX-F	Appeals under section 23 of Consumer Protection Act, 1986 (68 of 1986)	1-6	63

Original Petition

Original Petition, where value of the goods or services and compensation exceeds Rupees One Crore, can be filed with the Registry of this Commission within a period of Two Years from the date on which the cause of action has arisen. Petition can be filled on all working days between 10.00 A.M. to 5.00 P.M. at 7th Floor, 'B' Wing, Janpath Bhawan, Janpath New Delhi. Original Petition should be signed by the complainant and supported by an affidavit with Five copies, and One set each for Opposite Parties. The Original Petition along with all th copies should be paginated and duly indexed in the following seriatim:-

(a) the name, description and the address of the complainant;

(b) the name, description and address of the opposite party or parties, as the case may be, so far as they can be ascertained;

(c) the facts relating to complaint and when and where it arose;

(d) documents in support of the allegations contained in the complaint (all documents should be filed with legible English translation).

(e) the relief which the complainant claims.

FIRST APPEAL

If any person is aggrieved by an order made by the State Commission in exercise of its powers conferred by sub-clause (i) of clause (a) of Section 17 may prefer an appeal against such order to the National Commission within a period of thirty days from the date of the order on all working days between 10.00 A.M. to 5.00 P.M. at 7th Floor, 'B' Wing, Janpath Bhawan, Janpath, New Delhi. The Memorandum of Appeal in Original should be duly signed by the Appellant (s) and must be supported by An affidavit along with Five copies for the Commission and One set for each Respondent. Memorandum of appeal Shall be in legible handwriting preferbly typed and shall set forth concisely under distinct heads of the grounds of appeal. Paper books should be duly paginated and indexed as per the seriatim given below:

1. Name of Parties;
2. Certified copy of the order of the State Commission;
3. Memorandum of appeal with affidavit duly attested by Notary or Oath Commissioner;
4. Copy of complaint and written statement filed by opposite party (ies) before the State Commission;
5. Supporting document, if any.

The legible translation in English of all documents/ impunged orders should be filed along with all sets.

REVISION PETITION

Revision Petition as provided under Section 21 (b) of the Consumer Protection Act, 1986 can be filed with the Registry of this Commission on all working days between 10.00 A.M. to 5.00 P.M. at 7th Floor, 'B' Wing, Janpath Bhawan, Janpath, New Delhi. Petition must be supported by an affidavit along with Five copies for the Commission, and One set for each Respondent. Paper books of Petition and all the copies should be paginated and duly indexed in the following seriatim:-

1. Memo of Parties;
2. Certified copy of the order of the State Commission;
3. Order of the District Forum;
4. Copy of Memo of Appeal and reply before the State Commission;
5. Copy of complaint and written version filed before the District Forum;
6. Revision Petition with Affidavit duly attested by Notary or Oath Commissioner;
7. Supporting documents, if any.

BAGLA COMMITTEE REPORT

National Consumer Disputes Redressal Commission

The National Commission was set up in the year 1988. Initially, 37 posts of various categories were sanctioned by the Central Government for the Commission. Subsequiently, six more posts were created in terms of an order of the Supreme Court. There is a manifold increase in the filing of consumer cases in the Commission because of the steady growth of the consumer movement in the country. 17.805 cases have been filed in the Commission since its inception and presently 8,016 cases are pending for disposal. A statement showing the number of cases filed, disposed of and pending as on 1.11.1999 is annexed as Annexure 'B'. In order to cope up with the increase in work and for its smooth functioning, the National Commission had taken up the matter with the Ministry of Food & Consumer Affairs for the creation of 35 additional posts in June, 1996. The Ministry of Finance, Department of Expenditure has however, sanctioned five temporary posts, viz. one post of Assistant Registrar, one post of Assistant, two posts of LDCs and one post of Stenographer Gr. 'D'.

Section 20 of the Consumer Protection Act, 1986 deals with the National Commission. It consists of the President and four Members. The President of the Commission has to be a person., who is or has been a Judge of the Supreme Court and is entitled to salary and perquisites as available to him in the Supreme Court. A Judge of the Supreme Court is entitled to the following staff:-

Category of Staff	Scale of Pay	
AR-cum-PPS	Rs. 11360-16040	1
Sr. P.A.	Rs. 6500 – 10500	1
Staff Car Driver	Rs.3050 - 4590	1
Jamadar	Rs.2610 - 3540	1
Peons	Rs.2550 - 3200	6

Similarly, the four Members of the National Commission are either former High Court Judges or Secretaries to the Government of India. A Judge of the High Court is entitled to the following staff:-

Category of Staff	Scale of Pay	
PPS	Rs. 10000-15200	1
PA	Rs. 5500 – 9000	1
Staff Car Driver	Rs. 3050 – 4590	1
Peon	Rs. 2550 – 3200	3

In view of the above, the President of the National Commission should be provided the same number of staff as is made available to a sitting Judge of the Supreme Court because he enjoys the same salary and perquisites as are available to a sitting Judge of the Supreme Court. The Members of the National Commission should, likewise, be provided the same staff as is given to a sitting High Court Judge except that only one peon each be posted with the Members. Further a staff car driver may be provided to them after decision on the availability of independent staff car for each Member is taken. In other words, a Principal Private Secretary, one Personal Assistant and one peon should be posted with the Member.

Two Court Masters/Readers, preferably shorthand knowing, should assist the Commision in the hearing of matters. They should be Officers in the pay scale of Rs. 6500-10500.

The Office of the Commission is headed by the Registrar who is assisting the Commission in all administrative and judicial matters. He also functions as Head of Office and exercise financial powers delegated to him by the Head of Department. One Grade 'B' Stenographer has been provided to the Registrar. However, only one peon attends to the Registrar and the Deputy Registrar. It is essential that a peon is provided exclusively to the Registrar as per his entitlement.

The Commission has presently no post of Joint Registrar. Section 24B of the Act lay downs that the National Commission shall exercise administrative control over all the state Commissions and through the State Commission over the District Forums. As such, the services of an officer of the level of Joint Registrar are essential for assisting the National Commission in performing its function of administrative control.

There is only one post of Deputy Registrar in the Commission who looks after the Judicial, Administrative and Accounts Sections. Keeping in view the volume of work involved, it is essential that there should be at least two posts of Deputy Registrars; One Deputy Registrar may look after the work on the judicial side and the other for the administrative side.

Originally, only one post of Assistant Registrar was sanctioned. One more post of Assistant Registrar has now been created by the Ministry of Finance. Assistant Registrars supervise the work of Judicial and Administration branches as well as preparation of daily cause list.

The post of Joint Registrar may be created in the pay scale of Rs. 14,300-18,300. The post of Deputy Registrar in this Commission is in the scale of Rs. 12,000-16,500, and are equivalent to Director and Deputy Secretary in the Govt, of India who are entitled to a Personal Assistant/Grade 'C', stenographer in the scale of Rs. 5500-9000. Therefore, one Stenographer may be provided to the Joint Registrar and one each to the Deputy Registrars.

The posts of Assistant Registrar in this Commission are in the pay scale of Rs. 10,1000-15,200 which is equivalent to the pay scale of an Under Secretary to the Govt. of India. A Stenographer Grade 'D' in the pay scale of Rs. 4000-6000 is attached with an Under Secretary. Two posts of Grade 'D' Stenographers in the scale of Rs. 4000-6000 may, therefore, be created for the Assistant Registrars.

One peon each with the Joint Registrar and Deputy Registrars and one peon for two Assistant Registrars may be provided in terms of Govt. of India's instructions.

As the National Commission exercise three types of jurisdictions viz. Original, Appellate and Revisional, three independent Branches should be set up to deal with each of the three categories of cases. On the administration side, there should be an Establishment/Administration Branch and an Accounts Branch. An officer of the level of Section Officer in the scale of Rs. 6500-10,500 should be Incharge of the Judicial and Administration Sections respectively. The Establishment/ Administration Branch and Accounts Branch should be supervised by an Officer of the level of Section Officer.

Coming now to the staff strength in the Judicial Branches, it may be mentioned that as on 1.11.99. 1285 Original Petitions are pending. The entire work load is being handled by one UDC and one LDC. On account of acute shortage of staff, we are even utilizing the service of two Class –IV officials to assist the Original Branch staff.. Considering the volume of work and highly inadequate staff, there is an utmost need to augment the strength of the Original Branch. While determining the staff strength of the District Forum and the State Commission, it has been stated that not more than 250 files should be earmarked for a seat to be manned by a Dealing Assistant and LDC. Adopting the same criteria, five Assistant and five LDCs should be provided for the Original Branch. In other words, four more posts of Assistant and four posts of LDCs should be created to cope with the existing load of work.

2,627 Appeals are pending at present. There is only one Assistant in the Branch. Here again, the services of Class-IV officials are being utilized. Needles to say that the lone officials in the Branch is over-burdened and staff strength must be increased commensurate with the work load. The follow up action in Appeals and Revisions is somewhat less compared to Original Petitions. It, therefore seems appropriate that posts should be created on the basis of 500 files per seat. Considering the pendency, the work must be apportioned among five seats, each of which must be manned by an Assistant and LDC. To put it concretely, at least five Assistant and five LDCs should be posted in the Branch.

The pendency in the Revision Petition Branch is the highest. 4,104 Revision Petitions are pending. Only three LDCs assisted by a couple of Class-IV officials are looking after the work of the Branch. The Revision Petitions filed in the Commission are first listed before the Commission and depending upon the order passed, follow up action is taken by the officials. To handle this work load, there should at least be eight Assistant and eight LDCs.

In the Administration Branch, we have only one Upper Division Clerk. He is looking after the purchase of stores and stationery items. This Branch also deals with establishment matters which are dealt with by the Assistant Librarian because no official has been earmarked for establishment matters. Section Officers of Revision Petition Section is looking after the work of Administration/Establishment/Accounts Branch in addition to his duties. It is, therefore, incumbent that there should be an independent Section Officer, one Assistant and one UDC to look after Establishment/Administration/Accounts matters.

In Accounts Branch, only one Assistant has been provided. He does not possess any accounting qualification like S.A.S. It is pertinent to mention that deposits are made in this Commission by the contending parties, in accordance with the orders of the Commission. Handling of these deposits, viz. obtaining FDRs, enchasing them, making payment to parties etc. entails a lot of accounting work. Accounts Branch dealing with financial matters must, therefore, have an Officer of the level of Accounts Officer with requisite qualification and experience, one Assistant/Treasurer and one type knowing UDC.

There is no post of Translator in this Commission. Govt. of India has recently desired this Commission to forward a proposal for the creation of a post of Hindi Translator and Hindi typist. It is therefore, recommended that a post of Hindi Translator in the pay scale of Rs. 4000-6000 and one post of Hindi typist/LDC in the pay scale of Rs. 3050-4590 may be created.

The National Commission is an apex body deciding consumer complaints received from all over the country. Against the decision/order of the Commission, the consumers can approach the Hon'ble Supreme Court by way of an appeal. The Office has to maintain record of decided cases because the Registry of the Supreme Court calls for the original records from the Registry of the National Commission. Presently, there is no post of Record Keeper and the Commission has disposed of about 9680 cases. In order to maintain the record, one UDC, one LDC and one peon would be required.

A filing counter may be set up in the Commission for receiving complaints, Appeals and Revisions as well as for maintaining institution registers for issue/dispatch of Notices. One post of Assistant and one post of UDC may be created for the filing counter.

There is no satisfactory system of inspection of records by the Counsel/parties. A post of Assistant should be created and the incumbent appointed against this post may receive applications for inspection of records and make available the same under the supervision of the Registrar.

The National Commission is maintaining a Library for reference purposes, for which one Assistant Librarian and one Junior Library Attendant have been provided. As earlier stated, the Assistant Librarian is also looking after the establishment matters and, therefore,

Is unable to devote to his work whole-heartedly. A post of Librarian may be created in addition to the post of Assistant Librarian and Junior Library Attendant.

There are three cars and two posts of Staff Car Drivers in this Commission. One of the three cars is for the President and thus there is one driver for two staff cars. For the time being, a post of one staff car driver is required to be sanctioned, pending the decision on the availability of independent staff car for each Member.

A post of Despatch Rider is also essential for effecting service of notices issued by this Commission. This will result in considerable saving of postage used for issuing notices along with copies of Original Petitions. Appeals and Revision Petitions to the opposite parties for filing their version of case.

There are two photo-copier machines which are being operated by Class-IV officials. These machines are highly sensitive and unless these are handled by trained operators, there may be technical and operational problems. It is, therefore, proposed that two posts of photo-copier operators may be created.

One Daftry for each of the Judicial Sections, Administration Section and Accounts Section may also be provided for arranging the record in the Branches.

One peon each may be provided in the three Judicial Branches, one in the Administration Branch and one in the Accounts Branch. Thus five posts of peons may be created.

The Office of the Commission is located on the 5th Floor in 'A' Wing and 7th Floor in 'B' Wing of Janpath Bhawan. One sweeper may be posted on each of the two floors for cleanliness of the building. There should also be two posts of Chowkidar.

In view of the position, as explained above, the following staff will be necessary for the National Commission:-

Registrar	:	1
Joint Registrar	:	1
Deputy Registrar	:	2
Assistant Registrar	:	2
AR-cum-PPS	:	1
PPS	:	4
Sr. P.A.	:	1+4
Court Master	:	2
Accounts Officer	:	1
S Os	:	4
Librarian	:	1
Grade 'B' Stenographer	:	1 (for Registrar)
Grade 'C' Stenographer	:	3 (for Joint Registrar and Deputy Registrar)
Grade 'D' Stenographer	:	2 (for Assistant Registrar)
Assistants	:	22
Original Petition	:	5
First Appeal	:	5
Revision Petition	:	8
Establishment	:	1
Accounts	:	1
Filing Counter	:	1
Inspection Branch	:	1
U.D.C.	:	4
Record Room	:	1
Filing Counter	:	1
Administration	:	1
Accounts	:	1
L.D.C.	:	19
Original Petition	:	5
First Appeal	:	5
Revision Petition	:	8

Record Room	:	1
Hindi Translator	:	1
Hindi Typist	:	1
Asstt. Librarian	:	1
Junior Library Attendant	:	1
Daftry	:	5
Staff Car Driver	:	3 (one for President and two for the Office)
Jamadar	:	1
Peons	:	21
Despatch Rider	:	1
Photo-copier Operator	:	2
Sweeper	:	2
Chowkidar	:	2

STATE CONSUMER DISPUTES REDRESSAL COMMISSIONS

Section 16 of the Consumer Protection Act lays down that a State Commission shall consist of a President and two Members. The President of the State Commission has to be a person who is or has been a judge of the High Court.

A Judge of a High Court is entitled to the following staff; in addition to three peons

i) PPS/PS -1

(In the pay scale of Rs. 10,000-15,200)

ii) Personal Assistant -1

(In the pay scale of Rs. 5500-9000)

iii) Staff Car Driver -1

(In the pay scale of Rs. 3050-4590)

The President of the State Commission may be given this staff. As regards

Peons, a consolidated recommendation is being made separately, out of which the President may have peons.

For Members personal staff may consist of two Stenographers in the pay scale of Rs. 5500-9000 and 2 Peons in the pay scale of Rs. 2550-3200. A Court Master/Reader may be provided to assist the President and Members of the State Commission in the Court. This officer should be in the pay scale of Rs. 5500-9000.

The State Commission should have a Registrar in the pay scale of Rs. 8,500-13,500/-. He will assist the State Commission in all judicial and administrative matters. A shorthand knowing LDC in the pay scale of Rs. 3050-4590/- who may work as Personal Assistant to the Registrar and one Peon may be provided to him.

The State Commission exercise Original, Appellate and Revisional jurisdiction. Therefore, two sections may be created – one for the Original Petitions and the other for Appeals and Revisions. A post of Administrative Officer (Class-II) may be created for an overall charge of these Sections. Each section should be headed by an officer of the rank of Dy. Superintendent in the pay scale of Rs. 5000-8000.

In each of these judicial sections, seats of dealing assistant may be created to handle 250 files per seat. The dealing assistant should be assisted by an LDC. Thus one Assistant and one LDC should be provided in each of the two sections for every 250 files. The total number of staff in the judicial sections can, therefore, be worked out keeping in view the total number of pending files dealt with therein and adopting the criteria of 250 files for one Assistant and one LDC. Besides, one Peon may be posted in each section.

In the State Commissions, orders are at times dictated in regional language because the consumers are not conversant with the English language. We, therefore, recommend that a post of regional language, Stenographer in the scale of Rs. 4000-6000 may be created.

A Post of Assistant and a type knowing LDC may also be created for the Establishment/Administration Branch.

Accounts Branch of the State Commission should be supervised by an Accountant in the pay scale of Rs. 5500-9000. One Bill Clerk and a type knowing LDC may be provided in the Accounts Branch for its smooth functioning.

A good Library is absolutely essential for a quasi-judicial body like the State Commission. Therefore, a trained Librarian in the pay scale of Rs. 5500-9000 may be posted for manning the library.

A filing counter may be created for receiving complaints, appeals and revisions, for maintaining institution registers and issue/despatch of notices. There should be two clerks and one peons for the Filing Counter in the pay scale of Rs. 3050-4590 and Rs. 2550-3200 respectively.

An LDC and one Peon will be necessary for inspection of record which will be made available by them under the supervision of the Registrar.

A record room may be set up in each of the State Commissions for keeping files of decided cases. One LDC and one Peon may be posted in the record room for arranging files, entering in the Access register and for weeding out the record.

A Post of Despatch Rider is also essential for effecting service of notices issued by the State Commission. This will save considerable amount incurred on postage for sending copies of the complaints appeals revision petitions to enable the opposite party(s) to file its/their versions of the case.

Two posts of Daftry, two posts of Sweeper and two posts of Chowkidar may also be sanctioned, keeping in view the requirements of the office as well as the President and Members of the Commission.

To sum up, the staff requirement of the State Commission wil be as under:-

For President :

i) PPS/PS -1

ii) PA -1

iii) Staff Car Driver -1

For Members :

i) Stenographers -2

For Office :

i) Registrar -1

ii) A.O. (Group 'B') -1

iii) Dy. Superintendent -2 (1each for Original and Appellate/ Revision Sections)

iv) Court Master -1

v) Accountant -1

vi) Librarian -1

vii) Assistant (s) for Branches

viii) Regional language Steno. –1

ix) LDC(s) for Branches

x) P.A. to Registrar/Shorthand

Knowing LDC -2

xi) Filing Clerks (LDC) -1

xii) Inspection Clerk (LDC) -1

xiii) Record Keeper (LDC) -1

xiv) LDC for Estt. Branch -1

xv) Bill Clerk (LDC) -1

xvi) Typist (LDC for A/cs. Branch) -1

xvii) Despatch Rider -1

xviii) Daftry -2

xix) Peons -10 (for President, Members, Registry, two branches and five Offices)

xx) Sweeper -2

xxi) Chowkidar -2

Note : One Assistant and One LDC for every 250 pending files. The number of Posts may

Be sanctioned keeping in view the total pendency.

For the States which have a pendency of less than 500 cases, the staff strength shall be as follows : -

For President

1. PPS/PS : 1
2. P.A. : 1
3. Staff Car Driver : 1

For Members

1. Stenographer : 1

For Office

1. Registrar : 1
2. Court Master : 1
3. Accountant : 1
4. P.A. to Registrar : 1
5. Assistant : 1
6. U.D.C. : 1
7. L.D.C. : 1
8. Typist : 1
9. Peons : 1
10. Chowkidar : 1
11. Sweeper : 1

This staff shall look after the judicial, the administrative and the library work.

CONSUMER DISPUTES REDRESSAL FORUMS

Section 10 of the Consumer Protection Act lays down that each District Forum shall consist of a President and two other Members. The President of the District Forum has to be a person who is, or who has been, or is qualified to be a District Judge.

In Writ Petition (Civil) No. 1141 of 1988, Common Cause vs. Union of India & Ors. the Hon'ble Supreme Court on 7th January, 1993 directed that if the work load of a District Forum exceeds the minimum monthly load of 150 cases consistently for a period of six months, a regular independent District Forum as envisaged by Section 9 of the Act should be established.

A District Judge is an Officer in the scale of Rs. 18,400-22,400, which is equivalent to the scale of Joint Secretary to the Govt. of India. Govt. of India's instructions provide that a Joint Secretary is entitled to a Private Secretary in the scale of Rs. 6500-10,000 and a peon in the scale of Rs. 2550-3200. As regards the two Members of the District Forum, one stenographer in the scale of Rs. 4000-6000 and one peon in the scale of Rs. 2550-3200 may be provided for them. There should also be a post of Court Master in the pay scale of Rs. 5500-9000 to assist the President and the Members in the 'Court'.

The Registry of the District Forum should be headed by the Registrar who should be of the rank of Superintendent in the State Government, which post carries the pay scale of Rs. 5500-9000. His duties will involve assisting the Forum in Judicial and administrative matters.

The District Forum exercise only Original Jurisdiction. With a view to create seats of dealing hands in the Judicial Section, the work load should first be assessed in terms of pending files. These files may be assigned to various dealing hands who will be responsible for taking all follow-up action as per the orders of the Forum/Bench. Each dealing hand of the level of UDC, assisted by an LDC, should handle at least 250 files. Thus, taking into consideration the total number of pending files and the yardstick of 250 files for a nucleus of one UDC and one LDC, the staff requirement in the Judicial Section may be worked out. One peon will also be required for the Judicial Section.

The Registrar of the District Forum may also look after the work relating to maintenance of Library, preparation of pay bills, T.A. bills etc. and for maintaining the books of accounts and keeping the bank guarantees which are taken from the parties in pursuance of the orders of the District Forum. However, one accounts knowing UDC in the scale of Rs. 4000-6000 may assist the Registrar in the work.

Presently there is no satisfactory arrangement for receiving the complaints and for issue or dispatch of notices as well as inspection of cases in the Forum. There should be one post of Clerk in the scale of Rs. 3050-4590 for receiving the complaints, maintaining the institution registers and issue or dispatch of notices and inspection of cases.

A post of Despatch Rider is also essential for effecting service of notices issued by the District Forum. This will save considerable amount incurred on postage for sending copies of the complaints to enable the opposite party (s) to file its/their version of the case.

There is an absence of a Record Room in most of the District Forum, as a result of which the files are not properly arranged and entered in the Access Register. The decided cases, therefore, cannot be traced out without avoidable loss of time. To begin with, one LDC and one Peon should be provided with duties of arranging the files in the Record Room, entering the same in the Access register and to take follow up action for weeding out the old records.

One post of Safaiwala/Chowkidar be also sanctioned for cleanliness of the office of the forum.

In view of the position, as explained above, the following staff will be necessary for a District Forum :-

1. P.S. : 1
2. Registrar (in the scale of Superintendent) : 1
3. Court Master : 1
4. Steno : 1
5. U.D.C.
6. L.D.C.
7. Receipt & Despatch Clerk (LDC) : 1
8. Record Keeper (LDC) : 1
9. Accounts Knowing UDC : 1 (will look after the library work)
10. Peons : 4
11. Safaiwala : 1
12. Despatch Rider : 1
13. Chowkidar : 1

Note : One UDC and one LDC for every 250 pending files.

In the smaller districts where less than 150 cases are pending, the strength will be UDC-1, LDC-1, 3 Peons, 1 Chowkidar cum Safaiwala. The UDC will look after the library work also. Resolutions adopted in the Conference of the Presidents and the Secretaries, In-charge of Consumer Affairs in the State Governments/UTs held on 17th & 18th August, 2007 at Hall No. 5, Vigyan Bhawan, New Delhi. After deliberations, the following Resolutions were adopted:-

1. Resolved that all the Consumer Fora should take necessary steps for their computerisation under the 'Confonet Project' with the assistance extended by the Government through NIC. Further the State Commission/District Fora should co-ordinate with the State Information Officer (SIO) and District Information Officer (DIO) to make Consumer Fora fully computerized.
2. Resolved that the grants released by the Central Government under the One Time Grant of 1995-1999 and of 2004-05 and now under the 'Integrated Project' for construction of building and purchase of furniture/ prescribed equipment for the State Commissions and District Fora should be fully utilized. The Utilization Certificate of the grants be furnished to the Central Government at the earliest.
3. Resolved that the State Commissions should hold Conference of the Presidents & Members of the District Forums on half yearly/annual basis to ensure the effective functioning of the Consumer Fora.
4. Resolved that a Committee may be constituted to study the salary/honorarium being paid to the Members of other quasi-judicial bodies and suggest suitable salary/ honorarium for the Members of the State Commission/ District Forum.
5. Resolved that the process of selection of Presidents & Members of the State Commissions as well as District Fora should be initiated six months in advance and the Presidents of the District Fora be appointed from amongst the sitting/retired District Judges/Additional District Judges, who are eligible for appointment as President of District Forum.
6. Resolved that the concerned authorities of the State Governments/UTs would ensure that the Orders of the

Consumer Fora are implemented and the Warrants issued by them are executed.

7. Resolved that the Consumer Fora should maintain punctuality in attending the sittings.
8. Resolved that the Consumer Fora should upload on the website every month, data relating to filing, disposal and pendency of cases.
9. Resolved that the District Fora will dispose of at least 60 to 70 cases each month.

MINUTES OF THE CONFERENCE OF THE PRESIDENTS OF STATE COMMISSIONS AND THE SECRETARIES INCHARGE OF CONSUMER AFFAIRS IN THE STATE GOVERNMENTS/UTS, ORGANISED BY THE NATIONAL CONSUMER DISPUTES REDRESSAL COMMISSION ON THE OCCASION OF ITS "FOUNDATION DAY" ON 17TH & 18TH AUGUST, 2007 AT HALL NO.5, VIGYAN BHAVAN, NEW DELHI.

INAUGURAL SESSION

(17TH August, 2007 - 4.30 p.m.)

The Conference commenced with lighting of a lamp and honouring of guests by presenting bouquets.

Smt. Rajyalakshmi Rao, Member of the National Consumer Disputes Redressal Commission (NCDRC), on behalf of the National Commission, welcomed Shri Sharad Pawar, Hon'ble Union Minister for Agriculture, Consumer Affairs, Food & Public Distribution, Shri H.R. Bhardwaj, Hon'ble Union Minister for Law and Justice, Hon'ble Shri Justice Ashok Bhan, Judge, Supreme Court of India and other distinguished guests. She outlined the various developments in the functioning of the National Commission over the last 20 years and informed that housing development corporations, private builders, insurance companies and Government bodies are now slowly becoming responsive to consumers. She further observed that confidence of the consumer arises out of knowledge of his rights and a belief that there is a redressal mechanism available at his doorstep in each and every district. Due to landmark judgments rendered by the National Commission and the Hon'ble Supreme Court, Indian Industry and Government Departments are now paying attention to quality consciousness in goods and services. She quoted a few important judgments rendered by the National Commission in the fields of banking, insurance, medical negligence etc. She observed that increasing consumer awareness has empowered them in demanding that the Consumer Fora decide their cases as expeditiously as possible.

Shri Y.S. Bhave, Secretary, Department of Consumer Affairs Government of India after welcoming the participants observed that the deliberations over the two days would lead to a greater understanding of their roles and responsibilities by the States and redressal agencies and foster a spirit of mutual cooperation in working to ensure that the faith reposed by the consumers in the justice delivery system is not belied. He informed that C.P. Act is looked upon as model legislation by many other countries and has many a time been lauded by the highest court of justice of our country. He however, observed that the consumer dispute redressal agencies have sometimes not been measuring up to this expectation.

The important point to be borne in mind, as a cardinal principle in adjudicating on consumer complaints is disposal through summary trial even while providing an opportunity for hearing to both the parties. He emphasized that Consumer Fora should function successfully, retaining their unique character and effectiveness so that consumers do not lose confidence in their justice delivery system. He commended the work done by the Consumer Fora in achieving a disposal of 88% and emphasized the need that State Governments should ensure that all the Consumer Fora are functioning. Planning and action is required to fill up vacancies in time. He informed that a comprehensive amendment to the Act to speed up the disposal of cases so as to ensure protection of consumer interests in the wake of liberalized and globalized market is on the anvil. The Central Government has launched a Confonet Project as well as Integrated Project under which financial assistance is being provided to the Consumer Fora functioning in the country for computerization and for improving the infrastructural facilities to them. Besides, the training programme conducted through IIPA is funded by the Central Government. Hon'ble Mr. Justice M.B. Shah, President, National Consumer Disputes Redressal Commission first of all congratulated the participants for taking interest in consumer movement and welcomed the distinguished guests on the day of celebration of the Foundation of the National Commission. The President of the National Commission observed that generally it is stated that the consumer is king but taking into consideration the following aspects, there is a need to ponder and decide whether he is the king or the object of exploitation!

(i) Is there any protection to consumers (patients) against the spurious life saving drugs being sold in the market?

(ii) Is he protected against the exorbitant rate of interest being charged by the banks?

(iii) The victim of motor vehicle accident is not given immediate treatment by a hospital on the ground that the amount for treatment is to be deposited first.

(iv) An unfortunate person getting a massive heart attack is not treated till the requisite deposit is made.

(v) Statutory authority constituted for development of the city or town by providing housing accommodation- delays in constructing houses and, yet demands (cost) escalation charges.

(vi) Insurance company repudiating the claim on flimsy ground by taking undue advantage of the exclusion clauses which are in small print and which could not be read or understood by the insured.

In such circumstances, it is apparent that consumer is the victim and not the king. He emphasized the need for Consumer Protection Councils in the States and Districts and expressed a hope that these Councils will work more efficiently and effectively. He suggested that the Consumer Fora are exercising inquisitorial jurisdiction and rendering justice on the basis of equity, de-hors technicalities evolved under the procedural laws. He emphasized the need for the Consumer Fora to follow the principles of natural justice. On account of the establishment of the Consumer Fora in the country, 50% work of the Civil Courts is now diverted to the Consumer Fora.

Because of globalization and multinational companies entering the market, the Consumer requires more protection from aggressive advertisements and unethical marketing. It is the responsibility of the Government as well as Consumer Fora to protect the consumers against such practices. The President of the National Commission emphasized that despite limited infrastructure, the Consumer Fora are functioning effectively and have disposed of 25 lakhs out of 29 lakhs cases instituted. He cited a landmark judgment delivered by the Supreme Court in the case of Lucknow Development Authority vs. M.K. Gupta-(1994) 1 SCC 243 wherein the Apex Court has observed as under: "The importance of the Act lies in promoting welfare of the society by enabling the consumer to participate directly in the market economy It attempts to remove the helplessness of a consumer which he faces against powerful business, described as, "a network of rackets' or a society in which,' producers have secured power' to 'rob the rest' and the might of public bodies which are degenerating into storehouses of inaction where papers do not move from one desk to another as a matter of duty and responsibility but for extraneous consideration leaving the common man helpless, bewildered and shocked. The malady is becoming so rampant, widespread and deep that the society instead of bothering, complaining and fighting against it, is accepting it as part of life. The enactment in these unbelievable yet harsh realities appears to be a silver lining, which may in course in time succeed in checking the rot."

In order to achieve the above object, President, NCDRC suggested that we must try to evolve a procedure where the State Governments may not delay in making appointments of the President of the State Commissions or District Fora or the Members of the State Commissions and District Fora so that consumers of justice are not frustrated. Easy procedure can be evolved for appointment of the Presidents of the District Fora with the intervention of the Hon'ble Law Minister in seeing that the strength of the Additional District Judge/District Judges in each State is increased, so that High Courts could be in a position to send some of them on deputation to the Consumer Fora. He further informed that if proper infrastructure is not provided and the appointments are not made as provided in the Act, pendency of cases at all levels will increase which finally would frustrate the purpose of the Act and consumers. He also informed the participants that National Commission is also facing the same difficulty in respect of its own building.

However, he suggested that instead of criticizing the concerned authorities for not providing the necessary infrastructure, which delays disposal of cases at all levels, let us work in such a way that we are never caught in the traffic jam of pending arrears and discharge our functions effectively and efficiently with zeal. Finally, he summed up by saying that let us have a vision so that in the years to come 'Silver Lining' dreamt by the Apex Court for helping the little man – the Consumer Protection Act, becomes more and more visible and shines brightly in the cloudy sky.

Shri Sharad Pawar, Hon'ble Union Minister for Consumer Affairs, Food and Public Distribution, while inaugurating the Conference, welcomed the guests and observed that he is glad that the National Commission is celebrating its 'Foundation Day' by holding a Conference to discuss the working of the consumer redressal agencies and how they should be made more purposeful. He informed that the consumer protection programmes and the consumer movement received a significant boost after the enactment of the Consumer Protection Act, 1986. Perhaps, there is no such model provided exclusively for consumers anywhere else in the world till now. Our legislation is looked upon as model legislation in many countries.

The Act has provided an additional legal recourse in the form of Consumer Fora for redressal of their grievances. He expressed his happiness that the overall performance of the Consumer Fora so far is satisfactory. Over 28 lakh cases were filed and 88 per cent cases were disposed off. He however, cautioned that the need of the hour is to change the common man's perception that the Consumer Fora have slipped onto the path of civil courts, making litigation long drawn out and taking several years to dispose of even cases involving small compensation. Furthermore, even where orders have been passed, the same are not getting executed on time.

An equally common criticism that we come across is that while the orders of the Fora are not swift enough, they also do not hit the offenders where it hurts them most and as such, offenders may not take the Fora seriously. This perception has to change. It should change in such a way that the Consumer Fora become a role model in redressing the grievances swiftly and more effectively so that there is a check on exploiters. He assured his wholehearted support, wherever needed in achieving the object of the Act. Honourable Minister informed that as per the provisions of the Consumer Protection Act, the State Commissions and District Consumer Fora are the responsibility of the State Governments but in order to ensure that these fora are not hampered by lack of infrastructure, the Central Government has been extending liberal assistance in the form of grants so that there are no resource constraints.

The Department has provided Rs.72 crores as one time grant to States between 1995 and 2005. Now under the Integrated Project, the Central Government is providing assistance at the rate of 36 lakh per district forum and 90 lakh per State Commission. Under the scheme already Rs.98 crores has been sanctioned for 18 States and Rs.50.26 crores released to these State Governments as the first tranche of assistance. Government of India will look positively at proposals coming from the other States also.

The Hon'ble Minister further expressed that when Government of India is spending liberally on providing all requisite infrastructure to these fora and the State Governments are also spending considerable resources, it behoves each and every fora to ensure that cases are disposed off within the time lines specified under the Act. He expressed confidence that with Justice M.B. Shah, an experienced jurist heading the apex Consumer Forum, all the 607 District Fora and 35 State Commissions would follow his leadership and commitment to ensure that Consumer Fora becomes a role model of which we all can be proud. He assured his wholehearted support wherever needed in achieving the objectives of the Act.

Honourable Minister informed that as a result of the amendments made in the Act and Rules, the National Commission is now able to hold sittings in three Circuit Benches. The Central Government is in the process of increasing the number of Members from five to nine to further strengthen the Commission. The Central Government has always been giving priority to the needs of the National Commission. In so far as the State Commissions and District Fora are concerned, often vacancies have been an impediment to disposal of cases and, in some places poor remuneration to Members of the Fora has been a disincentive. He informed that the responsibility of the State Government has been emphasized recently even by the Supreme Court, in its judgment in Civil Appeal No.2740 of 2007 (arising out of SLP (Civil) No.6928 of 1999) wherein apex Court has directed the "Governments to consider fixing adequate salaries and allowances for Members of the Consumer Fora at all the three levels so that they can function effectively and with a free mind." Besides, the Court has also directed them "to fill up vacancies expeditiously so that the Fora can function effectively." There are glaring disparities in salaries/ honoraria of Presidents and Members of State Commissions and District Fora amongst States. He suggested that the Conference may consider adopting a uniform formula for all States. He advised that provisions like the senior most member of a District Fora acting as the President in case of a vacancy; maintaining of panels of members to fill up anticipated vacancies and pending regular arrangements, allowing a neighbouring forum to look after work in a forum, are being adopted to ensure that no forum remains non-functional on account of vacancies.

Honourable Minister mentioned that the efficient functioning and performance of the District Consumer Fora is crucial to the efficiency of the Fora. He informed that he had already requested the Chief Ministers/Lieutenant Governors of all States/U.Ts. In June, 2006 that during the selection and appointment of President of District Fora, preference should be given to serving District Judges, who have the requisite experience and background. The Minister informed that the Government is doing its best to provide necessary assistance to the National Commission as well as to the State Commissions and District Consumer Fora. The Planning Commission and the Ministry of Finance have provided adequate budgetary allocation for implementing important schemes for the Consumer Fora. He referred to the Confonet project for which the Government has approved Rs.49 crores. He expressed hope that before the year is over, every district fora and State Commission shall be fully computerized and networked. He directed NIC and the State Governments to ensure that all problems relating to site preparation, installation, connectivity and provision of trained manpower are resolved on a war footing. He advised the Consumer Fora to take a pledge to dispose of the cases within the prescribed time stipulated in the Act and exhorted all present to rededicate ourselves to work for the welfare of the consumers and resolve to make them aware of their rights and responsibilities as consumers.

Effective functioning of the consumer dispute redressal machinery for rendering quick justice is a very important ingredient in this framework. To reduce pendency and ensure time bound disposal of cases in the Consumer Fora, the need of the hour is for every Presiding Officer of the Consumer Fora to take a pledge that they will dispose off the cases within the prescribed time norm. They have to find ways and means to achieve this goal. What is to be kept in mind always is the primary objective of the Consumer Protection Act, which is to provide simple, inexpensive and quick resolution of consumer disputes without having to observe the somewhat lengthy civil court procedures. Unless the Consumer Fora function effectively, the fledgling consumer movement would hit a roadblock and could become counter productive. Hence, there is an imperative need for effective functioning of Consumer Fora, particularly in the light of the intensified multi media publicity programme of the Government. He expressed hope that with the cooperation of all, the Consumer Movement in the country will get a further boost and that all present will ensure that the consumer is not disappointed or disillusioned due to delayed or inadequate justice. Hon'ble Shri Justice Ashok Bhan, Judge, Supreme Court of India at the outset raised a query as to "who is the service provider and who is the consumer?" He also replied that each one of us is service provider, each one of us is a consumer. He.

therefore, suggested that we should improve ourselves. The fight is not between service provider and consumer. The remedy ultimately lies within ourselves.

There is no gain saying that consumer is the focal point in all activities in the world. He observed that in the absence of proper infrastructure, the Fora may not be able to provide service. So they may be provided infrastructure and all the facilities. Once an Act is enacted, it is the responsibility of the Government to make available infrastructure etc. to them. Proper persons should be appointed in the Consumer Fora and they should be paid reasonable honorarium/salary. He cited examples, where the consumers are being cheated. The workload in the Fora has increased tremendously and it is the responsibility of the Government to establish additional Benches where the pendency is large. He insisted that minimum requirement of the Consumer Fora should be taken care of for their effective functioning. Lastly, he emphasized the need for 'Jagriti' which has to come from within. Shri H.R. Bhardwaj, Hon'ble Union Minister for Law and Justice informed that he drafted the Consumer Protection Bill on the advice of the then Prime Minister, late Mr. Rajiv Gandhi for redressal of the consumer grievances. The provision for Consumer Councils was also kept in the Bill. He expressed his happiness that after passing of the Act, the law on Consumer Protection Act developed so much that people are getting quick justice and the Consumer Fora are disposing of cases quickly. These Fora should maintain a unique character rather than simply following the pattern of Civil Courts.

He praised the work done by Shri Sharad Pawarji and hoped that he would provide other facilities to the Consumer For a for their effective functioning. Hon'ble Minister further stated that we are standardizing the measurement, the whole concept of service is being changed because the earlier weights and measures were different, labelling was not there.

Now laws and regulations relating to weights and measures have been comprehensively amended to meet the challenges of globalization. Similarly consumer fora also need to reorient themselves to match the challenge of the future. He narrated his experience as Law Minister for more than 15 years and found it rather frustrating sometime, when funds are not provided to the judiciary for the infrastructure or for their improvement in the service conditions.

The Consumer Fora would be deciding cases on the principles of natural justice and on the basis of inquisition. Inquisition is an investigation so they would be doing an investigator's job rather than the trial work. That is far more difficult as the whole burden would be on the Fora to probe into the allegation made against a service provider. He observed that it is a unique system in and now we have to ensure that it becomes a powerful system. Unless we build that as a mass movement, few Presiding Officers and Members of the Fora would not be able to do justice to the cause.

He emphasized the need for putting in place Consumer Councils in the States which councils the citizens could approach for taking up their causes. He further stated that Government should take care that the institution is looked after properly. The Consumer Fora are just like Courts and the persons working in them should be given all facilities. He brought to the notice that when Judges are employed in the Court to any full time work, they have to be treated as sitting Judges. By getting meager salary, persons in these fora cannot perform their functions. There should be uniformity of pay scales or honorarium of the Presidents and Members at all levels so that proper people are made available to the Fora. We should appoint proper people so that they could take the work seriously by paying them suitable salary/honorarium. He further observed that he came to know that in some States political people are being appointed which is not a good sign At the end he advised that whatever suggestions come from the Conference, we should try to implement them.

On the occasion of the Foundation Day of the National Commission, Hon'ble Shri Ashok Bhan, Judge, Supreme Court of India released a Souvenir along with Annual Report of the Commission containing the important judgments rendered by the National Commission as well as the rate of institution and disposal of cases of the Consumer For a functioning the country.

6

Business Session

The Business Session was chaired by Hon'ble Mr. Justice M.B. Shah, President of the National Consumer Disputes Redressal Commission. The Hon'ble President, NCDRC, in his Introductory Address, touched upon the following:-

(i) Disposal of Cases

In view of the huge pendency in the Consumer Fora and more so in the State Commissions, greater attention is required to be given to dispose off cases within the stipulated time provided under the Act. It is expected that the District Fora shall dispose off at least 60 to 70 cases each month. Furthermore, these Fora should list only so many cases in a day as can be disposed off. This will help avoid unnecessary adjournments.

(ii) Appointment of the Presidents and Members of the District Fora

Though, as per the resolution adopted in the last Conference (March, 2007), the process of selection of the Presidents and the Members of the State Commissions and District Fora should be initiated at least six months before the vacancy is due to arise, it has often been observed that this is not being followed. It is necessary that this be strictly followed.

Furthermore, the Presidents of the District Fora should be appointed from amongst sitting District Judges/retired District Judges or from the Additional District Judges, who are eligible for promotion. The Chief Justice of Hon'ble High Court be requested to recommend such Judges for the appointment in the District Fora. The matter is also being taken up with the Chief Ministers of all the States.

(iii) Uniform Honorarium

There is a strong need for increasing the honorarium of the Members of the State Commissions and the District Fora; many State Governments are paying a very meager amount to the Members. A uniform formula could be adopted by all State Governments to the effect that in case of persons who had retired from the Government/ an organized service, he should be paid last pay drawn minus pension. The pay of Member with non-official background may also be fixed in a manner that is more or less commensurate with that of other Members. It was also emphasized that the pay of the Members of the State Commission should be more than the President of the District Forum as the Members of the State Commission hear an appeal against the orders passed by the President of the District Forum.

(iv) 'Confonet' Project

As per the figures supplied by NIC 1763 computers have been received out of which 1387 computers have been installed. These figures need to be confirmed. It is also noticed that there are several District Fora, where the hardware and software have not been installed. It is the duty of the State Governments and NIC to provide the infrastructure to install the hardware/ software. The Consumer Fora are responsible for ensuring that all their data is placed on the website to facilitate the general consumers at large to know the status of their cases.

(v) To Provide Paper Books to the Members

Many Members of the District Fora have, during interactions informed that they are not being provided paper books and due to the same they are unable to participate in preparing the orders. It is essential that the paper books are provided to all the Members before of hearing of the cases.

(vi) Payment of Fees

Members of District Fora have also reported that at the time of filing of complaint, consumers are being directed to deposit the fee in the Treasury of the State Government, which takes a lot of time. For the ease of consumers, District Fora should accept fee in the form of Bank Draft or Indian Postal Order as already provided in the Consumer Protection Rules.

(vii) Training

State Governments should in coordination with the State Commissions organize training to the Presidents and Members of the District For a as is being done in IIPA.

While celebrating the 20th Year of establishment of the National Commission, the President further emphasized that mostly case law under the Consumer Protection Act has been developed by the Hon'ble Supreme Court and NCDRC. Landmark judgments have been published by the National Commission from time to time and now also being placed on the website. All the State Commissions and the District Fora should make full use of connectivity being provided under the Confonet to access such judgements.

Shri Y.S. Bhave, Secretary, Department of Consumer Affairs, Government of India, while addressing the participants, stressed that the Consumer Fora should take interest in installation of computer and other hardware/ software provided and also requested the State Secretaries to look into the matter personally to monitor the progress and ensure that all the difficulties are removed. Mr. Bhave also requested the participants to fully utilize funds provided under the Integrated Project by the Government of India expeditiously so that the benefit be availed of by the Consumer Fora. He further assured that he would write to the Chief Secretaries of all the States to help in providing the land and allot funds to the State Commissions for construction of building.

Smt. Alka Sirohi, Additional Secretary, Department of Consumer Affairs, Govt. of India in her address gave an overview of the status of action in respect of main agenda issues and highlighted areas of concern which were as follows:-

- Under Confonet, out of 607 District Fora and 35 State Commissions hardware has been supplied as per NIC's report in 93% locations. Of these, installation of hardware is only 83% against supplies made and installation of software has been done in less than 49% of the placed provided with hardware. This being the final year of the project it is important to ensure that all problems relating to site preparation, installation, connectivity and manpower are resolved on a war-footing. Full operationalization of the project needs to be ensured by 31/3/2008.

- Though, the responsibility for the State Commission and the District Fora rests with the State Government, Government of India have been giving liberal assistance for infrastructure development of these Fora in the form of one time grant. Out of the Rs.62 crores released between 1995-99, 10 States/ UTs are yet to utilize the money.
- Similarly, out of the Rs.20.20 crores of one time grant released in 2004-05 to thirteen States, eleven have either utilized only part or have not reported any utilization whatsoever.
- Govt. of India have under the Integrated Project provided for assistance upto Rs.36 lakhs for District Fora and Rs.90 lakh per State Commission for construction / upgradation of building and for furniture and office equipment. The detailed guidelines have been circulated to all States/ UTs and a proforma for sending proposals has also being circulated. So far assistance amounting to Rs.98 crores has already been sanctioned to 18 States and Rs.50.26 crores released as first tranche of assistance. She clarified that to be eligible for assistance, State Governments must show utilization of earlier grants, and provide information in the prescribed format. She exhorted the other States to avail of this scheme and come forward with proposals early as the scheme is currently in force only upto 31/3/2008.
- State Governments should ensure that vacancies of President and Members do not exist and that even before a post falls vacant, selection and approval of the substitute should be completed, so that the person may join as soon as the post falls vacant.

- Delays on the part of the State Governments in appointment of Members recommended by the Selection Committee need to be scrupulously avoided as delays would mean vacancies which will affect resolution of disputes. Government of India is also considering a provision in the Consumer Protection Act to facilitate State Governments in taking a decision on the recommendations of the Selection Committee within a stipulated time.
- There is a need to provide the requisite supporting staff to the State Commissions/ District Fora. The core staff may be employed on a permanent basis while the peripheral work could be outsourced and thus reduce the long term burden on the Government.
- There is a very large variation between remuneration paid to Members in different Sates, as given in Annexure-VIII to the Agenda Notes. States Governments could consider universally adopting the formula of giving last pay drawn minus pension wherever persons who have retired from organized services are appointed as President/ Member.
- Wherever the case load of pendency is very high, State Governments may consider creation of additional benches. Experience has been that where the State Commission holds sittings at places other than State Headquarters, touring (Circuit) Benches are more useful than the fixed permanent Benches as they provide for greater flexibility. Experience also shows that in case of President of District Fora, sitting District Judges/ Addl. District Judges, and if they are not available, retired Judges are a better option as their performance is generally much better than others.
- Addressing the Presidents of the State Commissions, Additional Secretary suggested that Government may be taken by them as a 'consumer' since it not only represents the consumers but it is also paying for all facilities for the Consumer Courts and is therefore, in return entitled to 'good service' in terms of efficient and

timely disposal of cases. She suggested that attempt should be made to ensure that prescribed time limits for disposal of cases are strictly observed and the consumer does not have to attend repetitive hearings.

Dr. Dharam Prakash, Honorary Joint Secretary, Indian Medical Association (HQs) speaking on behalf of the Medical Profession, stated that a farmer can never think of destroying his own crops. Similarly, the patient is bread and butter for a qualified doctor and hence no doctor would expect his patient to become worse or die by his treatment. The Hon'ble Supreme Court held that a medical practitioner must act with a reasonable degree of skill and knowledge and must exercise a reasonable degree of care. He observed that the Consumer Courts, for just decisions, must be assisted by a Board of medical experts. The degree of negligence and injury caused are very important for determination of compensation.

Dr. Prakash stated that the basis of any treatment depends on a few criteria. He suggested that the Consumer Protection Act could be amended to provide for the following :-

(1) Appointment of a Committee of Medical Specialists to assist the Consumer Fora and consisting of the following:-
    - Representative of the State Medical Council (for State Commission & District Fora) & Indian Medical Council (for the National Commission).
    - Representative from Indian Medical Association.
    - Representative from the respective Medical Specialists' Association pertaining to the defendants' specialty.

(2) In cases where negligence is proved, the penalty should be in consonance with and proportionate to the negligent act.

(3) In case of frivolous & unscrupulous complaint against Medical Practitioners, the complainant should be penalized by imposing a penalty of at least 75% of the amount claimed as compensation in the complaint.

(4) There should be no fee for Appeal to a higher Forum for Medical Practitioners.

Dr. Yatin Mehta, Consultant, Indraprastha Apollo Hospital, New Delhi gave a slide presentation covering various terminology used in the medical profession and explained different aspects of Medical Negligence, the Bolam Test, Standard of Care Required, Medical Ethics, Principal of Biomedical Ethics, Proving Medical Negligence, Complaints, Standard of Medical Care, Wrongful Act (Criminal liability & Civil liability), Medical Errors and Informed Consent.

Dr. Mehta also referred to some landmark judgements of the Hon'ble Supreme Court and National Commission in respect of medical cases. He stated that it is the legal duty of a doctor to disclose all relevant information to the patients and other concerned persons. The risk involved in the treatment should also be conveyed to the patient by the doctor before commencing such treatment.

Thereafter individual items on the agenda were discussed

Agenda Item No.1 (Status of Computerization and computer networking of the Consumer Fora under the Confonet Project)

Dr. Ranjana Nagpal, Sr. Technical Director, NIC made a State-wise and District-wise presentation on the status of supply of hardware, its installation, installation of software, entry of records and availability of the Technical Support Personnel (TSP). A copy of the presentation is annexed. The President, NCDRC and State Secretaries were requested to respond to the information and to confirm that this was correct. State representatives responded as follows:-

Chhatisgarh and Haryana corrected the names of some Districts.

Madhya Pradesh informed that they have three more Districts viz., Ashok Nagar, Anuppur and Burhanpur which need to be included. Similarly, Punjab informed that they have 20 District Fora including three newly created Districts in Taran Taran, Barnala and Mohali. It was decided that hardware and connectivity may be provided to these Districts once the staff in position and the Fora becomes functional.

J&K informed that the State Commission has two offices at Jammu and Srinagar, as the Government shifts for six months in a year to each of these locations, it was decided to provide hardware and connectivity at both these allocations.

Andhra Pradesh informed that they are now almost ready for on-line registration of complaints in Hyderabad District Fora.

Karnataka informed that the names of North Kannada and South Kannada Districts may be deleted as they do not exist. They also explained that they have developed very good software which could also be used for national system. Sr. Tech. Director, NIC confirmed that migration will be effected.

Tamil Nadu informed that installation of software in all the Fora will be completed by 31/8/2007 and data entry shall be taken up thereafter.

Gujarat informed that the NIC database reporting that no District Fora exist at Anand, Dahod, Narmada, Navsari, Panchmahals, Patan, Porbandar and the Dangs is not correct. District Fora already exist at Anand, Navsari, Panchmahals, Patan and Porbandar and new forum have been created in the remaining three. Buildings have been sanctioned for all these District Fora. Hardware and software may be provided to all these Fora on priority and installed early. Installation of hardware and software may be provided to al these Fora on priority and installed early. Installation of hardware and software in the other 20 districts will be completed by 31/10 2007.

Maharashtra reported having 39 Districts. Moreover, there were circuit benches of the State Commission at Nagpur and Aurangabad. It was decided that NIC shall immediately provide hardware and software to the remaining six locations.

Bihar reported creation of a new District of Arwal where posts have also been created. This may be included in the Confonet.

Jharkhand commented on the very poor quality of TSPs. It was decided that the DIO will personally supervise training of TSPs in each of the Districts and that Sr. Tech. Director, NIC will also review.

Orissa reported that hardware has been installed only in 18 of the 32 locations. Installation in the remaining districts must be expedited.

Uttar Pradesh reported installation of hardware at the State Commission and each of the 70 Districts.

West Bengal reported that NIC officials are not cooperating in installation of hardware/ software even though it has been supplied everywhere. Sr. Tech. Director, NIC promised to resolve the matter on priority.

Assam reported that in all the 23 District Fora hardware has been supplied everywhere but only partial installation has been completed and that too only in 12 Districts. Site preparation has been delayed because NIC released money only in July, 2007.

Mizoram also commented on the complete lack of interest by local NIC officials.

Chandigarh (U.T.) reported that no TSPs have been provided to either the State Commission or two District Fora. Sr. Tech. Director, NIC assured that this will be attended to on priority.

Delhi reported that in South Delhi-II District, which a new District Fora has been set up. Hardware is yet to be installed.

Additional Secretary (CA) stressed that Confonet is not a project simply for procurement of computers but for complete computerization and networking of District For a/ State Commissions. Wherever State Governments have got site preparation done and sent bills for the same to the NIC , payment as per rules may be expedited by NIC.

Additional Secretary (CA) also requested the State Commissions to ensure that wherever hardware has not been provided by NIC, full address of the District Fora may be communicated to NIC before the end of August, 2007 so that they can place orders for supplies.

Agenda Item No.2 Measures for speedy disposal of cases and to review of the performance of the Consumer Fora

(a) Status of Disposal of Cases

(b) Creation of Additional Benches

(c) Preparation of advance Panel for the posts of Members of State Commissions and District Fora

(d) Punctuality in conducting sittings

(e) Adherence to Regulations

(f) Adjournments

(g) Benchmark for disposal of cases

(h) Delay in Execution of Orders passed by the Consumer Fora by the Implementing Agencies

The President of the National Commission enquired from the President of the each State Commission to inform about the pendency of cases. Each representative gave the figures of pendency and wherever the pendency was large, he requested that the State Commission should try to dispose of them quickly and steps should be taken to create additional benches. In the States of Haryana, Maharashtra, Orissa, Uttar Pradesh & Delhi, there is urgent need for creation of Additional Benches. The Presidents of the State Commissions should monitor the functioning of the District Consumer Fora. The participants suggested that the Act should be amended with regard to removal of Presidents & Members of District Fora. Another Suggestion was that the Member should continue until the joining of a new Member.

The President of the National Commission stated that unnecessary adjournments should not be granted. The Fora should adopt a case management system wherein such number of cases be listed which can be disposed of.

Additional Secretary (CA) suggested that disposal of cases needs to be reviewed on two parameters -

(a) Percentage of cases disposed as against those pending; and

(b) disposal within the time prescribed in the Act.

In so far as percentage of disposal is concerned, the national average for disposal of District Fora is 90.67%. The Presidents of the State Commissions and State Secretaries should jointly review and ascertain the reasons in those District Fora where disposal has been less than 90%. Similarly, the national average for disposal of cases by State Commissions is 73%. Those State Commissions where disposal is less than this figure need to introspect to ascertain the reasons and take quick remedial action. There are some fora where there are only very few cases but even then the pendency is high. These need to be especially looked into.

It was decided that Presidents SCDRC and State Secretaries will undertake a monthly review of all Consumer Fora in the State, using as far as possible video conference facilities and take appropriate remedial measures where pendencies are high/ disposal low. They should also organize a half yearly/ annual conference where all attend in person.

Agenda Item No.3 - Uniform payment of honorarium to the Members of State Commissions and District Consumer Fora

President, NCDRC suggested that a Member of the State Commission should not get less honorarium than the President of a District Forum since he hears appeals against the orders passed by the latter. He also felt that if we are to get persons of eminence to man these posts. State Governments must provide a reasonable remuneration. Additional Secretary (CA) suggested that a Committee comprising of representatives of some State Governments and the Registrar, NCDRC may go through the present salary/ honorarium structure in different States/ UTs and suggest a uniform structure for all the States/ UTs to adopt. This was agreed to.

Agenda Item No.4 - Training Programme for the Members of the State Commissions and District Forums by the Indian Institute of Public Administration

It was explained by Additional Secretary (CA) that IIPA is already running intensive courses for Members of the District Fora. However, at times there are problems in State Governments sponsoring Members for such training or Members themselves not being willing to travel to Delhi for training. At times language of instruction is also a constraint. As such, the training could be decentralized and be organized at State

Headquarters by the State Government with the help of State Training Institutions. It was deiced that IIPA module will be circulated to all State Governments.

Agenda Item No.5 - Status regarding declaring Presidents of the State Commission as Head of Department and President of District Fora as Head of Office

The States which have not declared the President of the State Commission as Head of Department and the President District For a as Head of Office were requested to reexamine the matter.

Agenda Item No.6 - Power vested with the President, NCDRC and State Commission to withdraw judicial work from any President/ Member of State Commission / District Fora

The resolution passed in the Conference of 17/8/2005 was again reiterated. It was also proposed that Government may consider providing through an amendment in the Act, powers to the Selection Committee to transfer President/ Members of District Fora from one District to another.

Agenda Item No.7 - Utilization of Government grants given by the Central Government under the 'Integrated Project' for strengthening the infrastructure of Consumer Fora

Additional Secretary (CA) explained the scheme of Integrated Project and also stated that to be eligible for sanction of assistance, the States/ UTs also have to show utilization of the earlier grants. The money will be released in two instalments with the second instalment being released only after satisfactory utilization of the first instalment. Addl. Secretary clarified that as per norms State Governments are required to provide land free of cost for construction of building under the Integrated Project. However, where land is not available, if the State Government wishes to purchase a ready built building, Government of India will provide upto 70% of the cost limited to the cost ceiling (Rs.75 lakh and Rs.30 lakh in case of State Commission and District Fora respectively). In special cases where the cost of construction is extraordinarily high this ceiling may be raised by another 10% if there is adequate justification. She advised that wherever State/ UT Governments anticipate further expansion of the activities of the Fora, they could construct the building on a modular pattern so that it can be expanded further in future.

Additional Secretary (CA) also invited attention to the fact that though through the Integrated Project all requisite infrastructure for Consumer Fora can be provided. Some States remain ineligible for assistance as they are yet to utilize the earlier grants.

- The position of utilization is especially worrisome in J&K (24%), Tamil Nadu (41%), Jharkhand (52%), Assam (71%) and Bihar (91%). The 5 UTs of Andaman & Nicobar Islands, Chandigarh, Dadra & Nagar Haveli, Daman & Diu, and Lakshadweep are reporting that they have not received the grant during 1995-99. Addl. Secretary directed the CPU Divn. to immediately investigate the matter in consultation with IF.
- Some States/ UTs mentioned that the State Finance Departments are advising that the grant may be revalidated so as to enable usage now. Addl. Secy. requested the States to immediately send it in the form of proposal so that it can be examined for revalidation.

Agenda Item No.8 - Levying Fee for filing Complaint

It was agreed that the Department of Consumer Affairs will examine where there is a case for raising the exemption limit for charging of minimum fee. It was also agreed that a Committee comprising of the Joint Secretary (CA) and Registrar, NCDRC will examine the legality and financial propriety of permitting District Fora to take the fee as a cash deposit directly from the applicant and also whether this fee can be used for legal aid by the State Commission.

Agenda Item No.9 - Alternative Disputes Resolution Mechanism in the form of Lok Adalat for speedy disposal of consumer cases

President, NCDRC praised the efforts of Punjab and Orissa in organizing Lok Adalats. He also suggested that all States may consider pre-litigation statement of disputes in similar cases.

VALEDICTORY ADDRESS

Hon'ble Mr. Justice C.K. Thakkar, Judge, Supreme Court of India in his valedictory address congratulated the Presidents of the State Commissions for their immense service to the society. He stated that the concept of 'let the buyer beware' has now changed to 'let the seller beware', due to the activities undertaken by the Consumer Fora. He reflected that the disposal rate of Consumer Fora has improved and he hoped that this progress will be maintained. He impressed upon the Presidents & Members of the Consumer Fora the need for maintaining absolute punctuality in attending Courts. The Consumer Courts should avoid adjournments and not more than three adjournments should be granted. Brief, concise orders should be passed by the Consumer Fora, however, they must cover the facts and circumstances of the particular case. He further stated that in the Indian litigation system, the difficulty of a litigant really begins after his suit/complaint has been decreed as the nature of execution proceedings is very clumsy. There are some lawyers, who specialize in stalling the execution proceedings for years. This needs to be guarded against so as to ensure that the litigant should get the fruits of justice. For a Presiding Officer/ Member devotion and dedication is a must and we do our job with devotion and dedication, it will go a long way in serving the society.

7

Cause Lists of Supreme Court and High Courts

Daywise Hits

COURT	13-06-2008	14-06-2008	15-06-2008	16-06-2008	17-06-2008
SUPREME COURT OF INDIA	02092	01459	01081	02660	02131
AP HIGH COURT	01187	02240	05211	02356	07407
CALCUTTA HIGH COURT	02283	01622	01212	04057	02814
MADRAS HIGH COURT	05967	00619	05808	01993	04270
GUJRAT HIGH COURT	01186	03405	01873	01631	03950
JAIPUR HIGH COURT	00947	00794	00860	01190	00866
JABALPUR HIGH COURT	02218	02286	01965	03417	00420
INDORE BENCH	01035	01521	00925	01581	01382
ALLAHABAD HIGH COURT	00579	00560	01138	00394	00228
BOMBAY HIGH COURT	04908	02339	04822	02713	07491
DELHI HIGH COURT	01381	00792	00432	01376	01307
KERALA HIGH COURT	05394	03557	02636	03233	00282
NAGPUR HIGH COURT	00903	00844	00695	01450	00940
JAMMU & KASHMIR HIGH COURT	00142	00046	00028	00048	00020
HIGH COURT OF BOMBAY-PANAJI BENCH	00641	00440	00199	00547	00387
HIGH COURT OF ORISSA-CUTTACK	01110	01192	00728	01798	00909
PATNA HIGH COURT	00793	00663	00465	00720	00357
AURANGABAD BENCH	01038	01144	00612	02013	00496

APAT	00739	00565	00658	00835	00599
CIRCUIT BENCH AT PORTBLAIR	00001	00001	00001	00001	00003
HIGH COURT IN GUAHATI	00575	00290	00174	01054	01168
HIMACHAL PRADESH HIGH COURT	00530	00821	00508	01034	00996
NCDRC	00168	00142	00166	00283	00209
LUCKNOW BENCH	00647	00522	00551	01378	00658
CHATTISGARH HIGH COURT	00468	01295	01090	01842	00901
JHARKHAND HIGH COURT	00168	00138	00071	00188	00123
GWALIOR BENCH	00650	00561	00489	00647	00575
IMPHAL BENCH	00037	00001	00009	00025	00068
HIGH COURT OF UTTARANCHAL AT NAINITAL	00463	00748	00535	00666	00370
HIGH COURT OF CHENNAI-MADURAI BENCH	02498	02379	01781	00519	02285
HIGH COURT OF RAJASTHAN AT JODHPUR	00563	00263	00427	00637	00359
HIGH COURT OF RAJASTHAN - JAIPUR BENCH	00947	00791	00860	01190	00866
DEBTS RECOVERY TRIBUNAL - ALLAHABAD	00006	00008	00002	00020	00004
CITY CIVIL COURTS, HYDERABAD	00077	00052	00008	00048	00026
TOTAL	42341	34103	38020	43544	44867

Introduction

When numerous persons join together
It'll give a new strength! Progress is sure
In the task that is performed!
Think of it, O Comrades!
Can a single hand produce
A noise so loud?
If numerous hands join together
Won't it be achieved, O Comrades?
By Pavendar Bharathidasan

The words of Pavendar Bharathidasan calling the comrades to join together for doing business, reflects the achievements made by the cooperative institutions in the country. Hon'ble Chief Minister while elucidating the principles of cooperation has mentioned that unlike crows which gather together cawing and then disperse, we should come together like clouds bringing prosperity and develop ourselves. We should approach cooperatives to invest in small, small amounts and work hard to increase the earnings and then share the benefit with others. This is the basic principle of cooperatives. Coming together is not for taking away the resources but to give; not to exhaust but to accumulate; not to divide but to share. In India, the cooperative movement started in a small village viz. Tirur in the present Tiruvallur district in 1904 which is the first step in starting of rural credit society there. Over the period the movement was transformed into full fledged movement. Following this in 1904 the first consumer cooperative society was started as Triplicane Urban Cooperative Society. Cooperative movement has spread to diverse economic fields giving birth to different types of cooperative societies and has contributed immensely to the improvement of socio economic status of millions of people especially the poor and downtrodden in the rural areas.

All types of cooperative societies in the State were under the administrative control of the Registrar of Cooperative Societies till 1955. From 1956-1957 onwards due to massive expansion in cooperative movement, certain categories of the societies were transferred to the control of the respective heads of department who are designated as the Functional Registrars of these societies. As on date, there are 15 Functional Registrars besides Registrar of Cooperative Societies. The Registrar of Cooperative Societies remains the authority for interpretation of Cooperative Societies Act and Rules for all types of societies.

The Cooperative Societies presently under the control of Registrar of Cooperative Societies are involved mainly in disbursement of agricultural credit in rural and non-agricultural credit in urban areas, marketing of agricultural produce, sale of consumer goods and provision of fertilisers and other agricultural inputs to farmers. There are other specialized cooperative institutions like Printing Cooperatives, Employees Cooperative Thrift and Credit Societies and Labour Contract Cooperative Societies serving the interests of their members. Of late, the cooperative societies have come under severe threats to their existence because of agricultural loan defaults, market competition and lack of member patronage. At this juncture, the decision of the Government to waive all agricultural loans in the year 2006-07 has given a new lease of life to the entire cooperative sector. While the scheme has broken the shackles of indebtedness among the farming community, it has greatly improved the cash flow within the cooperative credit sector, facilitated greater provision of credit and other inputs for agricultural production and improved their operational viability. Government has so far released Rs.3304.42 crores to cooperative credit institutions over the last two years and will release the balance amount in next 3 years as per its commitments. Such is the success of this scheme that the Government of India have chosen to follow its foot steps and to announce a massive waiver of agricultural loans of Rs.60,000 crores in 2008-09 budget.

Government is fully aware of the critical role played by cooperatives in the development and well being of agriculture and rural sector. Cooperatives provide credit, provide fertilizers and other inputs and also distribute essential commodities under public distribution system. More than that they are accessible to all sections of people. Therefore Government will continue to support these institutions in all possible manner. To that end, Government have signed Memorandum of Understanding with Government of India and National Bank for Agriculture and Rural Development for implementation of the scheme of revival of Short Term Cooperative Credit Structure based on the recommendations of Prof. A. Vaidyanathan Committee. State and District Level Committees have been constituted and special audit of the societies to arrive at the accumulated loss as on 31.3.2004 is in progress. A part of recapitalization assistance as per the scheme is expected in 2008-09 and this will infuse substantial liquidity back into the system. Similarly, Government will also take action for reviving Long Term Cooperative Credit Structure, {Tamil Nadu Cooperative State Agriculture and Rural Development Bank (TNCSARDB) and Primary Cooperative Agriculture and Rural Development Bank (PCARDB)} as and when a similar scheme is announced by Government of India. Government will also take steps to sign Memorandum of Understanding with Reserve Bank of India for improving the status of Urban Cooperative Banks. These efforts will enable the cooperative institutions to work more effectively.

The Cooperative institutions coming under the purview of this department can be broadly classified as follows:

(i) Cooperative Credit Institutions

(ii) Cooperatives for marketing agricultural produce

(iii) Consumer Cooperatives.

(iv) Cooperatives engaged in cooperative education, training and research.

(v) Special types of Cooperative Societies.

The current activities and future prospects of the above types of cooperative societies are elaborately discussed in the following chapters.

COOPERATIVE CREDIT STRUCTURE

Cooperative credit structure is the single largest institutional credit delivery system in the State. It provides credit to the people particularly in rural areas at reasonable interest rate thereby reducing the dependency of the farmers on the informal credit source and usurious rate of interest. Geographically and culturally it is the most convenient institutional arrangement for availing the credit by farmers.

The cooperative credit structure in Tamil Nadu comprises of the following:

(A) Short term and medium term credit structure consisting of Tamil Nadu State Apex Cooperative Bank at the state level, Central Cooperative Banks at the district level and Primary Agricultural Cooperative Banks at the village level.

(B) Long term rural credit structure consisting of Tamil Nadu Cooperative State Agriculture and Rural Development Bank at the state level and Primary Cooperative Agriculture and Rural Development Banks at taluk/block level.

(C) Urban credit structure comprising of Cooperative Urban Banks located in the urban and semi urban areas and catering to the credit needs of their members and the public.

(A) Short Term Credit Structure

The Short Term Cooperative credit structure in Tamil Nadu is a three tier structure with Tamil Nadu State Apex Cooperative Bank at State level with 45 branches, 23 District Central Cooperative Banks at the district level with 717 branches and 4474 Primary Agricultural Cooperative Banks at the grass root level.

(i) Tamil Nadu State Apex Cooperative Bank (TNSACB) Chennai

The Tamil Nadu State Apex Cooperative Bank is the federation of the District Central Cooperative Banks. Being the Apex Bank, it raises resources and channelises them through District Central Cooperative Banks for both agricultural and non-agricultural purpose. It also channelises the refinance provided by National Bank for Agriculture and Rural Development (NABARD) towards short term and medium term agriculture and allied sector loans to District Central Cooperative Banks.

As on 29.2.2008, the Tamil Nadu State Apex Cooperative Bank has a share capital of Rs.61.07 crores including Government's share of Rs.0.26 crore. It has the reserves of Rs.700.48 crores and deposits of Rs.3944.98 crores. Compared to the previous year's level of reserves at Rs.517.95 crores and deposits at Rs.3263.50 crores, the growth in the reserves and the deposits in the current year have gone up by 35% and 21% respectively. The bank has earned a net profit of Rs.42.80 crores during 2007-2008 upto 29.2.2008.

The Tamil Nadu State Apex Cooperative Bank maintains a fund called the Primary Cooperative Development Fund financed out of contribution of profit making Central Cooperative Banks and the Tamil Nadu State Apex Cooperative Bank. The fund is utilized to strengthen the infrastructure facilities of the Primary Agricultural Cooperative Banks in the State. As on 29.2.2008, Rs.29.84 crores is available in this account. A special scheme was launched by Hon'ble Chief Minister Dr. Kalaignar to rejuvenate about 1192 weak Primary Agricultural Cooperative Banks with the help of this fund. Most of the societies in the above category had fallen dormant because of lack of resources and had stopped lending and other operations. To help them to restart lending, a special cash credit at the rate of Rs.20 lakhs per society is being provided by District Central Cooperative Banks at a concessional rate of interest and the difference between cost of funds and the concessional rate is being reimbursed to District Central Cooperative Banks from out of this fund. It is expected that these 1192 Primary Agricultural Cooperative Banks through this scheme will resume their normal operation of lending and to become financially viable in a course of 3 years, by securing breakeven level of business and through this, will offer adequate institutional credit to the farmers in their area of operation. As on 29.2.2008, 631 Primary Agricultural Cooperative Banks have been sanctioned with cash credit to the tune of Rs.126.20 crores and the entire 1192 Primary Agricultural Cooperative Banks will be covered under this scheme before April, 2008.

(ii) District Central Cooperative Banks (DCCB)

There are 23 District Central Cooperative Banks in the State with 717 branches mostly in rural areas to serve the Primary Agricultural Cooperative Banks and the rural public. The District Central Cooperative Banks raise resources through public deposits and also from Tamil Nadu State Apex Cooperative Bank and channelise them through Primary Agricultural Cooperative Banks for agriculture and rural credit. In addition, they meet the credit needs of dairy, handlooms, sugar and such other affiliated cooperatives. They also lend directly to the public for non-agricultural purposes within the area of operation of their branches. As on 26.3.2008, the District Central Cooperative Banks have extended credit to Primary Agricultural Cooperative Banks to the tune of Rs.1323.20 crores for crop loan of which Rs.985.59 crores is from their own funds and Rs.337.61 crores from National Bank for Agriculture and Rural Development refinance.

The details of District Central Cooperative Banks' activities are given below:-

(Rs. in crores)

Year	Deposits	Direct Loans
2004-05	6275.78	1778.12
2005-06	6979.34	2005.33
2006-07	7286.62	2973.02
2007-08*	7666.70	3292.53

* As on 29.2.2008

Compared to the last year, upto February 2008 the amounts of deposit have increased by 5.22%. Due to concerted efforts, better financial discipline and also adequate credit flow through waiver, as per final audit of the year 2006-2007, out of 12 District Central Cooperative Banks which were classified under Section 11(1) of Banking Regulation Act with negative net worth, 7 District Central Cooperative Banks have come out of this problem and it is expected that remaining 5 District Central Cooperative Banks also will record positive networth and come out of Section 11(1) by 31.3.2009. Efforts are being made to computerize all the branches of the District Central Cooperative Banks.

(iii) Primary Agricultural Cooperative Banks (PACB)

In Tamil Nadu, there are 4474 Primary Agricultural Cooperative Banks which provide credit to the farmers, distribute inputs like fertilizers and also run outlets under Public Distribution System. These banks provide short term and medium term credit for agriculture and allied activities. The short term loans are repayable within a period of 12 to 15 months and the medium term loans are repayable within 3 to 5 years.

Crop loan is the prominent item of credit to the farmers by Primary Agricultural Cooperative Banks, provided without collateral security upto 10 acres in respect of registered sugarcane growers and upto Rs.1 lakh in respect of other crops. The loan amount exceeding this limit is secured with mortgage of property or pledge of jewels. Primary Agricultural Cooperative Banks also issue loans for other agricultural purposes like purchase of farm machineries and for non-agricultural purposes including loans for the purchase of consumer durables, housing loans, education loans and professional loans.

The details of the loans issued by these banks from 2004-05 are furnished below:

(Rs. In crores)

Year	Crop Loans	Other Loans
2004-05	1080.58	2609.07
2005-06	1132.18	2718.69
2006-07	1250.62	3082.20
2007-08	1323.20	3254.68
	(As on 26.3.2008)	(As on 29.2.2008)

Considering the importance of increasing credit flow into the agriculture sector, Government has reduced the interest rate for the crop loans from 9% to 7% per annum from 2006-07, the interest differential being compensated by the Government. For the year 2006-07, Rs.18.28 crores was released and a sum of Rs.15.04 crores has been released for the year 2007-08 to the cooperatives as compensation to make up this interest subvention.

The Government is taking all efforts to inculcate the habit of financial discipline among the farmers. As a special measure, Government have announced further reduction of interest from 7% to 5% for all crop loans being repaid promptly by the farmers. This has been further reduced to 4% in 2008-09.

The Government lays emphasis on the timely disbursement of crop loan in adequate quantity. It is proposed to disburse Rs.1500 crores as crop loan during 2008-09. It is further proposed that the lending through Farmers Group will be encouraged by forming Joint Liability Groups which will benefit the farmers to get additional assistance by way of revolving fund to the tune of Rs.10 crores. This is expected to benefit the farmers in a great way to consolidate themselves and pool their resources in arranging their inputs supply, organizing cultivation activities and making joint efforts in marketing to fetch a better price for their produce. Ultimately this will pave way for consolidation of the farming activities by the farmers facilitating appropriate technological intervention for improving the productivity of the farm sector.

As a policy, this Government is not for liquidation of any Primary Agricultural Cooperative Bank which has been set up for the specific purpose of serving the farmers in their respective operational areas. Though liquidation notices were issued for 199 Primary Agricultural Cooperative Banks upto 2005-06, as a follow-up of the announcement made in the year 2006-07 to revive them, all out efforts have been made to revive them and bring them back to normalcy. The Government is happy to inform that out of 199 banks, 197 banks have already been revived and an amount of Rs.17.23 crores were issued as loans during 2006-07 to the members. During 2007-08, Rs.13.07 crores were disbursed as loans upto 29.2.2008. The efforts of the Government will continue for reviving the remaining two Primary Agricultural Cooperative Banks.

Due to long years of neglect, several societies have been put into doldrums. The pathetic status of some of the societies have forced them not to pay even the salaries to their own employees for many months. Due to the efforts made by this Government, the condition of many of the societies have appreciably changed. Due to initiatives such as waiver of agricultural loan, revival of societies through the assistance from Primary Cooperative Development Fund (PCDF), subsidy for running public distribution system and through various other measures, the business of the societies have improved and the non payment of salary has been brought down significantly. The Government will continue its efforts to ensure that all the societies become financially viable and no employee in any of the societies goes without salary.

The Primary Agricultural Cooperative Banks were permitted to mobilize deposits from the public for issue of loans and were unable to refund the deposits on due dates of maturity to the depositors by the Primary Agricultural Cooperative Banks. If this chronic problem continues then the confidence of the people will be shaken. This Government have made all out efforts to ensure that the depositors credibility is restored and their matured deposit amount with the interest is paid back to them. In this regard, an amount of Rs.170.62 crores as public deposit was pending on 30.6.2006 due to be refunded to the depositors. A promise was made in the Assembly that efforts will be taken to settle these deposits at the earliest. Due to the initiatives taken by the Government, Primary Agricultural Cooperative Banks were able to refund Rs.117.68 crores as on 29.2.2008 and further efforts are being made to refund the entire amount fully with due interest to the depositors.

This Government considers that Primary Agricultural Cooperative Banks are the fulcrum on which integrated package of services such as credit, insurance, inputs, marketing and extension can be delivered to the farmers. Recognising the importance of increasing productivity in agricultural sector as envisaged in the XI Five Year Plan, Primary Agricultural Cooperative Banks will be actively engaged in provision of integrated service to the farmers and serve as a point of dissemination of the technology and the improved cultivation practices. It is expected to increase the prosperity of farmers by availing better services particularly in the area of technological intervention. In this process, Primary Agricultural Cooperative Banks will actively collaborate with Agriculture Department and the Research & Development organisations and provide all inputs and services under one roof.

The Primary Agricultural Cooperative Banks will also act as Paddy Procurement Centres on behalf of Tamil Nadu Civil Supplies Corporation and will procure paddy at the minimum support price announced by the Government in the non delta areas apart from Direct Purchase Centres operated by Tamil Nadu Civil Supplies Corporation. Primary Agricultural Cooperative Banks will also assist the Cooperative Marketing

Societies, Tamil Nadu Cooperative Marketing Federation and National Agricultural Cooperative Marketing Federation of India (NAFED) to procure the agricultural produce directly from the farmers. Primary Agricultural Cooperative Banks will expand their produce pledge loan operations substantially to prevent distress sale by the farmers during peak harvest. A target of Rs. 100 crores will be set for disbursal under produce pledge loan by Primary Agricultural Cooperative Banks in 2008- 09.

Most of the Primary Agricultural Cooperative Banks are operating under manual system of record maintenance and face a serious threat from the new generation banks using latest banking technology to penetrate the rural areas. To counter such threat, state-of-art banking technology will be introduced and all the Primary Agricultural Cooperative Banks will be computerized by the end of 2008.

(B) Long Term Credit Structure

Long Term Cooperative Credit Structure consists of Apex Bank viz., Tamil Nadu Cooperative State Agriculture and Rural Development Bank, Chennai and 180 Primary Cooperative Agriculture and Rural Development Banks at taluk/block levels. These credit institutions are providing investment credit to the members for activities like minor irrigation, horticulture, plantation crops and other agriculture and allied sectors.

(i) Tamil Nadu Cooperative State Agriculture & Rural Development Bank (TNCSARDB)

The Tamil Nadu Cooperative State Agriculture and Rural Development Bank raises the funds necessary for its lending by floating ordinary and special development debentures. As the National Bank for Agriculture and Rural Development refinance could not be availed from 2004, due to National Bank for Agriculture and Rural Development's insistence on automatic debit mechanism, Tamil Nadu Cooperative State Agriculture and Rural Development Bank could not make available required resources to Primary Cooperative Agriculture and Rural Development Banks for lending to agricultural sector. As on today the Bank is extending small quantum of loans for Non-

Farm Sector using its own resources. As on 29.2.2008, the share capital of the Bank stood at Rs. 40.29 crores and reserves Rs.566.10 crores and deposits Rs.1.19 crores. Due to virtual suspension of lending operations, the bank is in cumulative loss of Rs.143.84 crores as on 29.2.08.

(ii) Primary Cooperative Agriculture and Rural Development Banks (PCARDB)

There are 180 Primary Cooperative Agriculture and Rural Development Banks at taluk/block levels. The Primary Cooperative Agriculture and Rural Development Banks provide long term credit for purposes like minor irrigation, land development, purchase of agricultural machineries, horticulture, animal husbandry and other allied activities. The period of repayment of such loans ranges from 5 to 15 years.

Due to non-availability of refinance from National Bank for Agriculture and Rural Development, the lending activity by these Banks is practically nil for the last four years. During 2007-08, efforts were made to revive the activities of Tamil Nadu Cooperative State Agriculture and Rural Development Bank and Primary Cooperative Agriculture and Rural Development Banks by mobilizing resources through collection of overdues in Non-Farm Sector. From 1.4.2007 till 29.2.2008, Rs.72.91 crores was collected as against the overdue of Rs.278.43 crores under the Non-Farm Sector. Further through waiver, an amount of Rs.42.45 crores each for the year 2006-07 and 2007-08 were released to the long term credit structure as waiver compensation. This has increased the liquidity of both Tamil Nadu Cooperative State Agriculture and Rural Development Bank and Primary Cooperative Agriculture and Rural Development Banks.

As a result, during 2007-08, the Primary Cooperative Agriculture and Rural Development Banks have again started lending for the Non-Farm Sector including Jewel Loans. The Government will make all efforts to revive them by arranging refinance from National Bank for Agriculture and Rural Development during 2008-09. Activities like horticulture, organic farming, hi-tech farming, precision farming, micro irrigation project based activities like floriculture, cultivation of medicinal plants, plantations in waste land and farm mechanization will be given priority under agricultural investment credit during 2008-09.

The revival package for long term cooperative credit structure based on the recommendations of Prof. A. Vaidyanathan Committee is expected from Government of India soon. In principle, the Government has already agreed to implement the revival package. It is expected that the implementation of this package will help the long term lending structure to wipe out the accumulated loss and to regain its position as the pioneer of agricultural investment credit.

(C) Urban Cooperative Banks (UCB)

Urban Cooperative Banks provide banking and credit facilities to urban and semi urban population. As of now 120 Urban Cooperative Banks are functioning in the State. They mobilize deposits from the public and extend credit facilities for specified purposes. Their lending operations include provision of credit facilities to small traders, artisans and persons belonging to low and middle income group for purposes ranging from housing, business, education, consumer and other non-farm sector activities. During 2007-08, they have issued working capital and term loans to the extent of Rs.2144.29 crores. The deposit position in the Urban Cooperative Banks is Rs.2592.29 crores as on 29.2.2008 compared to Rs.2448.19 crores as on 31.3.2007. The Urban Cooperative Banks are expected to issue not less than 60% of their total lending to priority sector and to ensure that at least 25% of the priority sector lending is issued to the weaker section of the community.

Action will be taken to computerize all the branches of the Urban Cooperative Banks and Credit Societies during 2008-09, so as to improve operational efficiency and to provide better service to the customers in the lines of commercial banks.

Schemes Implemented by Cooperative Credit Structure

(i) Waiver of Agricultural Loans

The unprecedented move of the Government to waive the entire crop loan outstanding in the Cooperative Banks as on

31.3.2006 have benefited lakhs of farmers to break the debt trap besides giving a new lease of life to the cooperative credit institutions. Government have ordered to compensate the amount of waiver of agricultural loan in five equal instalments starting from 2006-07. So far waiver certificates have been issued to 2281617 farmers. The amount released so far to compensate the waiver of loan is as below:

(Rs. in crores)

Agency to which released	2006-2007			2007-2008		
	Princi pal	Inter est	Total	Princi pal	Inter est	Total
Government of India	12.29	3.53	15.82	6.94	2.12	9.06
NABARD	507.38	106.21	613.59	572.91	72.36	645.27
TNSC Bank	191.34	88.20	279.54	191.34	53.26	244.60
DCCBs	343.78	128.67	472.45	318.33	76.96	395.29
PACBs	172.43	60.78	233.21	215.92	66.13	282.05
TNCSARDB	42.45	16.98	59.43	42.45	11.66	54.11
Total	1269.67	404.37	1674.04	1347.89	282.49	1630.38

Following this path breaking efforts of the Government of Tamil Nadu, the Government of India has now made an announcement of massive agricultural loan waiver to the extent of Rs.60,000 crores during 2008-09 budget. This laudable initiative taken by the Government of India to redeem the farm sector from the stagnation is expected to trigger further growth in agricultural sector. It is expected that this loan waiver announced by the Government of India will be fully extended to Tamil Nadu and the amount released already by the Government of Tamil Nadu as loan waiver will be fully compensated by the Government of India on the eligible components.

(ii) Interest subvention for crop loan

The crop loan has been extended with the concessional rate of interest by reducing the effective rate of lending from 9% to 7% with effect from 2006-07. Further to imbibe the discipline of better repayment among the farmers, the Government of Tamil Nadu has ordered to give further interest subvention @ 2% from 2007-08 so that the effective rate of lending of crop loan to the farmers who are prompt in repaying the loans will be 5%. During 2008-09 budget, the Government have further reduced this rate to 4% for crop loan lending.

(iii) Interest reduction for Non-Farm Sector Loans

The Government have ordered to reduce the rate of interest to12% on all the outstanding non-farm sector loans as on 31.3.2001 availed from the cooperative credit institutions besides completely waiving the penal interest as a one time measure to wipe out the overdues. Under this scheme, the borrower has to remit 25% of the outstanding and avail the concessions extended and pay the remaining 75% within the stipulated period. In order to encourage the repayment, the scheme which originally ended on 31.3.2007 extended upto 31.3.2008 under various spells. Under this scheme upto 29.2.2008, 113252 beneficiaries availed the scheme and paid the dues. The benefit to the extent of Rs. 96.02 crores were passed on to these beneficiaries.

(iv) Jewel Loans

The cooperative banks issue loans on the pledge of jewels both for agriculture and non-agriculture purposes. The jewel loans are more popular among the public and banks are more secure and borrowing is hassle free for the beneficiaries. During 2007-08, Rs.8409.40 crores was disbursed as Jewel Loan upto 29.2.2008.

(v) Kisan Credit Card Scheme

The Kisan Credit Card Scheme is being implemented to provide timely credit to the farmers so that delay in disbursement of credit is minimized. As on 29.2.2008, the Primary Agricultural Cooperative Banks have issued Kisan Credit Cards to 17.13 lakh farmer members.

(vi) Credit supply to weaker sections

The Primary Agricultural Cooperative Banks are paying special attention to meet the credit needs of weaker sections. NABARD has stipulated to extend not less than 30% of short term lending by cooperatives to small farmers who own or cultivate less than 5 acres. Further, it is targeted to extend 14% of the quantum of loan issued under short term loans and 30%

under medium term loans to the members belonging to Scheduled Caste/ Scheduled Tribe.

(vii) Micro Credit Scheme

The District Central Cooperative Banks and Urban Cooperative Banks are implementing this unique scheme to benefit marginalized small and petty merchants and street vendors engaged in the business of selling flowers, vegetables, fruits and running petty shops. They are the most vulnerable group for exploitation by usurious money lenders. Their credit requirements are very small but critical. This scheme which was launched by this Government has been amplified and streamlined over the years. Under the scheme the loan amount upto Rs.5000/- is being provided without any security. It is proposed to improve the scheme further by issuing credit card to such beneficiaries and organize them as a self help group. During 2007-08 upto 29.2.2008, a sum of Rs. 27.79 crores has been issued to 67288 beneficiaries. It is proposed to issue such loan for Rs.50 crores during 2008-09.

(viii) Assistance to Self Help Groups

Lending through self help groups is considered extremely effective to ensure financial inclusion. It is also beneficial to the banks in terms of better repayment and lower transaction cost. Under various schemes and Government sponsored programmes, lending is extended through self help groups. During 2007-08, cooperative institutions have issued loans to the tune of Rs.170.13 crores to self help groups upto 29.2.2008. It is proposed to lend Rs.200 crores during 2008-09.

(ix) Women Entrepreneur Loan Scheme

The District Central Cooperative Banks and Urban Cooperative Banks are providing loans upto Rs.10 lakhs repayable in 60 monthly instalments at 12% interest to women entrepreneurs to start small industries and to take up service activities. During 2007-08, a sum of Rs.9.96 crores has been disbursed to 4848 women entrepreneurs till 29.02.2008.

(x) Working Women Loan Scheme

Under this scheme, the District Central Cooperative Banks and Urban Cooperative Banks are issuing loans upto Rs.1.00

lakh at an interest rate of 12% per annum to working women drawing monthly income. This loan is repayable in 36 instalments. As many as 5063 women beneficiaries were benefited to the extent of Rs.11.81 crores during 2007-2008 upto 29.2.2008.

(xi) Maternity Loan Scheme

Cooperative credit institutions are issuing maternity loan to pregnant women upto Rs.2000/- at an interest of 11%. During 2007-2008, a sum of Rs.0.39 crores has been disbursed to 1929 women beneficiaries upto 29.2.2008.

(xii) Professional Loan

The District Central Cooperative Banks are extending professional loan to doctors and engineers upto Rs.10 lakhs at an interest rate of 12% per annum. This loan is repayable over a period of 15 years.

(xiii) Interest free share capital loan to SC/ST members

In order to enhance the borrowing power of SC/ST members, interest free share capital loan is provided every year. During 2007-08, a sum of Rs.20 lakhs have been provided to 8000 SC/ST members of Primary Agricultural Cooperative Banks @ Rs.250/- per member and a sum of Rs.5 lakhs have been provided to 1000 SC/ST members of Urban Cooperative Banks @ Rs.500 per member.

It is proposed to continue the same and during the year 2008-09, a sum of Rs.20.00 lakhs will be provided to 8000 SC/ST members in the Primary Agricultural Cooperative Banks @ Rs.250 per member and a sum of Rs.5.00 lakhs will be provided to 1000 SC/ST members of Urban Cooperative Banks @ Rs.500 per member as interest free share capital loan.

(xiv) Interest free share capital loan to women members

The borrowing power of the members in the cooperative banks needs to be enhanced. This inevitably requires adequate step up in the share capital. Considering the poor financial condition of the rural women particularly to those belonging to weaker sections, the Government is providing interest free share capital loan as the normal level of borrowing is limited to 20 to 40 times of the share capital investment. This amount is repayable in five instalments commencing from the succeeding year in which loan is sanctioned.

The details of the share capital assistance provided during 2007-08 are furnished below:

(Rs. in lakhs)

Sl. No	Name of the Institution	Loan amount per individual	No. of bene ficiaries	Total loan amount
1.	Primary Agricultural Cooperative Banks	Rs.500/-	2000	10.00
2.	Primary Cooperative Agriculture and Rural Development Banks	Rs.1000/-	500	5.00
3.	Urban Cooperative Banks	Rs.500/-	1000	5.00
4.	Loans to physically handicapped by the above banks	Rs.500/-	1000	5.00
	Total		**4500**	**25.00**

It is proposed to extend the scheme of interest free share capital loan to the women members of Primary Agricultural Cooperative Banks, Primary Cooperative Agriculture and Rural Development Banks and Urban Cooperative Banks and physically handicapped persons during 2008 –09 also. Accordingly, it is proposed to issue interest free share capital loan to 2000 women members of Primary Agricultural Cooperative Banks at the rate of Rs. 500/-, five hundred women members of Primary Cooperative Agriculture and Rural Development Banks at the rate of Rs. 1000/- and thousand women members of Cooperative Urban Banks at the rate of Rs. 500/- and 1000 physically handicapped persons at the rate of Rs. 500/- through the above banks.

COOPERATIVE MARKETING SOCIETIES

The Cooperative Marketing Societies have been established with the object of facilitating the marketing of agricultural produce of its members at a remunerative price besides distributing farm inputs to them advancing pledge loan on agricultural produce and undertaking the processing and adding value to the agricultural produce handled.

The structure of Cooperative Marketing in Tamil Nadu is a two tier structure with the Tamil Nadu Cooperative Marketing Federation (TANFED) at apex level and 110 Primary Cooperative Marketing Societies (CMS) at district/taluk levels. Tamil Nadu Cooperative Marketing Federation was established in 1959 and is currently engaged in sale of fertilizers and other inputs through Cooperative Marketing Societies and Primary Agricultural Cooperative Banks. The federation owns a fertilizer mixing unit at Pamani near Mannargudi in Tiruvarur district. It also operates 38 owned godowns with capacity of 28,640 metric tonnes and two cold storage godowns one at Basin Bridge, Chennai with 1350 metric tonnes capacity and the other at Koyambedu with 2500 metric tonnes capacity. Tamil Nadu Cooperative Marketing Federation also undertakes price support operations on behalf of National Agricultural Cooperative Marketing Federation for Copra and for commodities like chillies as and when ordered by Government. During 2007-08, upto 29.2.2008, Tamil Nadu Cooperative Marketing Federation has distributed chemical fertilizer worth Rs.175.67 crores. This is 23% higher than the distribution of Rs.142.30 crores during 2006-07.

Apart from Tamil Nadu Cooperative Marketing Federation and Cooperative Marketing Societies, there are 3 special types of Cooperative Marketing Societies as detailed below:

The Nilgiris Cooperative Marketing Society

The Nilgiris Cooperative Marketing Society runs a potato auction yard at Mettupalayam and fertilizer mixtures to meet the specific requirement of selected crops in Nilgiris. It also supplies seed material to its members on demand basis and extends credit supplies as and when required.

Thanjavur Cooperative Marketing Federation

Thanjavur Cooperative Marketing Federation is fulfilling the needs of Thanjavur, Tiruvarur and Nagapattinam districts through 12 Primary Marketing Societies affiliated to it. These societies act independently from the Tamil Nadu Cooperative Marketing Federation.

Tudiyalur Cooperative Agricultural Service Society

This society is engaged in the production and distribution of seeds, distribution of fertilizers, pesticides and agricultural implements to the farmers. It also provides credit to its members on demand.

Functions of Cooperative Marketing Societies

(i) Marketing of Agricultural Produce

The Cooperative Marketing Societies perform the following two types of functions:-

(a) Providing agency service by making available the facilities like auction yards, drying facilities etc. and facilitate the traders and farmer members to transact their business. The marketing societies collect service charge for this purpose.

(b) Engaging in purchase, process and sale of agricultural produce. The processed products are also sold through consumer cooperative stores.

During 2007-08, cooperative societies have marketed the agricultural produce to the tune of Rs.907.94 crores upto 29-2-2008.

(ii) Linking of credit with Marketing

Cooperative Marketing Societies enroll the borrowers of Primary Agricultural Cooperative Bank as members and assist in the sales of the produce brought to the cooperative marketing society by the borrower member of the Primary Agricultural Cooperative Banks. These efforts helped the Primary Agricultural Cooperative Banks to recover loans besides assisting the farmers for selling their produce at remunerative price. In the year 2007-08, upto 29-2-2008, Rs.153.21 lakhs was recovered in this process.

(iii) Linking of Consumer Cooperative Stores with Marketing

Cooperative Marketing Societies have tie-up with the Cooperative Wholesale Stores. This enables the Cooperative Marketing Societies to procure the farmers' produce, process it and sell it to the Cooperative Wholesale Stores so that the wholesale stores get a quality product at a reasonable price and the farmers also get a good price. During 2007-08, the Cooperative Marketing Societies marketed produce worth Rs.16.48 crores upto 29-2-2008 to the Cooperative Wholesale Stores.

(iv) Issue of Produce Pledge Loan

During the peak harvesting season, farmers invariably resort to distress sale to meet their urgent need for cash. To protect the interest of such farmers, Cooperative Marketing Societies provide Produce Pledge Loan so that farmers are able to store the produce and dispose at later date to get a better price.During 2007-08 upto 29-2-2008, a sum of Rs.18.32 crores has been disbursed to the farmer members as Produce Pledge Loan.

(v) Processing of and value addition to agricultural produce

Some of the cooperative marketing societies are having processing units to process and add value to the agricultural produce transacted by them. They also provide processing facilities to the farmers at affordable rates. During 2007-08 upto 29.2.2008, cooperative processing units have processed agricultural produce to the tune of 16,500 metric tonnes.

(vi) Procurement of Copra under price support scheme

To protect the interest of the coconut farmers, cooperative marketing societies are implementing Price Support Scheme for copra at the minimum support price fixed by Govt. of India on behalf of National Agricultural Marketing Federation. The support price for the copra has been revised from Rs.36.20 to

Rs.36.60 per Kilo gram for the year 2008. During 2007-08 upto 29.2.2008, cooperative marketing societies have procured 5676.66 metric tonnes.

Despite the efforts of the Government, there are several cooperative marketing societies which are not functioning vibrantly. It is a great concern for the Government that these societies are not serving the intended purpose. Many of them are now confined to Public Distribution System operation instead of taking up agricultural marketing. A study by a special team has been conducted on the functioning of the Cooperative Marketing Societies and this Government will consider recommendation of this report and take appropriate action for the revival of these societies.

The global economic changes have boosted the prospects for the commodity trade and it is necessary that the benefits which accrue due to information revolution should ultimately reach the farmers. The Government is well aware of the importance of introducing a better price discovery mechanism and disseminating the price information and trends of the various major markets and to the farmers so that they can take appropriate decision in disposing of their produce and get better price.

As a new venture, this Government will take steps to provide a platform in the selected cooperative marketing premises to disseminate the information on the price trend in various markets and commodity exchanges. Tamil Nadu Cooperative Marketing Federation will also institutionalize the system of providing consulting service on the commodity price trend and link it up with these cooperative markets so that the farming community are guided properly to take appropriate decisions on their production and marketing. This is expected to help the farmers to find out the correct price for their produce, based on the assessment of market fluctuation and price forecast.

8

Consumer Cooperative Societies

The major objective of the consumer cooperatives is to serve the consumers by supplying quality products at reasonable prices. They play a vital role in containing the prices of commodities by market intervention at the time of crisis.

The consumer cooperatives in Tamil Nadu comprises of three tiers:

i. Tamil Nadu Consumer Cooperative Federation (at the apex level)

ii. Cooperative Wholesale Stores (at the district level) and

iii. Primary Cooperative Stores (at the grass root level)

(i) Tamil Nadu Consumer Cooperative Federation

Tamil Nadu Consumer Cooperative Federation at Chennai is the apex body. It procures paper and other stationery material in bulk and distributes them to the district cooperative wholesale stores, primary cooperative stores and cooperative printing presses. The Federation also purchases crackers during the festival season and distributes them to the cooperative wholesale stores and primary agricultural cooperative banks for sale to the general public. Though on a cumulative loss of Rs. 4.28 crores, the Federation has earned a current profit of Rs.62.00 lakhs in 2007-08 from a turnover of Rs.3.01 crores. In the current year, this organization has ventured into purchase of onions from Nasik through SAFAL (vegetables and fruits) National Exchange (SNX) and is distributing them throughout the state through Public Distribution System outlets. Action is being taken to enroll as a member of SNX so as to source fresh vegetables and fruits from all over the country. The Government will take steps to expand the operations of this Federation further and facilitate it to take up procurement and sale of wide ranging consumer products from upcountry locations during 2008-09.

(ii) Cooperative Wholesale Stores

At present 34 cooperative wholesale stores are functioning in Tamil Nadu. They are engaged in transporting the essential commodities from the Tamil Nadu Civil Supplies Corporation godowns as lead societies and deliver them to the public distribution system outlets run by cooperative societies. The wholesale stores also procure consumer goods in bulk directly from the producing centres, manufacturers and the marketing societies and offer the same to the consumers at reasonable prices.

During the year 2007–08, the cooperative wholesale stores had transacted business to the tune of Rs. 1015.71 crores on both controlled and non controlled commodities. In the year 2008–09, it is expected that the turnover will touch Rs.1100 crores. A high level committee has been constituted by the Government to identify the cause for the sickness of the five huge loss making Stores viz., Triplicane Urban Cooperative Society, Park Town Cooperative Wholesale Stores, Chennai, Madurai Pandian Cooperative Wholesale Stores, Trichy Chinthamani Cooperative Wholesale Stores and Coimbatore Chinthamani Cooperative Wholesale Stores and to suggest ways and means to rehabilitate these wholesale stores and to monitor their proper functioning. The report is expected soon and on the basis of this report action will be taken to rehabilitate these five stores and to set them on a growth path during 2008-09.

(iii) Primary Cooperative Stores

As on date, 3550 primary cooperative stores including students' cooperative stores at base level are functioning in Tamil Nadu. These primary cooperative stores are engaged in the distribution of quality consumer goods at reasonable prices, besides functioning as outlets for distribution of essential commodities under Public Distribution System.

During the year 2007-08, consumer cooperatives achieved retail sales to the tune of Rs. 318.93 crores.

COOPERATIVE EDUCATION, RESEARCH AND TRAINING

The Tamil Nadu Cooperative Union which was established in 1914 imparts cooperative education and training. The union also takes steps to propagate the ideals of cooperative movement through conduct of exhibition and other methods of publicity.

Cooperative Training

There are 20 cooperative training institutes in the State. Out of these 11 are independent and 9 are functioning as the units of Tamil Nadu Cooperative Union. All these units conduct Diploma course in cooperation of 36 weeks duration and award diploma to the candidates. During the year 2007-08, 866 students have been trained.

In addition, these institutes conduct short term courses on computer operation and jewel appraisal. These institutes also conduct correspondence courses for the employees of the cooperatives who are unable to undergo the direct training.

Higher Diploma in Cooperative Management

Two institutes of cooperative management, one at Chennai and another at Madurai are run by the National Council for Cooperative Training, New Delhi. These institutes conduct, higher diploma course in cooperative management. They also run a number of short term courses for the staff and officers of cooperative department and societies including those under the Functional Registrars. In the year 2007-08, these 2 institutes conducted 172 courses till 29.2.2008. They have planned to conduct 195 courses in 2008-09.

Technical Education

Three cooperative industrial training institutes at Bargur in Dharmapuri District, Pattukottai in Thanjavur District and Tiruchuzhi in Virudhunagar District and one cooperative Polytechnic at Lalgudi in Trichy District are run by Tamil Nadu Cooperative Union. These institutes provide technical training to the youths for their self-employment. An average of about 400 students get technical education every year through these industrial training institutes and polytechnic.

Cooperative Research

In order to encourage the students who are doing research in cooperation, the Tamil Nadu Cooperative Union has created a chair of Rs. 5.00 lakhs each in the Madras University, Madurai Kamarajar University, Bharathiar University and Annamalai University. Out of the interest earned on the investment of this deposit, scholarships are awarded to the research students.

Mobilising the Resources

The Tamil Nadu Cooperative Union collects 3% of the net profit of cooperative societies for Cooperative Research and Development Fund and 2% of the net profit for Cooperative Education Fund and maintains these funds. As on 29.2.2008 the amount available in this corpus fund of CRDF and CEF are Rs.65.80 crores and 44.15 crores respectively. Proceeds from such corpus is being utilized for development of cooperative movement, development of societies through infusion of new technology, research in critical areas, conduct of member education programme and training and carrying out publicity and propaganda.

In the year 2008-09, it has been proposed to meet the cost of development of common banking software for all the cooperative banks and Employees' Cooperative Thrift and Credit Societies (ECS). Further it has been proposed to give appropriate grants to unviable and financially weak Primary Agricultural Cooperative Banks and Employees' Cooperative Thrift and Credit Societies to purchase computers and other accessories for taking up computerization.

SPECIAL TYPES OF COOPERATIVES

Cooperative Printing Press

There are 26 cooperative printing press in our State with a total membership of 12645 with share capital of Rs. 2.09 crores. They fulfill the printing needs of all cooperatives, Government, quasi-Government and general public.

Salt Workers Cooperative Production and Sale Societies

In our State 10 Salt Workers' Cooperative Production and Sale Societies are functioning at present. Out of these, 5 societies are functioning exclusively for the welfare of Adi Dravida members. These societies are engaged in the production of iodised salt with financial assistance from the Government under TAHDCO scheme.

Labour Contract Cooperative Societies

As of now, 115 Labour Contract Cooperative Societies are functioning in our State with a total membership of 34,431 labourers. These societies are formed to raise the standard of living of SC/ST by providing employment opportunities to the members by securing contract works. The members of these societies are availing the benefits in full as the middle man between the management and the labourers are eliminated. These societies are provided with financial assistance in the form of share capital, working capital and managerial subsidies from the funds obtained from the Government of India.

Barbers and Washermen Cooperative Societies

In our State, six Barber Cooperative Societies and three Washermen Cooperative Societies are functioning with the object of improving the conditions of barbers and washermen who belong to the economically weaker sections.

Large Sized Multi-Purpose Cooperative Societies (LAMPS)

At present 17 LAMP cooperative societies under Integrated Tribal Development Programme areas and two societies under non-Integrated Tribal Development Programme areas are functioning in the State. These societies provide single window service for production credit, consumption credit, supply of agricultural inputs, marketing of agriculture produce, collection and marketing of minor forest produce and supply of essential commodities under Public Distribution System to the Tribals.

These societies have 81955 tribal members and 9364 non-tribal members. In order to enable the Tribals to undertake agricultural operations, LAMP societies provide short term loans for cultivation and medium term loans for allied activities of agriculture. In order to avail the loan facility, share capital subsidy has been provided to the members of the society. As these loans are provided free of interest, interest subsidy to compensate the interest loss has also been provided. In addition, financial assistance in the form of subsidy for transport, drivers' pay and maintenance of vehicles have also been provided. An amount of Rs. 90 lakhs each for the year 2006-07 and 2007-08 has been sanctioned by the Government as subsidy to these LAMP societies for the above purposes. Presently most of these LAMP societies are not healthy. The Government took special efforts during 2007 – 08 to rejuvenate LAMP societies in Kolli Hills area by infusing funds, increasing lending activities and taking up marketing of tapioca directly to the mills, it being the major produce in that area. In the process, besides increasing turnover and profits, higher price for tapioca to the tribal farmers could be ensured on a sustainable basis. This experiment will be repeated in other LAMP societies to improve their performance during 2008-09.

Other Type of Societies

35 Cooperative canteens are also functioning for providing food at economic cost to students, workers and staff of various institutions.

ROLE OF COOPERATIVES IN PUBLIC DISTRIBUTION SYSTEM

The Cooperative societies play a major role in the distribution of essential commodities in public distribution system. Cooperatives run 21630 fair price shops which accounts for 93% of the Public Distribution System outlets. These shops are run by 5060 cooperative societies comprising of 86 lead societies, 4540 link societies and 434 self lifting societies. In addition to this the cooperatives are also running 5898 part time fair price shops to serve the families in far-flung and remote areas and 36 mobile fair price shops to serve the people in hilly areas to deliver essential commodities at the door steps of people. At present 266 kerosene bunks are also run by cooperatives in order to streamline the distribution of kerosene. The Government has been compensating the loss met out by the fair price shops on account of the sale of essential commodities at subsidised prices under public distribution system over and above the present retail margin provided by the Government. During the year 2006-07 and 2007-08 an amount of Rs. 97.05 crores and Rs.106.90 crores respectively have been sanctioned to the cooperatives as subsidy.

Control of Price and Sale of Non-controlled Commodities in Public Distribution System Outlets

There has been increase in the prices of certain daily used commodities such as pulses, edible oil, wheat products etc., In order to protect the poor and middle income families from the spiralling price rise, the Government as a measure of price control has been selling these commodities through the fair price shops at reasonable prices. Besides, more than 20 non-controlled commodities are being sold through the Public Distribution System outlets at reasonable prices. The required products are purchased in bulk through wholesale stores to reduce intermediary margins. During 2007-08 upto 29.2.2008, non controlled goods worth of Rs.842.87 crores have been sold through Public Distribution System outlets.

Supply of Electronic Weighing Machines

The supply of essential commodities in correct weighment to the cardholders under public distribution system is accorded top priority by this Government. Accordingly an amount of Rs. 11.50 crores has been sanctioned in 2007 - 08 for the supply of modern electronic weighing machines to all cooperative shops. The supply and installation is in progress. It is expected that by end of May 2008, all the fair price shops run by cooperatives will have electronic weighing machines.

Revision of Pay Scales to the Employees of Fair Price Shops

The Government has considered the plea of the employees of fair price shops and issued orders revising the scales of pay of salesmen and packers working in the fair price shops run by the cooperatives as announced while moving the demand on Cooperation in the last Budget Session. Giving effect to this, all the regularized salesmen and packers were brought under regular time scale of pay.

Sale of Ooty Tea

In order to alleviate the sufferings of the small tea growers in the Nilgiris District, the Government has ordered to sell tea processed by INDCOSERVE under public distribution system through fair price shops. The Government have fixed a target of 250 metric tonnes per month and the cooperatives have distributed a total quantity of 2673 metric tonnes of Ooty tea from April, 2007 upto February, 2008 through cooperative fair price shops.

Sale of Iodised Salt

With a view to minimize the health hazard caused by iodine deficiency, the Government has decided to promote the sale of iodised salt produced by the Tamil Nadu Salt Corporation and has ordered to sell the iodised salt through fair price shops in all districts of Tamil Nadu. Iodised salt is being sold at Rs.2.50 per Kg. During 2007-08, upto 29.2.2008, 28562 metric tonnes of Arasu salt were sold.

Sale of Khadi Products

Government has announced that soap products of Tamil Nadu Khadi and Village Industries Board will be sold through fair price shops run by the cooperative societies. Initially it was proposed to sell 4 varieties of toilet and washing soaps, to start with 11 districts. The scheme has now been extended to all the districts in the State with a view to sell 10 varieties of Khadi products through fair price shops. The value of Khadi products sold through cooperatives during 2007 – 08 upto 29.2.2008 is Rs. 152.59 lakhs.

INTEGRATED COOPERATIVE DEVELOPMENT PROJECT

The Integrated Cooperative Development Project is implemented for the overall development of the cooperatives in the selected districts of this State. This scheme has an integrated area based approach for cooperative development in rural areas. It aims on the development of functional linkages between cooperatives to promote their overall development to cater to the needs of rural community in an effective manner. Emphasis is laid on the strengthening and turning the primary cooperatives into multi-purpose entities. The State Government have been receiving financial assistance from National Cooperative Development Corporation in the form of loan and the funds are channalised to the district central cooperative banks concerned which are acting as Project Implementing Agencies. The Integrated Cooperative Development Project scheme had been implemented in the following 8 districts as shown below:

Sl.No	Name of the District	Year of implementation	Outlay (Rs. in lakhs)
1.	Virudhunagar	1989-1995	862.51
2.	Cuddalore Integrated		
3.	Villupuram South ArcotDistrict	1992-1997	1506.97
4.	Coimbatore	1995-2001	1080.99
5.	Dharmapuri	1995-2001	1160.25
6.	Tiruvannamalai	1996-2001	816.58
7.	Kancheepuram	1998-2005	1123.88
8.	Ramanathapuram	2000-2004	687.03
	Total		**7238.21**

At present Integrated Cooperative Development Project is being implemented in the following six districts.

The detailed project reports prepared by the consultants in respect of Salem, Erode, Madurai and Pudukottai have been cleared by the State Level Coordination Committee and the National Cooperative Development Corporation. The administrative approval for implementation of the scheme in the above districts is under consideration of the Government. As regards Tirunelveli district, the National Cooperative Development Corporation has given its approval and the detailed project report is under examination.

(Rs. in lakhs)

Sl.No	Name of the district	Total outlay	Amount released by Government
1	Tiruchirapalli	1216.98	1216.98
2	Thanjavur	1101.09	1101.09
3	Perambalur	937.81	937.81
4	Tiruvarur	1222.44	1222.44
5	Theni	987.73	695.75
6	Thoothukudi	942.08	638.49
	Total		

The Government has selected Dindugul, Karur, Vellore, Sivaganga and Nagapattinam districts for implementation of Integrated Cooperative Development Project in the next stage of assistance. The National Cooperative Development Corporation has given its concurrence for implementation of the scheme in these districts. Draft Project Reports for implementation of the scheme are under preparation by the appointed consultants. The Government have also selected the Nilgiris district for implementation of Integrated Cooperative Development Project and the National Cooperative Development Corporation has given its approval in principle.

CHAPTER IX: COOPERATIVE ELECTIONS

This Government is keen to conduct polls to cooperatives in a fair and democratic way so that they function independently in an effective and efficient manner under the guidance of the elected representatives. Consequent on the cancellation of the elections a spate of petitions were filed in the High Court and the final verdict of the Court in this matter is still awaited. After the receipt of the verdict of High Court and in consultation with the political parties in the Legislature, necessary further action will be taken for the constitution of separate Election Commission and to conduct election to cooperatives in a fair and free manner.

9

Department of Consumer Protection

2007 LEGISLATIVE SUMMARY

The following public acts, enacted during the 2007 Regular Session and 2007 Special Session of the General Assembly, affect the work of the Department of Consumer Protection or the persons and industries regulated by the Department. These legislative enactments have been signed into law by Governor Rell, and are therefore available in final public act form.

Where a section of a public act modifies existing statutory language, a reference is made to the specific section of the Connecticut General Statutes being modified. Where a public act is wholly new, it becomes inserted as a new section upon being codified as part of the Connecticut General Statutes. The codification process is undertaken by the Legislative Commissioner's Office ("LCO") .

The new laws are conveniently grouped below according to the division within the Department having jurisdiction over the topic area. Selecting any link below will take you to the text of the new law.

Drug Control Division

AN ACT CONCERNING REVISIONS TO STATUTES RELATING TO THE DEPARTMENTS OF PUBLIC HEALTH AND SOCIAL SERVICES AND TOWN CLERKS PA 07-252 §73 (Sharing of license, registration and investigatory information)

This Departmental proposal helps to protect the public from individuals who have violated the laws and regulations related to prescription drugs. It enables the Drug Control Division to share additional types of information with other state and federal authorities, and may help prevent unscrupulous individuals from working with prescription drugs. The ability to obtain more information about individuals will assist regulatory agencies in their mission to protect the public health and safety. (Effective October 1, 2007)

AN ACT CONCERNING REVISIONS TO STATUTES RELATING TO THE DEPARTMENTS OF PUBLIC HEALTH AND SOCIAL SERVICES AND TOWN CLERKS PA 07-252 §74 (Use of the term "pharmacy" and similar words)

This Departmental proposal helps to avoid confusion among consumers by clarifying which business entities are allowed to use terms such as "pharmacy" or "drug store" in their business advertising. The new language allows the use of these terms by businesses that perform services directly to pharmacies or pharmacists, but do not engage in business activities with the general public. (Effective October 1, 2007)

AN ACT CONCERNING REVISIONS TO STATUTES RELATING TO THE DEPARTMENTS OF PUBLIC HEALTH AND SOCIAL SERVICES AND TOWN CLERKS PA 07-252 §75 (Controlled substance registrations)

This Departmental issues controlled substance registrations to many types of health care practitioners. Controlled substances include addictive pain medications and narcotic-type prescriptions. This new law helps protect the public safety by providing additional enforcement tools to the commissioner. These new tools help the department to protect the public health and safety through its jurisdiction over prescription medications, which include controlled substances. With this new law, the commissioner may place registrations on probation, place conditions on registrations, and assess civil penalties for cause. Fraudulent billing practices and failure to maintain records are added as potential reasons for action by the commissioner. (Effective October 1, 2007)

Liquor Control Division

AN ACT CONCERNING ALCOHOL SERVER AND SELLER TRAINING

PA 07-41 (Training for servers and sellers of alcohol)

This Department-supported proposal will assist the commissioner in the enforcement of state liquor control laws. For any alcohol permit holder whose license has been suspended or revoked, this new law allows the commissioner to require that business to have their employees participate in an alcohol seller and server training program. Completion of the program may be a condition for the license to be returned. This law helps to protect the general public, and minors in particular, by helping to assure that those who serve alcoholic beverages do not serve minors, and do not continue to serve intoxicated patrons. (Effective October 1, 2007)

AN ACT CONCERNING NOTICE IN DRAM SHOP ACTIONS INVOLVING DEATH OR INCAPACITY AND MANUFACTURER PERMITS FOR BREW PUBS

PA 07-165 (Dram shop actions)

The Dram Shop statute holds the server of alcoholic beverages responsible when an intoxicated patron injures a third party. This public act modifies the Dram Shop statute where intoxication results in a death or incapacity. It allows more time for an aggrieved person to give notice that a cause of action is to be filed in Superior Court. This change benefits the families of a person killed or incapacitated as a result of intoxication.

Occupational & Professional Licensing Division

AN ACT CONCERNING THE ENFORCEMENT OF CERTAIN PROFESSIONAL AND OCCUPATIONAL LICENSING, CERTIFICATION AND REGISTRATION LAWS

PA 07-188 (Enforcement of occupational licensing laws)

This important Departmental proposal helps to protect consumers from substandard and unscrupulous contractors by instituting a criminal penalty for those working without a proper occupational license. Occupational licenses, including for example the plumbing, electrical, and heating trades, are administered by the Department, and are coordinated by the Occupational and Professional Licensing Division. Licensing laws protect the public by requiring specific educational training, a period of supervised work experience, and a comprehensive examination prior to obtaining a trade license. This Departmental initiative will help protect the public safety. (Effective October 1, 2007)

AN ACT CONCERNING LICENSURE FOR HEATING, PIPING, AND COOLING WORK

PA 07-183 (Heating, piping, and cooling licenses)

This public act expands the group of individuals needing heating, piping, and cooling licenses issued by the Department. The new law requires licensure for individuals who operate on-site heating or air conditioning systems of a certain capacity. This new law protects the public safety by helping to ensure that qualified individuals operate heating and cooling systems using high-pressure steam or large quantities of refrigerants. (Effective July 1, 2007)

AN ACT CONCERNING REAL ESTATE LICENSURE AND MAINTENANCE OF LISTS OF PRIVATE HUNTING GROUNDS BY TOWN CLERKS

PA 07-214 (Real estate licensing fees; Broker entities)

Section one, a Departmental proposal, removes the requirement that a Five Dollar fee be paid annually to remain eligible to take a real estate license examination. (Effective July 1, 2007)

Section two, a Departmental proposal, eliminates the current Twenty-Five Dollar fee for obtaining a duplicate real estate license from the Department. (Effective July 1, 2007)

Section three, a Departmental proposal, establishes a "grandfather clause" to allow certain real estate broker entities (companies) to remain licensed despite a recent legislative change requiring that each such company be majority-owned by a Connecticut-licensed real estate broker. All other entity requirements remain in full force. (Effective July 1, 2007)

Section four, a Departmental proposal, allows the Real Estate Commission to authorize the department's third party testing vendors to charge a fee to applicants who sit for a section of a real estate examination. (Section four is effective upon passage)

Trade Practices Division

AN ACT CONCERNING THE ENFORCEMENT OF CERTAIN PROFESSIONAL AND OCCUPATIONAL LICENSING, CERTIFICATION AND REGISTRATION LAWS

PA 07-188 (Enforcement of occupational licensing laws)

This important Departmental proposal helps to protect consumers from substandard and unscrupulous contractors by instituting a criminal penalty for those working without a proper license. Occupational licenses, including for example the plumbing, electrical, and heating trades, are administered by the Department. Licensing laws protect the public by requiring specific educational training and a period of supervised work experience prior to obtaining a trade license. This Departmental initiative will help protect the public safety. Complaints against contractors are investigated by the Trade Practices Division. (Effective October 1, 2007)

AN ACT CONCERNING THE NEW MOTOR VEHICLE LEMON LAW

PA 07-212 ("Lemon Law" program improvements)

This Departmental proposal improves the administration of the new motor vehicle "Lemon Law" program, which is administered by the Trade Practices Division. This program settles disputes between consumers who have purchased a new vehicle and the vehicle's manufacturer.

This program provides an avenue for consumers to obtain restitution if a new vehicle has had mechanical problems and meets certain requirements. The changes in this law provide for a single professional arbitrator to decide each case, instead of a panel of three volunteer arbitrators. This change will greatly improve the efficiency of the program. (Effective October 1, 2007)

AN ACT INCREASING PENALTIES FOR THE SALE OF CIGARETTES OR TOBACCO PRODUCTS TO MINORS

PA 07-175 (Preventing tobacco sales to minors)

This new law allows the commissioner to investigate the sale of tobacco products to minors. The commissioner may hold hearings, levy fines against tobacco distributors, and may forward complaints to the State's Attorney for prosecution. (Effective October 1, 2007)

AN ACT CONCERNING THE ENFORCEABILITY OF AUTOMATIC CONTRACT RENEWAL PROVISIONS

PA 07-215 (Automatic renewal of consumer contracts)

This new law provides protection to consumers by specifying how automatic contract renewal provisions must be disclosed. The change helps to prevent a consumer from being charged for goods or services where they took no active steps to renew a contract. If the required notice is not provided, the goods or services become the consumer's at no charge. Violations of this provision are violations of the Connecticut Unfair Trade Practices Act. (Effective October 1, 2007)

AN ACT CONCERNING ELECTRICITY AND ENERGY EFFICIENCY

PA 07-242 §3 ("Energy Star" certified air conditioner rebate program)

Section three of this new law requires the commissioner to certify retailers to participate in a program that allows rebates to be issued upon the purchase of an "Energy Star" compliant (energy efficient) air conditioner as a replacement for another non-compliant model. A fine may be imposed by the commissioner if a non-compliant model is not taken out of use. (Effective upon passage, but program start date is prior to January 1, 2008)

AN ACT CONCERNING THE RELEASE, SALE AND ACCURACY OF CONVICTION INFORMATION, THE ISSUANCE OF A REARREST WARRANT OR CAPIAS FOR FAILURE TO APPEAR, THE DUTIES OF BOARDS OF DIRECTORS AND EXECUTIVE BOARDS OF

CONDOMINIUMS AND OTHER COMMON INTEREST COMMUNITIES, AND THE DEFINITION OF COMMUNITY ASSOCIATION MANAGER

PA 07-243 §§3-8 (Community Association Managers)

Community Association Managers are registered with the Department. Sections three through eight of this public act modify the existing statutes related to Community Association Managers and were supported by the Department. The new law assists condominium owners by providing for improved disclosure of records, particularly financial records, by condominium associations and third-party management companies. Also, the definition of "Community Association Manager" has been expanded in section eight of the new law to include individuals who are the directors or managers of a management company, or who directly provide management services. (All sections effective October 1, 2007)

About ConsumerOnline

Consumer Online is an initiative launched by Consumer Online Foundation (COF) to interlink and integrate a comprehensive database of information related to consumers, consumerism and the digital economy.

Consumer Online Foundation, is a registered Trust formed with the motive of ensuring that modern technologies and communication medium are used to sub serve the greater common good. COF advocates the use of these effective communication tools to ensure improved productivity, enhanced information delivery, reduced transaction costs and efficiency in society. COF manages one of the country's largest resource centres on Consumer law and policy in India and its dedicated band of researchers have been involved in addressing various legal remedies affecting consumers.

The COF has adopted a four-pronged strategy of providing (i) Research support; (ii) Information dissemination; (iii) Advocacy support; and (iv) Litigation support to achieve its mandate.

COF has conceived, managed and implemented the CORE Centre project on behalf of the Consumer Co-ordination Council and the Ministry of Consumer Affairs, Food and Public Distribution. It has also helped build the countries largest resource centres on Consumer law and policy in India and its dedicated band of researchers have been involved in addressing various legal remedies affecting consumers.

COF has spear headed several public interest litigations including the PILs on issues, like the banning of Internet E-groups like yahoo; improper implementation of the FM radio policy; and the arbitrary introduction of the Conditional Access System(CAS).

The present COF website has been designed to interlink and integrate content relating to consumer issues in a digital economy and provides specific information of the activities, events, press releases, and campaigns on the subject. Such information would help the consumers in understanding the evolving role of policy and law in consumer awareness.

INTELLECTUAL PROPERTY RIGHTS IN INDIA

There is a well-established statutory, administrative and judicial framework to safeguard intellectual property rights in India, whether they relate to patents, trademarks, copyright or industrial designs. Well-known international trademarks have been protected in India even when they were not registered in India. The Indian Trademarks Law has been extended through court decisions to service marks in addition to trade marks for goods. Computer software companies have successfully curtailed piracy through court orders. Computer databases have been protected. The courts, under the doctrine of breach of confidentiality, accorded an extensive protection of trade secrets. Right to privacy, which is not protected even in some developed countries, has been recognized in India.

Protection of intellectual property rights in India continues to be strengthened further. The year 1999 witnessed the consideration and passage of major legislation with regard to protection of intellectual property rights in harmony with international practices and in compliance with India's obligations under TRIPS. These include:

1. The Patents (Amendment) Act, 1999 passed by the Indian Parliament on March 10, 1999 to amend the Patents Act of 1970 that provides for establishment of a mail box system to file patents and accords exclusive marketing rights for 5 years.
2. The Trade Marks Bill, 1999 which repeals and replaces the Trade and Merchandise Marks Act, 1958 passed by the Indian Parliament in the Winter Session that concluded on December 23, 1999.
3. The Copyright (Amendment) Act, 1999 passed by both houses of the Indian Parliament, and signed by the President of India on December 30, 1999.
4. A *sui generis* legislation for the protection of geographical indications called the Geographical Indications of Goods (Registration & Protection) Bill, 1999 approved by both houses of the Indian Parliament on December 23, 1999.
5. The Industrial Designs Bill, 1999 which replaces the Designs Act, 1911 was passed in the Upper House of the Indian Parliament in the Winter Session which concluded on December 23, 1999 and is presently before the Lower House for its consideration.
6. The Patents (Second Amendment) Bill, 1999 to further amend the Patents Act, 1970 and make it TRIPS compliant was introduced in the Upper House of Indian Parliament on December 20, 1999.

In addition to the above legislative changes, the Government of India has taken several measures to streamline and strengthen the intellectual property administration system in the country. Projects relating to the modernization of patent information services and trademarks registry have been implemented with help from WIPO/UNDP.

The Government of India is implementing a project for modernization of patent offices at a cost of Rs.756 million incorporating several components such as human resource development, recruiting additional examiners, infrastructure support and strengthening by way of computerization and re-engineering work practices, and elimination of backlog of patent applications. An amendment to the Patent Rules was notified on June 2, 1999 to simplify the procedural aspects.

The Trade Marks Registry is also proposed to be further strengthened and modernized. A project for modernization was earlier implemented during 1993-96. Further strengthening of the Registry is being taken up at a cost of Rs.86 million. The main thrust now is to strengthen the infrastructure of the Trade Marks Registry and the early removal of backlog of pending applications, transfer of records to CD-ROM's, re-engineering of work processes, appointment of additional examiners, etc.

As regards the aspect enforcement, Indian enforcement agencies are now working very effectively and there has been a notable decline in the levels of piracy in India. In addition to intensifying raids against copyright infringers, the Government has taken a number of measures to strengthen the enforcement of copyright law. Special cells for copyright enforcement have been set up in 23 States and Union Territories. In addition, for collective administration of copyright, copyright societies have been set up for different classes of works.

Concerns Expressed over IPR Protection & India's Response

It has been alleged that there is absence of effective patent protection in the pharmaceutical sector. India does provide for patents in the pharmaceutical sector.

However, in terms of Section 5 of the Patents Act, the patents are presently restricted to the methods or process of manufacture and not extended to the substances/products themselves. In terms of the TRIPS Agreement, India has time till January 1, 2005 to extend patent protection to this area. The ten year transition period available for providing product patents to pharmaceutical products is within WTO rules.

It has been further alleged that India has failed to meet its current obligations required under Articles 70.8 and 70.9 of the TRIPS Agreement by implementing appropriate, conforming mailbox and exclusive marketing rights procedures. However, the Government of India has taken the following steps to meet its obligations under Articles 70.8 and 70.9:

1. On December 31, 1994, Government of India promulgated an Ordinance to provide a means to receive product patent applications in the fields of pharmaceutical and agricultural chemical products and also for grant of exclusive marketing rights. Pursuant to this measure the Indian Patent Office has been receiving product patent applications in those fields.
2. India has established a mail box system through administrative instructions. Numerous applications have already been filed in this mail box system, and many of them have been filed by US companies;
3. India has also made changes to its Patents Act to put in place a machinery for implementation of Articles 70.8 and 70.9 by providing for establishment of a mail box system to file patents and according exclusive marketing rights for 5 years. This provision was made in the Patents (Amendment) Act of 1999.

Concern has also been expressed over the compulsory licensing provision in the Patents (Amendment) Act, 1999. It may be noted that as per the provisions of Section 84 of Patents Act, 1970 and Clause 35 of Patents (Second Amendment) Bill, 1999, a compulsory license may be granted in case the patented invention has not met the reasonable requirement of the public at a reasonable price.

This provision is intended to provide for necessary and adequate safeguard for the protection of public interest taking in to account the specific needs of a developing country like India.

This fact is supported by the US Health GAP Coalition. In their submission to the USTR, they have drawn attention to the announcement by President Clinton on December 1, 1999, that the US would henceforth take health concerns into account when formulating trade policies. They state that overly restrictive intellectual property regimes can - and have - lead to situations in which patent holders price commodities above levels at which they can feasibly be purchased in the developing world.

When this happens with pharmaceuticals, a public health crisis ensues. Health GAP Coalition, therefore, requests USTR to view IPR decisions made by foreign governments in the context of their health concerns, especially those countries that are simply trying to ensure that their citizens have adequate access to medicines.

Furthermore, the compulsory licensing system has been in place since the inception of the Patents Act, 1970 in India. It is noteworthy that not a single case of misuse of this provision has been observed during the last 30 years.

An application for compulsory license may be granted only after the applicant has approached the patentee prior to the application with an offer to grant license on reasonable terms and conditions (as per Clause 36 of Patents (Second Amendment) Bill, 1999).

In determining whether or not to grant a compulsory license, the Controller of Patents is required to take in to account, the nature of the invention, the time that has elapsed since the sealing of the patent and the measures already taken by the patentee or any licensee to make full use of the invention (Section 85 of Patents Act, 1970).

In settling terms of a compulsory license, the Controller of Patents is required to secure that the articles manufactured under the patent shall be available to the public at the lowest prices consistent with the patentees deriving a reasonable advantage from their patent rights (Section 97(1)(ii)). These provisions substantiate the extant of a non-discriminatory administration of compulsory licenses.

In addition, the Patents (Second Amendment) Bill, 1999 has provided for an appeals process, before an Appellate Board, on any decisions by the Controller of Patents including a grant of compulsory license (Clause 54) before approaching the Indian Courts. The Patents Law provides for compulsory license to avoid misuse of an Exclusive Marketing Right by the right holder. This provision meets a larger public interest, keeping in mind the specific Indian conditions and are in compliance with Article 31 of TRIPS.

The Indian Patent laws are neutral in their application to domestic or foreign inventions. Any disqualification, compulsory licensing, and exclusion from patentability, are provided for only in the larger interest to provide therein necessary and adequate safeguards for the protection of public interest, national security, bio-diversity, traditional knowledge, etc. These provisions are within the sphere allowed under Article 27, 30 and 31 of TRIPS.

It is to be noted that 1999 has been a year of great coherence of political will, resulting in the passage of major IPR laws and work toward the establishment of an effective administration mechanism.

Copyright Protection in India

India has one of the most modern copyright protection laws in the world. Major development in the area of copyright during 1999 was the amendment to the Copyright Act of 1957 to make it fully compatible with the provisions of the TRIPS Agreement. Called the Copyright (Amendment) Act, 1999, this amendment was signed by the President of India on December 30, 1999 and came into force on January 15, 2000.

The earlier 1994 amendment to the Copyright Act of 1957 had provided protection to all original literary, dramatic, musical and artistic works, cinematography, films and sound recordings. It also brought sectors such as satellite broadcasting, computer software and digital technology under Indian copyright protection.

The Copyright Act is now in full conformity with the TRIPS obligations.

The other important development during 1999 was the issuance of the International Copyright Order, 1999 extending the provisions of the Copyright Act to nationals of all World Trade Organization (WTO) Member countries.

Concern has been expressed about the allegedly slow judicial system in India and the procedural issues involved in trial and conviction. The Indian judiciary is handling cases as expeditiously as possible.

The year that has gone by has again witnessed the versatility of the impartial and independent Indian judiciary when it comes to the issue of protection of intellectual property rights, amplified by the encouraging trends with Indian courts plugging in gaps in the statute with the common sense of the common law.

The Copyright Act, 1957 prescribes mandatory punishment for piracy of copyrighted matter commensurate with the gravity of the offense with an effect to deter infringement, in compliance with the TRIPS Agreement.

Section 63 of the Copyright Act, 1957 provides that an offense of infringement of copyright or other rights conferred by the Act shall be punishable with imprisonment for a term which shall not be less than six months but which may extend to three years with fine which shall not be less than fifty thousand rupees but which may extend to two lakh rupees (Rs. 200,000).

Section 63A provides for enhanced penalty on second or subsequent convictions, i.e. imprisonment for a term which shall not be less than one year but which may extend to three years and with fine which shall not be less than one lakh rupees (Rs. 100,000) and which may extend up to two lakh rupees (Rs. 200,000). Section 63B provides that any person who knowingly makes use on a computer an infringing copy of a computer program shall be punishable with imprisonment for a term which shall not be less than seven days but which may extend to three years and with fine which shall not be less than fifty thousand rupees but which may extend to two lakh rupees (Rs. 200,000).

For India where the per capita income at current prices is Rs.14,682/- or US $349, the quantum of the fines, which works out to be 14 times the per capita income, is quite a burden on an individual and would act as a strong deterrent.

As regards the reported requirement that actual knowledge be proved in criminal cases, the expressions "knowingly infringes or abets infringement" in Section 63 and "knowingly makes use" in Section 63B are included to protect *bona fide* users.

It may be noted that the expression "knowingly" was there even in the analogous Section 7 of the Indian Copyright Act, 1914. Bringing the principle of *"ignoratia juris reminem excusat"* may not be apprcpriate in the case of copyright as there are quite a large number of works which are in the public domain that a person can use freely, and it is natural for many to presume that such works are outside the copyright regime.

Copyright is a special right created by law to protect certain rights of authors while keeping a balance of the interest of the society. It will be too much to expect an ordinary user to sit in judgment like a court of law as to every single aspect of the right which may or may not be applicable to a work before using the same.

So far as Article 41 and 61 of the TRIPS Agreement are concerned, India has a modern and efficient judicial system that fits in with the general obligations provided in Article 41. Article 61 of the TRIP Agreement provides that remedies available shall include imprisonment or monetary fines sufficient to provide a deterrent consistent with the level of penalties applied for a crime of corresponding gravity.

The Indian Copyright Act, provides for both imprisonment and fine which in the Indian context would be a sufficient deterrent.

Civil proceedings against piracy have been quite effective - a result unique in the global enforcement against copyright piracy. For instance, in 1999, the Motion Pictures Association (MPA), filed 3 civil actions against 3 Indian cable networks and obtained injunctive relief covering 45 cities and 8 million cable homes. MPA has estimated that by these injunctions alone, cable piracy has been brought down by 50%.

Further, provisional measures, such as injunctions and *'Anton Piller'* orders, are available through the Indian courts to stop infringement and to contain any damages. Both foreign and domestic IPR holders are created equally under Indian law.

Indian enforcement agencies are working effectively and there is a decline in the levels of piracy in India.

In addition to intensifying raids against copyright infringers, the Government has taken a number of measures to strengthen the enforcement of copyright law. A summary of these measures is given below:

1. During the year the government continued to stress the need for strict enforcement of the Copyright Act and Rules. State governments and other Ministries were regularly requested to lay special attention to ensuring copyright protection in their functioning. Instructions were issued to officers in the government requesting them to ensure copyright protection, particularly of software, in their work situation.
2. The Government also brought out A Handbook of Copyright Law to create awareness about copyright amongst the stakeholders, enforcement agencies, professional users like the scientific and academic communities and members of the public. Copies of the Handbook were circulated free of cost to the state and central government officials and police personnel and also provided to participants in various seminars and workshops on IPR matters held during the year.
3. National Police Academy, Hyderabad and National Academy of Customs, Excise and Narcotics conducted several training programs on copyright for the police and customs officers. Modules on copyright have been included in their regular training programs.
4. The Department of Education, Ministry of Human Resource Development, Government of India has initiated several measures in the past for strengthening the enforcement of copyrights that include constitution of a Copyright-Enforcement Advisory Council (CEAC), creation of separate cells in state police headquarters, encouraging setting up of collective administration societies and organization of seminars and workshops

to create greater awareness about copyright law among the enforcement personnel and the general public.

5. The CEAC is reconstituted from time to time to review periodically the progress of enforcement of the Copyright Act and to advise the government on measures for improving the enforcement. Additional Secretary, Department of Education is the chairman of the CEAC. The CEAC members include representatives of copyright industry organizations and chiefs of state police forces. The CEAC meets at least twice every year. It discusses in detail issues of enforcement, piracy, etc.
6. Special cells for copyright enforcement have so far been set up in 23 States and Union Territories, i.e. Andhra Pradesh, Assam, Andaman & Nicobar Islands, Chandigarh, Dadra & Nagar Haveli, Daman & Diu, Delhi, Goa, Gujarat, Haryana, Himachal Pradesh, Jammu & Kashmir, Karnataka, Kerala, Madhya Pradesh, Meghalaya, Orissa, Pondicherry, Punjab, Sikkim, Tamil Nadu, Tripura and West Bengal. States have also been advised to designate a nodal officer for copyright enforcement to facilitate easy interaction by copyright industry organizations and copyright owners.
7. For collective administration of copyright, copyright societies have been set up for different classes of works. At present there are three registered copyright societies. These are the Society for Copyright Regulations of Indian Producers of Films & Television (SCRIPT) for cinematography films, Indian Performing Rights Society Limited (IPRS) for musical works and Phonographic Performance Limited (PPL) for sound recordings. These societies, particularly the PPL and the IPRS, have been quite active in anti-piracy work. The PPL has even set up a special anti-piracy cell under a retired Director General of Police, and this cell has been working in tandem with the police.
8. The Government also initiates a number of seminars/ workshops on copyright issues. The participants in these

seminars include enforcement personnel like the police as well as representatives of industry organizations.

9. Several other measures to create general awareness about copyright and for encouraging study of intellectual property rights in the educational system, besides modernizing the Copyright Office, are on the anvil.

Consequent to the number of measures initiated by the government, there has been more activity in the enforcement of copyright laws in the country during the last year compared to previous years. As per the data relating to copyright offenses available with the National Crime Records Bureau, the number of copyright cases registered has gone up from 479 in 1997 to 802 in 1998. The number of persons arrested has increased from 794 in 1997 to 980 in 1998. The value of seizures has gone up from Rs.2.88 crore (28.8 million) in 1997 to Rs.7.48 crore (74.8 million) in 1998. These figures reflect the general improvement in the enforcement of the copyright law.

10

Copy Right Law in India

INTRODUCTION

The Copyright Act, 1957 came into effect from January 1958. This Act has been amended five times since then, i.e., in 1983, 1984, 1992, 1994 and 1999, with the amendment of 1994 being the most substantial.

Prior to the Act of 1957, the Law of Copyrights in the country was governed by the Copyright Act of 1914. This Act was essentially the extension of the British Copyright Act, 1911 to India. Even the Copyright Act, 1957 borrowed extensively from the new Copyright Act of the United Kingdom of 1956.

The Copyright Act, 1957 continues with the common law traditions. Developments elsewhere have brought about certain degree of convergence in copyright regimes in the developed world.

The Indian Copyright Act today is compliant with most international conventions and treaties in the field of copyrights. India is a member of the Berne Convention of 1886 (as modified at Paris in 1971), the Universal Copyright Convention of 1951 and the Agreement on Trade Related Aspects of Intellectual Property Rights (TRIPS) Agreement of 1995. Though India is not a member of the Rome Convention of 1961, the Copyright Act, 1957 is fully compliant with the Rome Convention provisions.

Two new treaties, collectively termed as Internet Treaties, were negotiated in 1996 under the auspices of the World Intellectual Property Organization (WIPO). These treaties are called the 'WIPO Copyrights Treaty (WCT)' and the 'WIPO Performances and Phonograms Treaty (WPPT)'. These treaties were negotiated essentially to provide for protection of the rights of copyright holders, performers and producers of phonograms in the Internet and digital era. India is not a member of these treaties as yet.

The Section 9 of the Copyright Act requires for establishment of an office to be called the Copyright Office for the purpose of the Act. The Copyright Office is to be under the immediate control of a Registrar of Copyrights to be appointed by the Central Government, who would act under the superintendence and directions of the Central Government. The Copyright Office is currently located at the following address:

B-2/W-3, Curzon Road Barracks

Kasturba Gandhi Marg

New Delhi - 110001

Section 11 of the Copyright Act requires the Central Government to constitute a Copyright Board headed by a Chairman with not less than two and not more than 14 other members. Registrar of Copyrights is to be Secretary of the Copyright Board.

Section 12 of the Copyright Act also lays down the powers of the Copyright Board and deems it to be a civil court for the purposes of Sections 345 and 346 of the Code of Criminal Procedure, 1973 and also that all the proceedings of the Board would be deemed to be judicial proceedings within the meaning of Sections 193 and 228 of the Indian Penal Code.

THE MONOPOLIES AND RESTRICTIVE TRADE PRACTICES ACT, 1969 BARE ACT

36A. DEFINITION OF UNFAIR TRADE PRACTICE.

In this Part, unless the context otherwise requires "unfair trade practice" means a trade practice which, for the purpose of promoting the sale, use or supply of any goods or for the provisions of any services, adopts any unfair method or unfair or deceptive practice including any of the following practices, namely :-

(1) the practice of making any statement, whether orally or in writing or by visible representation which, -

(i) falsely represents that the goods are of a particular standard, quality, quantity, grade, composition, style or model;

(ii) falsely represents that the services are of a particular standard, quality or grade;

(iii) falsely represents any re-built, second-hand, renovated, reconditioned or old goods as new goods;

(iv) represents that the goods or services have sponsorships, approval, performance, characteristics, accessories, uses or benefits which such goods or services do not have;

(v) represents that the seller or the supplier has a sponsorship or approval or affiliation which such seller or supplier does not have;

(vi) makes a false or misleading representation concerning the need for, or the usefulness of, any goods or services;

(vii) gives to the public any warranty or guarantee of the performance, efficacy or length of life of a product or of any goods that is not based on an adequate or proper test thereof : Provided that where a defence is raised to the effect that such warranty or guarantee is based on adequate or proper test, the burden of proof of such defence shall lie on the person raising such defence;

(viii) makes to the public a representation in a form that purports to be -

(i) a warranty or guarantee of a product or of any goods or services; or

(ii) a promise to replace, maintain or repair an article or any part thereof or to repeat or continue a service until it has achieved a specified result. if such purported warranty or guarantee or promise is materially misleading or if there is no reasonable prospect that such warranty, guarantee or promise will be carried out;

(ix) materially misleading the public concerning the price at which a product or like products or goods or services, have been, or are, ordinarily sold or provided, and, for this purpose, a representation as to price shall be deemed to refer to the price at which the product or goods or services has or have been sold by sellers or provided by suppliers generally in the relevant market unless it is clearly specified to be the price at which the product has been sold or services have been provided by the person by whom or on whose behalf the representation is made;

(x) gives false or misleading facts disparaging the goods, services or trade of another person.

Explanation : For the purposes of clause (1), a statement that is -

(a) expressed on an article offered or displayed for sale, or on its wrapper or container; or

(b) expressed on anything attached to, inserted in, or accompanying, an article offered or displayed for sale, or on anything on which the article is mounted for display or sale; or

(c) contained in or on anything that is sold, sent, delivered, transmitted or in any other manner whatsoever made available to a member of the public, shall be deemed to be a statement made to the public by, and only by, the person who had caused the statement to be so expressed, made or contained;

(2) permits the publication of any advertisement whether in any newspaper or otherwise, for the sale or supply at a bargain price, of goods or services that are not

intended to be offered for sale or supply at the bargain price, or for a period that is, and in quantities that are, reasonable, having regard to the nature of the market in which the business is carried on, the nature and size of business, and the nature of the advertisement.

Explanation : For the purpose of clause (2), "bargain price" means -

(a) a price that is stated in any advertisement to be a bargain price, by reference to an ordinary price or otherwise, or

(b) a price that a person who reads, hears, or sees the advertisement, would reasonably understand to be a bargain price having regard to the prices at which the product advertised or like products are ordinarily sold;

(3) permits -

(a) the offering of gifts, prizes or other items with the intention of not providing them as offered or creating the impression that something is being given or offered free of charge when it is fully or partly covered by the amount charged in the transaction as a whole.

(b) the conduct of any contest, lottery, game of chance or skill, for the purpose of promoting, directly or indirectly, the sale, use or supply of any product or any business interest;

(4) permits the sale or supply of goods intended to be used, or are of a kind likely to be used by consumers, knowing or having reason to believe that the goods do not comply with the standards prescribed by competent authority relating to performance, composition, contents, design, constructions, finishing or packaging as are necessary to prevent or reduce the risk of injury to the person using the goods;

(5) permits the hoarding or destruction of goods, or refuses to sell the goods or to make them available for sale, or to provide any service, if such hoarding or destruction

or refusal raises or tends to raise or is intended to raise, the cost of those or other similar goods or services.

REVIEW OF THE PROPOSED AMENDMENT TO THE COPYRIGHT ACT

The Government of India is planning to amend the Copyright Act 1957. We believe that some of proposed changes may have serious public interest implications, and we provide our review of the same.

Summary of the Review

Access to knowledge and cultural goods is critical to ensure full participation of the public in political and cultural life and to ensure benefit to them from any scientific and technological advancement. The copyright system seeks to promote the efficient dissemination of knowledge in the public domain by maintaining a balance between enabling rewards to producers of knowledge on the one hand, and access to these copyright goods for the public, on the other. It is therefore critical that laws pertaining to copyright in any country be drafted in a manner that best ensures an ideal balance between public and private interest.

This review seeks to examine the implications of the proposed amendments, as well as to re-examine some of the existing provisions from a public interest perspective.

The copyright law of a sovereign nation is influenced by the status of that nation's accession to the major international conventions, treaties and trade rules, which in the case of India, are:

(i) The Berne Convention for the Protection of Literary and Artistic Works ("Berne Convention")

(ii) The agreement on trade related aspects of intellectual property rights ("TRIPs") which also incorporates the Berne Convention

Additionally, there are a number of other copyright-related treaties like the WIPO Copyright Treaty ("WCT") and the WIPO Performances and Phonograms Treaty ("WPPT") which bind signatory nations to additional changes to their copyright law. It is to be noted that India is only bound to the terms of the Berne Convention and the TRIPs agreement, and not to either the WCT or the WPPT. We are therefore not legally obliged to any commitments beyond those obligated under TRIPs and Berne.

We note that some of the proposed amendments to the Act seek to introduce provisions related to the WCT and WPPT, and we need to be extremely cautious before introducing any amendments that may be detrimental to public interest. For instance the current proposals seek to introduce Digital Rights Management ("DRM") into the Act, and we review why this is not in the best interests of a developing country.

We also note that it is important for government to recognize and rely on flexibilities of the Berne Convention and the TRIPs agreement which enable access to knowledge and information, by ensuring easy access to copyrighted materials in respect of educational, private or general use, and via any media or form. For instance, we note that the present amendment seeks to promote greater access to knowledge and information for persons with any sensory disabilities. This is a welcome move, especially if enacted with a thorough review of the details of the need, and the enabling provision thereof.

Lastly, a short note on who we are. This review was drafted at the Alternative Law Forum ("ALF") by Lawrence Liang, Achal Prabhala and Nirmita Narasimhan, and is supported by important consumer-rights organisations, disabled-rights groups, film producers' associations, NGOs and universities from across India, namely:

Citizen consumer and civic Action Group ("CAG")

Independent Documentary Producers Association ("IDPA")

National Association for the Blind ("NAB")

Centre for the Study of Developing Societies ("CSDS")

Voice (Voluntary Organization In Interest of Consumer Education)

Consumer Online Foundation

Drishtiviklang Sangh (Association of the Visually Handicapped)

M S Swaminathan Research Foundation

Mahiti (International Open Source Network - India)

Tata Institute of Social Sciences ("TISS")

It is also supported by the renowned legal scholar and former Vice Chancellor of Delhi University, Professor Upendra Baxi. More details on the organisations, and the designated contact with respects to this review, follow on the next page. We trust that you will find our suggestions useful, and we look forward to clarifying any part of this document, as necessary.

THE PURPOSE OF COPYRIGHT *BY LYDIA PALLAS LOREN*

Lydia Pallas Loren is Associate Professor of Law, Northwestern School of Law of Lewis & Clark College.

The newspaper you read this morning, the television show you watched last night, the movie you are going to see this weekend, the computer software you use to prepare your letters or send your email, the music you listen to in the car on your way to work: they are all copyrighted. Copyright permeates our lives and yet, despite its impact on our lives, relatively few people, including lawyers, have sufficient knowledge or understanding of what copyright is. And far too many people, including lawyers, have major misconceptions concerning copyright. These misconceptions are causing a dangerous shift in copyright protection, a shift that threatens the advancement of knowledge and learning in this country. This shift that we are experiencing in copyright law reflects a move away from viewing copyright as a monopoly that the public is willing to tolerate in order to encourage innovation and creation of new works to viewing copyright as a significant asset to this country's economy. The most recent example of this shift is the new Digital Millennium Copyright Act, sign by the President on October 28, 1998.

Understanding the root cause and the dangers of this shift requires exposing the most fundamental and most common misconception concerning the underlying purpose of the monopoly granted by our copyright law. The primary purpose of copyright is not, as many people believe, to protect authors against those who would steal the fruits of their labor. However, this misconception, repeated so often that it has become accepted among the public as true, poses serious dangers to the core purpose that copyright law is designed to serve.

The core purpose of copyright law is not difficult to find; it is stated expressly in the Constitution. Article I, section 8, clause 8 of the United States Constitution provides that Congress shall have the power: "to promote the Progress of Science and useful Arts, by securing for limited times to Authors and Inventors the exclusive Right to their respective Writings and Discoveries."

This clause is the constitutional basis for the Copyright Act and also the Patent Act. It is the only clause in the grant of powers to Congress that has a stated purpose. Section 8 of Article I gives Congress the power to take such actions as declare war, coin money, raise and support Armies, and provide and maintain a navy. Yet none of these other grants say for what purpose the power is to be exercised. The copyright clause, in contrast, is very specific about its purpose. The exclusive rights that are granted to authors are "to promote the Progress of Science and useful Arts." To fully appreciate this clause, one must understand "science" in its eighteenth century meaning. At the time of the writing of the Constitution "science" denoted, broadly, knowledge and learning. So the core purpose of copyright law, as expressly stated in the Constitution is: to promote the progress of knowledge and learning.

Why did the founding fathers feel the need to state the purpose of copyright and patent, expressly, when none of the other enumerated powers has an express purpose stated? One probable reason lies in the history of the monopoly of the copyright.

A Quick Trip Back in History

When the printing press was introduced into England in 1476, the need for protection of printed works was inevitable. The probable genesis of copyright law was the crown's grant of a letters patent, the printing patent, giving one entity a monopoly on the printing of certain works. Of course, a fee for that monopoly was paid to the crown, thus making the letters patent a source of revenue for the crown.

If the crown could grant these patents, the guild of booksellers, called the Stationers' Company, found that they could agree among themselves to allow a monopoly on works. The members of the Stationers' Company were almost all of the printers in England; if they agreed to respect one another's claims to particular works it was a de facto monopoly. Thus, the idea of a "copyright" started out as a member of the guild registering the title of the manuscript or "copy" with the guild. Registering a copy with the guild gave that printer the exclusive right in the copy. Thus copyright as first used was a noun - the exclusive right in the copy, whereas today many think of copyright more as a verb - the exclusive right to copy.

A bookseller's registration of the copy with the guild gave the bookseller the exclusive right to print and vend the work as a matter of private law, agreed to by members of the guild. The problem with private law, however, is that it can only be enforced among those who have agreed to it. The bookseller's private law copyright was no exception. It was enforceable only among the members of the Stationers' Company. Because of this limitation, the booksellers often sought public affirmation or codification of their private law.

In 1557, the desires of the booksellers and the desires of the crown coincided. The crown perceived the need to gain greater control over "the dangerous possibilities of the printed word" and so granted a royal charter to the Stationers' Company that limited most printing to only members of the company. This charter also empowered the company to search out and destroy "unlawful" books, which gave the guild the public enforcement mechanism for its private law. If a nonmember was printing a work that had been registered with the company by a member, the nonmember could now be stopped. It also meant that if a work which was disagreeable to the crown was being published, it too could be stopped. This arrangement provided the crown with added policemen to enforce its goal to control printed works. Censorship was born. The power of censorship and press control through the Stationers' Company copyright lasted for over 150 years. Finally, in the early 1700s parliament refused to continue to support the monopoly that the stationers had enjoyed for centuries and the power of censorship that the crown had enjoyed along with it.

Copyright in the United States

The framers of the United States Constitution, suspicious of all monopolies to begin with, knew the history of the copyright as a tool of censorship and press control. They wanted to assure that copyright was not used as a means of oppression and censorship in the United States. They therefore expressly provided for the purpose of copyright: to promote the progress of knowledge and learning.

With the stated goal firmly fixed in the Constitution, the task of accomplishing that goal was given to Congress. The means for achieving that goal are also stated in the Constitution. The promotion of the progress of knowledge and learning was to be accomplished by "securing for limited times to Authors .... the exclusive Right to their ... Writings." The monopoly of the copyright would be tolerated, but only as a means to an end. The Constitution adopts a Field of Dreams approach to the creation of works of authorship - the idea that "if you protect it, they will come." By establishing this marketable right to the use of one's expression, copyright supplies the economic incentive to create and disseminate ideas. As the Supreme Court has recognized: "The immediate effect of our copyright law is to secure a fair return for an 'author's' creative labor. But the ultimate aim is, by this incentive, to stimulate artistic creativity for the general public good."

In fulfilling the constitutionally mandated goal of copyright law, Congress has had to ask, as one early legislative report did, two questions: "First, how much will the legislation stimulate the producer and so benefit the public; and second, how much will the monopoly granted be detrimental to the public?" As Judge Walker of the Second Circuit recently summarized: "The copyright law seeks to establish a delicate equilibrium. On the one hand, it affords protection to authors as an incentive to create, and, on the other, it must appropriately limit the extent of that protection so as to avoid the effects of monopolistic stagnation." The founding fathers wanted copyright to be a mechanism by which our democracy would grow and flourish - a way in which our storehouse of knowledge is stocked.

THE DARK SIDE OF COPYRIGHT TODAY

Modern-day copyright harbors a dark side. The misunderstanding held by many who believe that the primary purpose of copyright law is to protect authors against those who would pilfer the author's work threatens to upset the delicate equilibrium in copyright law. This misunderstanding obviously works to the benefit of the content owning industries, such as the publishing industry, the music and motion picture industries, and the computer software industry. This fundamental misunderstanding is perpetuated by the stern FBI warnings at the beginning of video tapes, by overly broad assertions of the rights in the copyright notices, and by the general lack of public discourse about the balance required in copyright law if copyright is to fulfill its constitutionally mandated goal of promoting knowledge and learning.

This dark side, this pervasive misconception, is turning copyright into what our founding fathers tried to guard against - a tool for censorship and monopolistic oppression. This may sound extreme to some, but consider the beginnings of copyright in this country. The first Copyright Act in the United States granted only the exclusive right only to print, publish, and vend a copyrighted work, and it lasted for only fourteen years, with the possibility of a second fourteen-year term. No exclusive rights to perform the work or to create an adaptation of the work were granted, only the right to print, publish, and vend for, at most, twenty-eight years.

Under current copyright law, not only do copyright owners have the right to publish and distribute the work, but copyright owners also have the right to control the public performance of a work, to control the making of adaptations of the work, and to control the reproduction of the work independent of what is done with that new copy. And, as a result of the Copyright Term Extension Act passed in October, 1998, now the basic term of copyright lasts for the life of the author plus seventy years. This new term is a far cry from the original maximum term of twenty-eight years, and results in a much larger monopoly and a much longer time that the public must wait for any given work to enter the public domain.

Congress also has created additional criminal sanctions for copyright infringement with the passage in December 1997 of the No Electronic Theft or "NET" Act. Under this new legislation, an individual who is engaging in willful infringement can be held criminally liable even if that person is not engaging in the infringement for profit or commercial advantage. For the previous century a profit motive had always been the touchstone of criminal infringement. Now, if, over the course of any 180-day period, someone willfully infringes copyright by reproducing or distributing one or more copies of one or more works which have a retail value over $1000, they can be found criminally liable.

Most recently, in October 1998, the President signed the Digital Millennium Copyright Act. Among other additions to the Copyright Act, the Digital Millennium Copyright Act provides both civil and criminal legal sanctions for the circumvention of technological measures employed by copyright owners to control access to their works. Except in narrow and specifically prescribed circumstances, a violation of federal law occurs regardless of why such circumvention is undertaken. This legislation seriously impedes the access to copyrighted works and the non-copyrighted elements of those works, thereby threatening the ultimate aim of copyright, the promotion of the progress of knowledge and learning. The Digital Millennium Copyright Act also permits copyright owners to force internet service providers to remove material from the internet and the world wide web when the copyright owner believes the material is infringing.

The Importance of Balance in Copyright Law

The ever-expanding scope of rights granted to copyright owners and lengthy duration of this statutory monopoly leads necessarily to an added importance of the rights granted to users of copyrighted works during the term of copyright if copyright law is to remain consistent with its constitutionally mandated goal. While the rights granted to copyright owners are broad, those rights are expressly made subject to rights of the users of copyrighted works which are detailed in 14 separate sections of the Copyright Act.

The most important of the rights of users is that of fair use. Yet fair use is the least specifically defined and least understood of users' rights. The Copyright Act provides that certain kinds of uses of copyrighted works, called fair uses, are not an infringement of copyright, despite the fact that the use may involve copying, adapting, performing, or displaying the copyrighted work. If a particular type of an activity is a fair use, then the copyright owner of the work has no right to demand that the use first be authorized by the copyright owner or to demand the payment of a fee for engaging in that type of use. The Act lists four non-exclusive factors for courts to consider in determining whether any particular use is a fair use and thus not an infringement of copyright. (The four factors are: (1) the purpose and character of the use, including whether such use is of a commercial nature or is for nonprofit educational purposes; (2) the nature of the copyrighted work; (3) the amount and substantiality of the portion used in relation to the copyrighted work as a whole; and (4) the effect of the use upon the potential market for or value of the copyrighted work.) A court is required to examine these factors in adjudicating an assertion of infringement by the copyright owner on the one hand and the assertion of fair use by the alleged infringer on the other.

Of the four factors to be considered in a fair use analysis, two concern money, and, in the fair use analysis of most courts, the two non-monetary factors are often not that relevant to the outcome of the case. But this focus on money, coupled with the general misconception that copyright's primary purpose is to protect authors against those who would pilfer their work, threatens further detriment to achieving the constitutionally mandated goal of copyright. If the use at issue is something for which the copyright owner desires to charge a fee and is able to show the court a simple and efficient means of paying the fee, the copyright owner can often defeat an assertion of fair use. This results in a situation that permits the copyright owner to narrow the rights of fair use by providing a licensing scheme for the types of uses that should not require permission from the copyright owner. If copyright is to continue to be the engine of the progress of knowledge and learning in this country, Congress and the courts should not permit the right of fair use to be limited in this manner.

An argument in favor of more rights for users of copyrighted works and correspondingly fewer rights for copyright owners, often is countered by the copyright owning industries with an argument based on an economic analysis of copyright law. The argument goes like this: the greater the monopoly you permit, the greater are the financial rewards and therefore the greater the incentive to create. Thus, with broader monopoly rights, greater numbers of works are created and disseminated resulting in greater knowledge. To this there are, at least, three responses.

First, the conclusion that a greater numbers of works will be created when there are greater monopolies fails to account for the negative implications of broad monopolies on creative expression. When the scope of the copyright monopoly becomes too great, the creation of new works is, itself, hampered. After all, each creator of a new work builds in some way on the works of the past. With overly broad monopolies, new works that build upon old are not created, creativity is stifled, and thus the net value to society is lessened. We have, what Judge Walker referred to a "monopolistic stagnation."

Related to this first response is another concerning the conclusion that greater monopolies will result in greater levels of creativity. Creative individuals produce new works for a variety of reasons. The kinds of increases in monopoly rights of copyright owners empirically have not been shown to increase the production of new works. It seems unlikely that a creative individual, in determining how to spend her limited time and resources thinks, "ah, now that my copyright lasts for seventy years after my death I will invest more in creating more works." The greater scope of these monopolies instead benefits large corporate owners of significant numbers of copyrights. The majority of the copyrights are obtained by assignment from the original creators of the copyrighted works, after the works have been created. The amount paid for the assignment of the copyright depends, in part, on the projected profitability of the exploitation of the work, but it has not been shown that greater monopolies necessarily result in a net gain of new creative works.

Finally, even if greater monopolies would result in greater numbers of new works being created, the conclusion that greater knowledge will result also is flawed. When the scope of the copyright monopoly becomes too great, there are uses which would result in a net gain to society, but the benefits of those uses are dispersed among all members of society. Because of this dispersion of benefit, it is extremely difficult for the full value of that particular use to be internalized in any bargained-for exchange between the copyright owner and the would be user of the copyrighted work. If the scope of the copyright owner's monopoly is too broad, then those beneficial uses will not occur. The kinds of uses which have those disperse external benefits are the uses that, if permitted, would in fact further the goal of copyright, to promote the progress of knowledge and learning.

Copyright interpreted not with a focus on the ultimate aim of the progress of knowledge and learning, but instead with a focus on the monetary rights of copyright owners, results in uses that would be a net gain to society not taking place. The recent paradigm shift reflects a short term view of the copyright monopoly. If the monopolies granted to copyright owners are larger, then obviously the content owning industry can generate more revenue. This increase in revenue results in a larger gross national product, a smaller trade deficit, and greater employment. However, the threat of monopolistic stagnation looms very real and the ability of the content owning industry to charge monopolistic prices increases as competitive works are cabined in by broader monopolies granted to everything from literature and motion pictures to computer software.

Copyright and Censorship

Copyright interpreted in light of the fundamental misconception of copyright and a focus on monetary issues also poses a serious threat of censorship, private censorship, enforced by our federal courts through assertions of copyright infringement and enforced by internet service providers who will remove material from cyberspace to appease a copyright owner and maintain a statutory exemption from copyright infringement liability. To bring this theoretical discussion down to concrete examples, the stories of two cases, one litigated and one not litigated, are illuminating.

The first is the story of the litigated case concerning a parody version of Roy Orbison's song "Oh, Pretty Woman" recorded and distributed by the rap group 2 Live Crew. Before recording its parody, 2 Live Crew sought authorization to use the song from the copyright owners of Pretty Woman, but their request was rejected. 2 Live Crew went ahead and recorded their parody anyway and, as a result, found themselves sued for copyright infringement. 2 Live Crew asserted the defense of fair use and the district court agreed and dismissed the lawsuit. The district court held that the parodic nature of 2 Live Crew's song was meant as commentary and criticism of the original, and thus was a fair use and not an infringement of the copyright. 2 Live Crew was not as fortunate in front of the court of appeals, which reversed the finding of fair use, finding that the harm to the copyright owner's market for the copyrighted work outweighed any parodic purpose that might be found in 2 Live Crew's song. 2 Live Crew, however, had the financial wherewithal to file a petition for certiarori with the Supreme Court, and fortunately for 2 Live Crew the Supreme Court was willing to review their case.

In its opinion, the Supreme Court emphasized that parody can provide social benefit by shedding light on an earlier work, and in the process, creating a new one. The Supreme Court recognized that "2 Live Crew's song 'was clearly intended to ridicule the white-bred original' and 'reminds us that sexual congress with nameless streetwalkers is not necessarily without its consequences. The singers . . . have the same thing on their minds as did the lonely man with the nasal voice, but there is no hint of wine and roses.'" Another way to understand the Court's ruling is that the Court determined that commentary and criticism in our society has disperse external benefits that must be taken into account when determining fair use. The value to society of permitting people to comment on other people's work through parody has general benefit in society that is spread among all people. That aspect of the value of parody cannot be captured by the creator of the parody to assist in paying a license fee to the copyright owner in order to obtain permission to use the work that is being parodied. The general value of permitting parody is a disperse external benefit that cannot be internalized in any bargained-for exchange.

Someone aware of this case prior to reading this article, unless extremely knowledgeable in this area, would probably think the Supreme Court ruled 2 Live Crew's parody constituted fair use. While the Supreme Court did reverse the court of appeals ruling that 2 Live Crew's song was infringement, the Supreme Court did not rule that the parody was fair use. The Court remanded for further proceedings. And, on remand, the district court was directed to consider the possible market harm for the non-parody rap versions of Pretty Woman that might be licensed by the copyright owner. There were no proceedings on remand; rather, the case settled with 2 Live Crew entering into a license with the copyright owners of the song for future sales of their parody.

While the Supreme Court in the 2 Live Crew case repeatedly warned against overemphasizing monetary issues in the context of a fair use analysis, lower courts have continued to focus on harm not only to the market for the original, but also on harm to markets for other uses of the work that the copyright owner might be interested in licensing. These courts focus on protecting the copyright owners in various, yet to be exploited markets. These courts are focusing on the misconception of copyright - that it is intended to protect authors from those who would pilfer their works.

2 Live Crew was fortunate. The group had the resources to fight all the way to the Supreme Court that repeatedly

emphasized the importance of the promotion of the progress of science and the useful arts as the ultimate aim of copyright. But, in the end, even for 2 Live Crew's parody, a license from the copyright owner was the result. The need for a license, of course, grants to the copyright owner the power to deny that license which is the power to censor certain kinds of speech.

If doubts remain about the validity of the argument that copyright is increasingly being used as a tool of censorship dangerously threatening to impede rather than promote knowledge and learning, a second story should be considered. This story provides an example of a loss to the general storehouse of knowledge, sought to be stocked, not locked, by copyright.

David Stowe, a professor in the Department of American Thought and Language at Michigan State University, sought to show the conflicted cultural politics of big band jazz in the 1940's. Specifically, he wanted to show the sexism and racism that was pervasive in the big band culture of that time through the use of various cartoons that had appeared in Down Beat, a jazz monthly magazine. Down Beat normally grants permission for use of excerpts from its magazines and doesn't even charge a fee. However, in Professor Stowe's case, upon reviewing the content of the material, the magazine declined to grant permission, at any price. The reason? The drawings made the magazine "look bad." Unlike 2 Live Crew, for Professor Stowe the risk of going ahead and using that material and having to litigate his rights, with the risk also of being found to be an infringer, were too high. Society lost out on an enhanced scholarly work because a copyright owner was able to censor Professor Stowe's work.

Stories like those of Professor Stowe abound in academic circles. The amorphous application of the four fair use factors and their unbalanced emphasis on money, given that the pervasive misconception of copyright's purpose is shared by some judges, makes reliance on the doctrine of fair use unsavory to those who we would most like to see use it - scholars writing works to benefit the general public storehouse of knowledge. The risk of a suit are high, the costs of litigation enormous, and the risk of being found to be an infringer not negligible. All of this leads to a power of censorship in the hands of copyright owners.

This power of censorship at the hands of copyright owners has recently entered the realm of digital technology, and again the copyright owners have been given a very large stick with which to convince others to assist them in censoring potentially critical works. Under the recent Digital Millennium Copyright Act, copyright owners are given a very effective tool for censoring speech in cyberspace. Copyright owners can, in effect, force internet service providers to remove material from the internet and the world wide web posted by anyone simply by sending the internet service provider that is storing the material a written notice asserting a good faith belief that the material is infringing. If the internet service provider fails to expeditiously remove or disable access to the claimed infringing material, the internet service provider itself can become liable for any infringement that might be found. Clearly internet service providers will err on the side of removing any material claimed to be infringing. But this removal occurs without an independent judgement of whether infringement is in fact occurring. The only judgement is that of the copyright owner. While a counter notification to the service provider from the person who posted the alleged infringing material requires the service provider to replace the disputed material fourteen days later, the copyright owner can stop the reposting merely by filing a court action within those 14 days. Adjudication is not required to keep the material out of the public's reach.

The significance of the ability to censor speech in cyberspace is extremely important. Cyberspace empowers individuals to reach millions of others with their messages without having to rely on expensive and often content-selective publishing entities. Yet in this potentially equalizing forum we now have legal rules in place that permit copyright owners to halt speech merely by asserting a claim of copyright infringement.

The Future of Copyright

I am not advocating an elimination of copyright protection. The protection granted to copyright owners is essential in providing the economic incentive for the creation of works. But in determining the scope of the monopoly rights granted to copyright owners, given the extreme length of the monopoly, we must not lose sight of the true purpose of copyright - to promote the progress of knowledge and learning - and we must all realize that too broad a monopoly will impede rather than promote that progress on which this country was founded.

Initially the base of this country's economy was land; there was, after all, so much of it. Then, the base of the economy became manufacturing, the industrial age. Now, we have begun what is referred to as the information age. The way information-based products are protected is through intellectual property, including copyright. The economic importance of copyright has led to additional rights for copyright owners, longer terms of copyright protection, and legal protection for the technological locks put on works in digital media.

With each request for an expansion of the copyright monopoly, whether an expansion in scope or in length, the question must be asked: will the significant cost to the public of the increased monopoly be outweighed by the additional works that will be created and disseminated as a result of a greater incentive provided by that increase in the scope or duration of the copyright monopoly? In this equation the disperse benefits generally of a greater informed citizenry achieved through limits on the copyright monopoly must be factored in.

The economic importance of copyright will only continue to grow and the contours of the rights of copyright owners and users will continue to change with much debate about the direction that change should take. In all of this debate, however, we should not let a fundamental misconception of the primary purpose of copyright law in this country shape our rules to the detriment of the true constitutional aim of the limited statutory monopoly of the copyright: to promote the progress of knowledge and learning.

Bibliography

Ahmad, Imtiaz: *State and Foreign Policy: India's Role in South Asia*, New Delhi, Vikas, 1993.

Baxi, Upendra: *The Crisis of the Indian Legal System*, New Delhi, Vikas, 1982.

Bhatia, B.M.: *Indian Agriculture: A Policy Perspective*, New Delhi, Sage, 1988.

Bookman, Zarkovic: *The Political Economy of Discontinuous Development: Regional Disparities and Inter-regional Conflict*, New York, Praeger, 1991.

Bose, Sugata: *Peasant Labour and Colonial Capital: Rural Bengal since 1770*, Cambridge, Cambridge University Press, 1993.

Chaudhuri, Pramit: *The Indian Economy: Poverty and Development*, New York, St. Martin's Press, 1979.

Desai, Vasant: *A Study of Rural Economics: A Systems Approach*, Bombay, Himalaya, 1983.

Dhingra, C.: *The Indian Economy: Resources, Planning, Development, and Problems*, Delhi, Sultan Chand, 1983.

Kashyap, C.: *National Policy Studies*, New Delhi, Tata McGraw-Hill for the Lok Sabha Secretariat, 1990.

Kishore, K.: *Economic History of Mughal India: An Annotated Bibliography, 1526-1875*, Calcutta, Santiniketan, 1991.

Kohli, Rajan: *Structural Change in Indian Industries*, New Delhi, Capital Foundation Society, 1994.

Little, I.M.D.: *India: Macroeconomics and Political Economy, 1964-1991*, Washington, World Bank, 1994.

Raj, K.N.: *New Economic Policy*, Delhi, Oxford University Press, 1986.

Terence, J.: *The State and Development Planning in India*, Delhi, Oxford University Press, 1994.

Index

□□□